Zhang Wenguang's Chaquan Volume III

Representative Weapons of the Chaquan System

Available from **tgl books**

Translated from the Chinese by Andrea Mary Falk
Jiang Rongqiao's Baguazhang
Li Tianji's The Skill of Xingyiquan
Yan Dehua's Bagua Applications
Di Guoyong on Xingyiquan: Volume I, Foundations
Di Guoyong on Xingyiquan: Volume II, Forms and Ideas
Di Guoyong on Xingyiquan: Volume III, Weapons
Zhang Wenguang's Chaquan
Zhang Wenguang's Chaquan: Volume II, Further Styles
Zhang Wenguang's Chaquan: Volume III, Representative Weapons

Researched and written by Andrea Mary Falk
A Shadow on Fallen Blossoms: The 36 and 48 Traditional Verses of Baguazhang
Falk's Dictionary of Chinese Martial Arts
Beijing Bittersweet
Shadowboxing in Shanghai

www.thewushucentre.ca

Zhang Wenguang's Chaquan

Volume III
Representative Weapons of the Chaquan System

张文广

中国查拳典型器械套路

translated and edited

by Andrea Mary Falk

霍安娣翻译，主板

Translation copyright © 2025 by Andrea Mary Falk

All Rights Reserved

ISBN 978-1-989468-42-5

Originally published by Zhang Wenguang as Zhongguo Chaquan Dianxing Qixie Taolu. Published by Zhongguo Renmin Gongan Daxue Chubanshe, Beijing, China, 1995.

Translated and edited by Andrea Falk,

in Morin-Heights and Quebec City, QC, Canada.

This is volume three of a three volume translation set on Chaquan.

The techniques described in this book are performed by experienced martial artists. The author, translator, and publishers are not responsible for any injury that may occur while trying out these techniques. Please do not apply these techniques on anyone without their consent and cooperation.

TABLE OF CONTENTS

Zhang Wenguang's Preface vii
Translator's Preface xi
Editor's Preface   xii

CHAPTER ONE: INTRODUCTION 1
CHAPTER TWO: CHA SABRE 7
CHAPTER THREE: KUNWU SWORD.. 33
CHAPTER FOUR: LOCKING SPEAR... 63
CHAPTER FIVE: SHEPHERD'S STAFF... 95
CHAPTER SIX: CHA HOOKS.. 127
CHAPTER SEVEN: HORSE CONTROLLING BATONS................... 155
CHAPTER EIGHT: TWO-HANDED CUTTER 183
CHAPTER NINE: CRESCENT MOON BLADE............................... 211

Mandarin Pronunciation of *pinyin* 241
About the translator   243

ZHANG WENGUANG'S PREFACE

I was born May 15th, 1915, in a Hui nationality household in Tongxu county, Henan province. I loved martial arts from an early age, and in 1928 sought out the famous Chaquan master Zhang Fengling, from Guan county, Shandong province, becoming his disciple to learn Tantui and Chaquan. From 1929 on, I also learned from the modern master Chang Zhenfang, to further my studies in Chaquan and the Chaquan weapons. My teachers were very strict and I trained very rigorously, so I achieved excellent basic skills. Everything I did, I did with particular accuracy and exactness. In 1933 I was accepted at the Nanjing Central Wushu Academy. There I would learn Changquan, Taijiquan, Xingyiquan, Baguazhang, and other styles of martial arts, including their weapons. I also trained the fighting arts of wrestling, boxing, sparring, and short  and long weapons sparring. During this period, I obtained a systematic mastery of the characteristics and flavour of many styles of martial arts. I became a martial art professional, and gradually gained skill at performing forms, though my long suit was still the combative events. At the Academy I gained much real life experience, and also learned a great deal of theory and learned to love research, building a good foundation for my teaching career. I learned the essence of many styles of martial arts, nevertheless, my specialty remained Chaquan.

Throughout the 1930s, I won national championships in forms and sparring many times. In 1935, I was selected to the Chinese national wushu team, with whom I performed many times on trips to Hong Kong, Singapore, Malaysia, the Philippines, and other places. In the spring of 1936, I won first place in the wushu selection competition prior to the Olympic Games, held to select the team that would perform. Thus, in June 1936, I took part in wushu performances at the Eleventh Olympic Games, held in Berlin, Germany. During that trip, we did performances in Berlin, Frankfurt, Hamburg and other cities. I performed Chaquan, Meihua sabre, locking spear, and other vigorous forms that, with their fast movement and sudden stops, and unique characteristics, made people gasp in admiration. The barehand versus spear partner form that I did with Wen Jingming was the most popular, receiving great rounds of applause. This was the first time that Chinese wushu had seen such success on the international stage. Although the Chinese Olympic team failed dismally at this Olympic Games in the official events, the wushu team's performances of our traditional people's sport brought glory to our country. Foreign friends loved and praised the three characteristics of China's wushu – that it was a health building sport, that it was practical, and that it was aesthetically pleasing to watch.

In August 1936, I took up teaching, research, and organisational leadership in wushu, beginning my long term involvement in the sport's 'battlefront'. I worked at the Shanghai Sports Science School, the State Maintained Sports Research School, the Tianjin Hebei Sports Normal College, and finally the Beijing Sports Institute. Of these, I have spent the longest time at the Beijing Sports Institute, starting there in 1953, indeed from its founding until now – so that is over forty years. Wushu has undergone immense development during this time. During this period, I have done, or participated in, teaching, research, coaching, and other work with great success. It doesn't need mentioning that Chinese wushu could only have seen this fast, extensive, and deep development in the New China, with the great, glorious, and correct leadership of the China Communist Party.[1] Only in this way has wushu become ready for promotion throughout Asia and the world.

I have been responsible over many years for teaching wushu in the educational system. I have been on the panel of judges and the professorship appraisal group at the Beijing Sports Institute for many years. Since 1963 I have made innovations in developing the nation's first graduate students and starting foreign students' wushu classes, in addition to cultivating and training a great many wushu and coaching professionals. Among these students, some became professors, associate professors, high level coaches, and ministry level cadres. They are currently working diligently in their individual positions to advance the sport of wushu. I am very pleased to see this.

As well as my teaching, I have done a great deal of work in the community. I participated in the committees that developed the standardised fist, spear, sabre, sword and staff forms, that developed the new style competition rules, and that developed the judging criteria for wushu competitions. I have been the head judge at national and international wushu competitions, and chairman of arbitration committees. I am an accredited national judge

---

[1] Translator's note: The author skips the years from 1966 to 1972 that he, and many other wushu masters, were sent down and re-educated for being wushu professionals and teachers. From 1969 to 1972, Zhang was sent down to rural Shanxi for re-education through labour. He preferred that to the constant criticism sessions on campus, and was able to practice wushu on the sly. The Sports Institute re-opened in 1972, and Zhang was able to return to Beijing. Saying that the Party was working constantly on the development of wushu is a bit 'playing it safe' for publication, I feel.

in wushu, weight lifting, and wresting. I have worked tirelessly towards making the sport of wushu more rational, standardised, and systematic. During the same time, I also researched into and tried to put in order materials on the traditional styles. I have written over ten books, the main ones being *China's Chaquan, An Aggregate Form For Chaquan, A Youth Form, Broadcast Taijiquan, Chinese Style Wrestling*, and *Spring Kicks*. I have published articles on research results, such as *Research Into Sparring Techniques*, and *Origins of China's Chaquan*. I have worked as editor-in-chief, and also written some of the materials in works such as *Collection On China's Olympic Games: Wushu Volume*, and *Sports Encyclopedia, Wushu Volume*. I feel that this work has gone some way in contributing to the development of wushu, the enrichment of theoretical knowledge about wushu, and bringing new rationalisation to the contents of traditional styles of wushu.

In order to carry on and develop China's wushu, the national sports governing body asked people in the key sports institutes to take part in the project of searching out and organising traditional wushu. I enthusiastically responded to this call. Because my main style was Chaquan, I took part in the work on Chaquan. In the winter of 1983, I took a small group of researchers to the homeland of Chaquan, throughout the North-west. We paid no heed to the winter's cold or the distances traveled, and set up many meetings, courtesy calls, and observations of many different teachers, saw many flavours of performances, found many writings about Chaquan, discovered some grassroots histories, collected many materials, and wrote up *China's Chaquan Forms*, and *Primary Exploration Into The Origins Of Chaquan*. Much of this material has made it into this book, for the enjoyment of the general readership. It is the result of a relatively systematic and complete research into Chaquan as a whole.

Over the past thirty years, I also took part in exchanges and promotion of wushu on the international stage. I have acted as coach, referee, expert, and team leader in many trips abroad. In 1960 I was an athlete in the troupe that travelled with Premier Zhou Enlai on the friendship trip in Myanmar (formerly Burma). Between 1980 and now, I have visited Japan five times. In February 1990, at the request of Hong Kong Chinese University, I took part in the report, *Development And Trends In China's Wushu*. I've experienced a wide variety of learning exchanges of all types, passed on and promoted China's wushu, and have also made many friends and helped spread wushu in Asia, Africa, North America, and other areas. I gathered together my experience in this work in teaching wushu abroad over many years, and in 1985, wrote *An Examination Of Teaching Methods Abroad, Recollections Of The View From Under Mount Fuji – Memoires Of Teaching In Japan* and other articles. In these, I expressed my ideas on how to better promulgate wushu teaching and exchanges abroad. In 1990, the formation of the International Wushu Association showed that the sport of wushu is making its way onto the world stage. Wushu has already been made an official event in the Eleventh and Twelfth Asian Games. I have seen with own eyes how wushu has developed quickly, and believe that it will one day make it into the Olympic Games as an official sport, and become popular around the word. Wushu began in China, but belongs to the world.

On July 25, 1980, I became a member of the Chinese Communist Party, becoming a new soldier in the vanguard of the proletariat. This realised a thirty-year desire of mine. On the eighth of November, 1986, the Beijing Sports Institute held a celebration of my fiftieth year anniversary of teaching wushu. I was most moved by this, and most grateful. I am just an ordinary wushu teacher, who, with the cultivation of the Party, was able to do the work that I ought to do. But the Party and the people have given me great credit and honour. I have received an award for working in Beijing Sports for thirty years, a medal for national sports, a medal for international wushu, and an award from the New China Sports, among others. I have also been given a special award from the government for intellectual contributions. I have been a committee member of the National Sports Assembly, the vice-chairman of the National Wushu Association, a committee member of the National Science Association Training Sub Committee, vice-director of the National Wushu Association, director and professor of Beijing Sports Institute Wushu Department, committee member of National Elderly Sports Association, and committee member of the National Gerontology Committee, among others.

Now, as I approach my eightieth year, I am gratified to see that, thanks to the diligence of many wushu workers, wushu has developed with deep roots and new growth, and has a vital life. Wushu, a valued cultural treasure of China, has not only developed, but is moving out into the world. I will certainly, with all my force, continue to do my best to help wushu develop.

Zhang Wenguang

May, 1994

TRANSLATOR'S PREFACE

I published the Chaquan forms of Zhang Wenguang's 1985 book *China's Chaquan* in 2023 as *Zhang Wenguang's Chaquan*, then the remaining forms in that book in 2024 (Huaquan, Paoquan, Hongquan, and Tuiquan) as *Zhang Wenguang's Chaquan Volume II*. I then found a book in my shelves that professor Zhang published in 1995 on the Cha system weapons. So, here it is, as *Zhang Wenguang's Chaquan Volume III*.

Professor Zhang (1915-2010) was the head of the martial arts department at the Beijing Physical Culture Institute (Beijing Sports University) from 1953 to 1994, and was actively involved in researching and writing about Chaquan when I was a wushu student there, from 1980 to 1983. I learned the Chaquan fourth form at the Beijing Physical Culture Institute in 1982, but did not learn its particular weapons. I saw a lot of Chaquan, enough to appreciate the style and want to help professor Zhang promulgate it.

As usual, while going through the book I corrected some typos and errors that were in the original Chinese text. I would like to mention that in the text 'forward' and 'in front' sometimes means 'in the direction of travel' and sometimes 'in relation to the way the torso is facing'. You can usually tell which by context and the images, but sometimes I have made a comment to clarify.

I hope that you enjoy this book.

Andrea Falk

(Aka Huo Andi 霍安娣)

Morin-Heights and Quebec City, QC, Canada

January 2025

EDITOR'S PREFACE

Chaquan is one of the more complete systems of martials arts in China, and as such is very popular among the people. The system includes the five categories that comprise many martial arts: basics, empty hand forms, weapons forms, partner forms (bare handed and weapons), and sparring training.

Chaquan has had weapons forms for a long time, but they have been transmitted traditionally, from one person to another, and not been written down. Because of the lack of systematic and complete records, some forms have been gradually lost, and research to discover complete information on weapons is difficult. This book endeavours to document the flavour and characteristics of Chaquan weapons by following the national sports federation guidelines: "Beijing Physical Education Institute, and the other six core sport institutes, should carry out research into the major martial styles and their weapons". We have spent many years studying and practising Chaquan and its weapons. We have investigated traditional Chaquan and weapons, completed surveys, held conferences, done analyses, and undergone many methods of study. Finally, we have gained a complete picture of representative Chaquan weapons and have been able to organise this in a coherent manner.

There are many weapons in the Chaquan system, generally called the 'big eight', which refer to the sabre, spear, sword, staff, hooks, batons, trident, and cutter. Each of them has a number of forms. From among the most popular Chaquan weapons – how to we pick those that seem easier to make popular? How do we continue to develop these forms? We compared them, trying them all out. We felt that the trident was too heavy and sluggish, not terribly popular among the masses, and so would present difficulties in popularization, so we took courage and omitted it. The crescent moon blade, on the other hand, is very popular among the people, so we have included it. We have selected eight representative weapons forms to propagate: the Cha sabre, Kunwu sword, locking spear, shepherd's staff, Cha hooks, horse controlling batons, two-handed cutter, and the crescent moon blade. These we can call 'the new eight' main weapons.

During our work on researching and organizing the Chaquan representative weapons, we held to two principles. One, to not have moves that go against wushu competition rules. That is, to take out repetitive moves, to keep a clean structure, to have the forms stay within a rectangular area, and to ensure that all the moves connect in a natural, harmonious, manner. Two, to make sure that each weapon maintains its own flavour and characteristics. Each one – whether the standard weapons such as sabre, spear, sword, and staff, or the unusual weapons such as hooks, batons, cutter and crescent blade – has its own techniques that are combined with the methods, footwork, and bodywork of Chaquan. Each form fully reflects the training value and artistry of both Chaquan and the weapon. For example, the Cha sabre, locking spear, and shepherd's staff all show characteristics standard to those weapons – 'a sabre is as fierce as a tiger', 'the spear stabs in a straight line', and 'the staff swings in a big circle'. The Kunlun sword and Cha hooks reflect the artistry of 'a sword is like a flying phoenix', 'hooks are lively, powerful, and floating'. These Chaquan weapons forms keep the expansive postures, the precise movements, the quickness and agility, the clear rhythm, the mixture of hard and soft, and the lively movements of Chaquan. They also add the specific weapon techniques such as pierce, chop, stab, slice up, flowers, spins, and jumps. All of these forms are true to life, aesthetically beautiful, bold and powerful, and expansive.

This book, then, is the culmination of a great deal of work, during which time we sought out the genuine, cleared out the chaff, and kept the essentials. We counted on our own experience and referred to many resources. Finally, we can present the results to the martial arts readers. We thank, among many others, comrades Zhang Manli and Zhang Wuyuan for their help.

We have worked hard during the process of writing this book, but there cannot help but contain some insufficiencies. For this we beg the indulgence of the readers, and ask for critiques.

Editorial Committee

May, 1994

INTRODUCTION TO THE REPRESENTATIVE WEAPONS OF THE CHA SYSTEM

Chaquan is one of the more complete systems of Chinese martial arts, and as such is very popular. It has foundational exercises, empty hand forms, weapons forms, partner forms (barehand, and weapons), and sparring training, indeed, five important categories that comprise martial arts. Its main training exercises include hand folding (involving pulling and sliding), the ten spring kicks lines, sandbag training, stone weights, stone locks [tr. note: like kettlebells], twisting poles, and snapping leather straps. Its barehand forms include ten Chaquan forms, four Huaquan forms, three Paoquan forms, four Hongquan forms, and two Tuiquan forms. These have already been written up in a book. [Tr. note: *China's Chaquan*, translated by myself as *Zhang Wenguang's Chaquan* and *Zhang Wenguang's Chaquan Volume II.*] In this book, we will introduce Chaquan's representative weapons forms.

The Past And Present of Weaponry Training

During the vigorous development of wushu as a sport, weapons have become more and more popular and the skill level has risen considerably. The construction and difficulty level of the forms has been continuously developing. The conventional weapons of sabre, spear, sword and staff, particularly, now have standardised weights, heights, diameters, and components, making the sport of weaponry better structured. In 1957, the National Sports Commission set up a wushu work group, which created many weapons forms, based on traditional forms of the sabre, sword, spear, and staff. This served to promote and popularise the sport of wushu weaponry. In 1979, after the National Sports Commission promulgated the circular *Unearth and Collate The Wushu Legacy*, widespread and deep work around the country began seeking out and classifying all sorts of wushu treasures. Many weapons forms, buried for many years, once again regained their lustre. This year, in May, at the National Wushu Exchange Meet held in Nanning, a galaxy of talents converged to show their once-hidden skills. Each weapon form had undergone some work to 'weed out the old to bring forth the new'. The composition of the forms was well-knit, and the flavour outstanding. The spectators enjoyed them immensely.

The Type And Characteristics Of These Chaquan Representative Weapons

There are many types of weapons in wushu, with the usual saying that there are eighteen standard weapons. The most commonly seen are sabre, spear, sword, and staff. To complete the eighteen, there are also the dagger-axe, halberd, hooks, crutch, shield, whip, mace, axe, shovel, and trident, among others [tr. note, not always the same eighteen in all lists, also often included are mallet, pole, pike, rake]. They are generally placed into one of three categories according to their characteristics – long, short, or soft. Long weapons include the spear, staff, and halberd. Short weapons include the sabre, sword, and hooks. Soft weapons include jointed weapons such as the nine-section whip and the three-section staff. Chaquan system weapons are a subdivision of this overall categorisation, and include sabre, spear, sword, staff, batons, cutter, hooks, and trident. These are called the 'big eight' weapons. They each have more than one form for training the needed skills. For example, the sabre has a Cha sabre and a crescent moon sabre. The sword has a Kunwu sword and a Cha sword form. The spear has a locking spear, a Cha spear, and a big spear form. The staff has a shepherd's staff, and a 108 staff form. The hooks have a Cha hooks and a walking hooks form. In addition to these are a horse cutter, a two-handed cutter, and batons. There is a trident, but it is heavy and awkward, and difficult to make, so very few practise it. We chose the crescent moon blade to popularise instead of the trident. We have thus as the representative Chaquan weapons in this book: the Cha sabre, Kunlun sword, locking spear, shepherd's staff, two-handed cutter, crescent moon blade, horse controlling batons, and Cha hooks. These, we can call the 'new big eight' weapons.

These 'new big eight' weapons build on all the main characteristics of Chaquan. Each has its own flavour, according to the weapon, as each weapon has its own characteristics that are added to the Chaquan flavour. In this way each one is unique.

The Cha sabre form emphasises the techniques of wrapping the head, chopping, hacking, stabbing, slicing up, parrying, hiding, and flowers. There are five sections with forty-eight moves, with many techniques interspersed throughout. It is quick as the wind, and calls for lively footwork and bodywork. It brings to mind the phrase 'the sabre is like a fierce tiger'. The Cha sabre form fully exhibits the sabre characteristics of boldness, speed, imposing manner, and power.

The Kunlun sword form emphasises the techniques of piercing, slicing up, snapping, dabbing, chopping, and parrying. There are six sections with fifty-six moves. Sword skills involve many techniques, footwork, and bodywork that call for a highly integrated dexterity. The form shows the aesthetically pleasing imagery of alternating stillness with motion, quickness with slowness, rise with fall, and the qualities of turning, lightness, floating, and 'swallow and spit' moves. It is rich in rhythmical imagery.

The locking spear form is a seven section form of fifty-four moves. The main emphasis is on the straight level stab, as 'the spear stabs in a line'. On the foundation of outer trap, inner trap, and stab, it also trains the techniques of flowers, jumping, and other techniques. It utilises many techniques that wrap the throat, and thread through near the neck, so it is called the 'mouth

INTRODUCTION

locking spear'.

The shepherd's staff form is also called 'five tigers flock of sheep staff'. It contains swinging, chopping, slicing up, poking, snapping, dabbing, flowers, and other techniques. It is fifty-eight moves in six sections. In performance, the staff is quick, powerful, and fierce, done with a bold and unrestrained manner. A verse says, "Five tigers mount the wind to leave Shaolin, on the wind Yaksha is seeking the dead; He searches everywhere, overturning flowers and scattering them all over, he occupies a body to carry a willow to search either side; A lone racoon dog hits out to the four gates. Take care as a wild goose lands on the beach. A jade girl threads the shuttle by stepping forward and back. A white ape shoulders the staff and enters a cave". These metaphors describe how the staff form hits to all four corners, swings in large arcing movements, and how its strikes come as densely as falling rain.

The Cha hooks is a double weapon with a multitude of cutting edges. The form has five sections with forty-nine moves. It emphasises hooking, brushing aside, parrying, slicing up, and pushing. Hooking and parrying are particularly utilised. In performance of this weapon, we emphasise 'the hooks move like breaking waves'. That is to say, one move after another combines smoothly with bodywork. It is said that the hooks move with the body, and the body follow the hooks. The body must be agile and the stepping light, to bring about lively and floating hooks.

The horse controlling batons form is forty-six moves in five sections, which emphasise chopping, stabbing, slicing up, poking, sweeping, and flowers. The structure is compact, the flavour unique. It contains a lot of jumps and spins, and thoroughly uses the fighting technique of sticks. The horse controlling batons form truly has a style of its own.

The two-handed cutter, also called the Pudao [tr. note: in English, often called a horse cutter], trains mostly chopping, hacking, slicing up, smearing, parrying, brandishing, and flowers. The form is fifty-one moves in six sections. The use of the long handle with the blade makes for clear and precise techniques, combined hard and soft movements, rolling and turning, and a full coordination of the body with the weapon.

The crescent moon blade, also called the big blade or the eighteenth blade [tr. note: in English, often called a halberd or General Guan's blade, though the crescent moon blade is more curved than the Guan's blade], has a form of six sections containing fifty-five moves. Because it is a long, heavy, weapon, it uses a lot of big chops and big hacks. The form is long, and shows an imposing mien, and is powerful and rigorous. Its main techniques are chopping, hacking, slicing up, parrying, smearing, sweeping, and flowers.

CHAQUAN, VOLUME III

The Main Skill Requirements Of The Chaquan Representative Weapons Forms

1. The methods are clear and cleanly done.

Each different weapon has its own particular techniques, and each has strict performance requirements. Weapons techniques change as the moves change. Each technique in a Chaquan weapons form, such as chop, hack, slice up, stab, parry, and flowers, must be done according to specific requirements. The changes from one to the next must be clean and clear, and the methods must not be messy or disorderly. Only by mastering the specific requirements for each technique with each weapon, can you hope to use them in real situations. Then you can move adeptly, use them with a degree of naturalness, and bring out each one's unique character. With mastery, the rich contents of the forms and their character will stand out. For example, the locking spear's main combination of outer trap, inner trap, and stab is a basic move of the spear. The saying 'the spear stabs in a straight line' means that the stab is level and fast, going directly in and directly out, with power reaching the tip of the spear. The stab has a high level stab, a middle level stab, and a low level stab, but the mid level stab is the main one. Thus the saying, 'the middle level spear, the spear is the king, one strike of the middle is hard to defend against'. Because of this, the same 'level stab' that shows up in many different combinations is done with varying requirements. The practitioner must master each and every one.

2. The weapon must work in coordination with the body.

Chaquan weapons are done with long range, expansive movements. This makes for high requirements in terms of the flexibility and elasticity of all muscle groups, tendons, and ligaments. In addition, the forms are performed in one flowing whole, and quickly, which requires a high degree of endurance and speed. Furthermore, the moves are comparatively difficult, with extensions and flexions, twists and turns, balances, leaps, rollovers, jumps, and tumbling. Moves are continuous and may be repeated, which takes a great degree of coordination. The techniques in each form require that the handwork, bodywork, and footwork are well practiced. Both high and low, upper and lower, must be considered, while front and rear must link together seamlessly. In addition to this, each specific technique of each individual weapon must be understood, and everything must be coordinated with the breath. The hands (weapons) must work with the eyes, to show that spirit and body combine as one. The weapons must be integrally combined with the actions and footwork, so that body and weapons become one. For example, the Cha sabre does many moves in which the left hand assists the action of the sabre in the right hand – the left arm may extend out or gather in, open or close, so that the overall move is harmonious, aesthetically pleasing, and adds to the power of the sabre. This is why there is the saying, 'to judge the single sabre, watch the left hand'. As another example, in the form of the locking spear, it is not enough to do the basic spear techniques correctly. They must be fully and strictly coordinated with the footwork and bodywork. The footwork must be light but stable – 'move like the wind, stand still like a nail'. The bodywork must be agile and varied and show that 'the spear is like a swimming dragon'. Furthermore, the spear requires strength in the waist and legs, arms, and wrists that combines the spear and body as one so that power penetrates through to the spear tip. Only in this way can the each and every move be coordinated and perfect.

3. Hard and pliant power interact and interchange.

'Hard and pliant' is a law of wushu power that is fully achieved in Chaquan weaponry. Hard and pliant, often comparable to attack and defence, combine to work together. In general, defensive actions use pliant power while attacking actions use hard power. When using a weapon, if one wants to utilise the interaction of hard and soft or pliant power, one cannot ignore the principle of attack and defense. For example, in the first section of the Cha sabre form, the sixth move, 'retreat with a head wrap', and the seventh move 'empty stance smear', the retreating step and the coiling around the back are defensive and pliant, while the smearing and stabbing are a flat sweeping hack – attacking and hard. Sometimes you need to use both hard and pliant within what is called one move. For example, in the second move of the first section, 'step forward cradle the sabre', the opening of the move is pliant, while the completion of the move is hard. If this move doesn't start out softly, then it cannot finish with hard power. Within each move of the weapons forms, you must master the correct and proper use of the interaction and interchange of hard and pliant.

4. There is a distinctive rhythm.

Chaquan weapons forms have very strict requirements as to the rhythm that occurs in the transition between fast action and stillness. All the moves of all the forms, and all the individual moves, show a clear rhythm of fast and slow, moving and stillness. That is to say, each these two elements must be present. Firstly, a movement should be fast and fierce, while a position should be still and stable. In addition, the whole form has three phases. In the opening phase, the movements should be stable and clear. In the peak phase, the movements should gradually accelerate. Every rise and fall, every turn, every dodge and jump, and every difficult move should progressively give place to the next. In the closing phase, the speed can decelerate, and gradually settle down.

CHAQUAN, VOLUME III

Points To Focus On During Performance

1. How to chose which weapon to practise.

If you want to train a Chaquan weapon, you must master the open hand forms first, to build a base on which to work. As for beginners, the weapon choice will vary with each individual, according to their preference and body type. A short person may choose a short weapon. A well conditioned person with good strength might chose a large weapon. An agile person may choose the hooks or spear. Among all the weapons, the spear is perhaps the most difficult, certainly not easy to master. It is said, 'it takes years to learn empty hand methods, months to learn the staff, and a long, long time for the spear'. No matter which weapon you chose, you must practice the basics. For example, learning the Cha sabre, practise chopping slicing up, and hacking. Learning the Cha hooks, practice hooking and parrying.

2. How to pick an individual weapon.

There is a large variety of weapons, made from varying materials. So, before starting to train with one, you must take care to pick one that is well made and able to withstand training in Chaquan. Make sure that the sabre blade and spear head have no nicks and are solidly in place, to prevent injury to yourself or standers by. In addition when training, pay attention to safety, don't play with weapons as if they are toys, and certainly don't aim them at people.

3. Do a thorough warmup before practising weapons.

The actions of the weapons use large range of movement and consume considerable energy and strength. You must do a proper general warm up, then practise some movements that your weapon requires. For example, do wrist and waist movements to warm up and relax those muscles.

4. Don't wear over-loose clothes.

The movements in weapons forms are expansive, and weapons have a certain weight, so be sure not to wear very loose clothing, so that your clothes don't get caught on a weapon and perhaps cause injury.

CHA SABRE

查刀

ABOUT THE CHA SABRE

The sabre is made up of a grip, a guard, and a curved, single-edged blade. The parts of the blade are the spine, the cutting edge, and the tip. The whole blade can be differentiated into the fore-section – the half nearest the tip – and aft-section – the half nearest the guard. Silks, or flags, may be attached to the end of the grip.

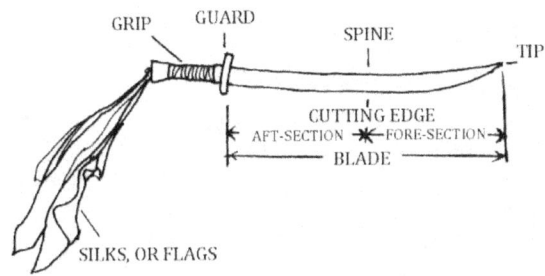

The length of the sabre that an individual will use is determined by cradling the sabre by the guard, upright at the side with the arm straight, the spine of the blade tucked into the elbow crease. The tip should reach at least the top of the ear.

The blade is curved and single-edged, and may be made of metal, wood, or bamboo. There is no weight restriction. The silks should not be longer than the blade, and may be left off entirely.

Cradling means to place the palm at the guard, tucking the thumb and forefinger on one side and the other fingers on the other side, so that all fingers cradle the guard. The wrist is held straight so that the spine of the blade is tight to the forearm.

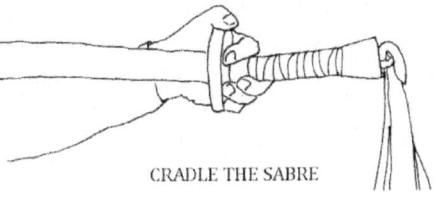

CRADLE THE SABRE

Holding, or grasping, means to hold the grip with the thumb web close to the guard and on the topside – facing the spine of the blade.

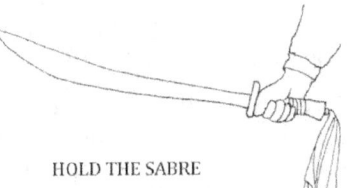

HOLD THE SABRE

The hand not holding the sabre (usually the left hand) generally holds the shape of an open palm or a hook. The palm is held with the thumb bent and tucked in, or straight and opened out. The fingers are held together, straight, and pulled back. The hook is made by bending the wrist and pinching the fingers and thumb together or pressing the thumb, index and middle fingers together and leaving the other fingers together and straight within the hook.

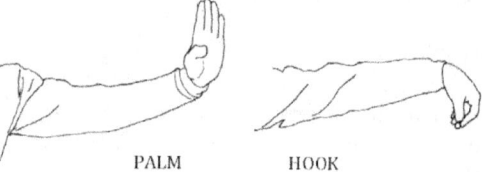

PALM   HOOK

THE MAIN TECHNIQUES OF THE CHA SABRE

Coil the Head and Wrap the Brain: Coil the Head is to hang the blade upside down, the blade spine lies on the left arm, then circles around the upper back to pass the right shoulder, keeping the head straight. The Wrap the Brain is to hang the blade upside down, the blade spine lies on the right shoulder, then circles around along the upper back to pass the left shoulder, keeping the head straight.

Chop: Come down from above with the power going to the cutting edge of the blade, the arm and blade forming a straight line. A swinging chop follows a vertical circle at the right or left side of the body, finishing with a chop into the cutting edge of the blade. A rear swinging chop is done by coordinating a full turn of the body with the swinging chop.

Hack: Chop down at an angle to the right or left side with the wrist cocked, putting power to the middle of the cutting edge.

Slice up: Slice forward and up with the cutting edge turned up, power going to the fore-section. An upright slice up is when the forearm is laterally rotated to turn the palm up, so that the blade circles at the right side, keeping close to the body, slicing up in front with power going to the fore-section. A reverse slice up is when the blade circles at the left side of the body to slice up in front, the forearm medially rotated, power also going to the fore-section.

Stab: Pierce directly forward with the tip, the arm and blade aligned straight. The cutting edge may be up, down, or left. A flat stab is when the tip is at shoulder height. An upwards stab is when the tip is above head height. A downward stab is when the tip is at knee height.

Parry: Hook by moving the tip up then back, or down then to either side, the power going to the spine of the blade. An upper parry is when the blade goes up and back, hooking tightly to the body. A lower parry is when the blade goes down and to either side towards the rear, also keeping tight to the body. A swinging parry is when the blade draws a full vertical circle tight to the body while hooking with the spine.

Hide: A wrapping hide is to wrap the blade around the waist, drawing it flat across until it is on the left side, the tip facing back, edge facing out. A standing hide is when the blade is vertical behind the left arm. A flat hide is when the blade is standing with the tip pointing forward and the cutting edge down, tucked in behind the right hip.

Flowers: Pivoting around the wrist, circle the blade vertically close to the body. This may be done normal or reversed, behind the body or in front. 'Chopping flowers' is when the circle is done with the cutting edge coming down when moving forward at the sides. 'Slicing flowers' is when the circle is done with the cutting edge coming up when moving forward at the sides. No matter which flowers are being done, there must be a clear distinction between the blade spine and the cutting edge, and the cutting movement must be smooth.

NAMES OF THE MOVEMENTS OF THE CHA SABRE FORM

Position Of Preparation
Section One
1. Step Forward, Cradle The Sabre
2. Empty Stance Carry The Sabre
3. Raised Knee Framing Block
4. Jump To Bow Stance Smear
5. Bow Stance Stab
6. Retreat, Coil The Head And Wrap The Brain
7. Empty Stance Smear
8. Raised Knee Framing Block
9. Jump To Bow Stance Stab
10. Turn Around, Bow Stance Chop
11. Empty Stance Cradle The Sabre
12. Jump To Bow Stance Stab
13. Drop Stance Press Down
14. Jump To Bow Stance Push
15. Drop Stance Press Down
16. Bow Stance Coil The Head
17. Jumping Turn, Empty Stance Smear

Section Two
18. Right Empty Stance Slice Up
19. Left Empty Stance Slice Up
20. Right Empty Stance Slice Up
21. Right Bow Stance Stab
22. Turn Around, Framing Block

CHAQUAN, VOLUME III

23. Jumping Turn, Empty Stance Smear

Section Three

24. Hastening Step
25. Right Bow Stance Stab
26. Hastening Step
27. Jumping Turn, Bow Stance Stab
28. Turn Around, Bow Stance Framing Block
29. Jumping Turn, Empty Stance Smear

Section Four

30. High Empty Stance Framing Block
31. Hastening Step
32. Jumping Turn, Drop Stance Chop
33. Drop Stance Press Down
34. Jump To Bow Stance Framing Block And Push
35. Jumping Turn, Drop Stance Smear

Section Five

36. Back-Cross Step, Cradle The Sabre
37. Side Thrust Kick
38. Step Forward, Chop
39. Flowers, Horse Stance Tuck The Sabre At The Back
40. Tornado Kick With The Sabre Tucked At The Back
41. Horse Stance With The Sabre Tucked At The Back
42. Turn Around, Bow Stance Framing Block
43. Jumping Turn, Empty Stance Smear
44. Bow Stance Stab
45. Bow Stance, Coil And Wrap The Head, Framing Block
46. Turn Around, Bow Stance Carry
47. High Empty Stance Flash Palm
48. Withdraw And Cradle The Sabre
49. Closing Posture

0. Position Of Preparation   yùbèi shì   预备势

Stand to attention with the heels together and feet turned slightly out. Hold the guard in the left hand with the blade's spine tucked inside the left forearm, the tip pointing up. Let the arms hang in a relaxed manner. Look forward. (image 1.0a) Medially rotate the arms slightly, bending the elbows. Turn the right palm down and turn in the fingers. Look to the left side. (image 1.0b)

1.0a   b

CHA SABRE

Section One

1. Step Forward, Cradle The Sabre   shàngbù bào dāo   上步抱刀

Step the left foot forward and shift forward, lifting the right heel, keeping both legs almost straight. Separate the hands out to either side to raise them with the arms slanting downwards. Look to the left side. (image 1.1a) Step the right foot forward and shift forward, lifting the left heel, still keeping the legs almost straight. Continue to raise the hands at the sides until they are level, turning the left palm forward so that the blade edge turns up. Continue to look to the left side. (image 1.1b) Bring the left foot up beside the right foot and stand up, reaching the torso forward slightly. Circle the hands forward to cradle the sabre in front of the chest, palms in. The right hand is placed on the back of the left hand. The sabre spine lies on top of the left forearm with the blade edge up and the tip pointing left. Continue to look to the left. (image 1.1c)

Keep the stepping light, and bring the left foot in to meet the right with a quick and light step. The arms should make a natural circle. The completion of the closed stance coordinates with the cradling of the sabre.

1.1a   b   c

2. Empty Stance Carry The Sabre   xūbù tuō dāo   虚步托刀

Turn to face left and withdraw the right foot, touching down the ball of the foot and bending both knees. Separate the hands to either side, lowering them. Look forward [tr. note: in the direction that the form will travel]. (image 1.2a) Shift back and settle the right heel, lifting the left heel slightly and bending both knees further, to take a left empty stance. Carry the sabre up in front of the chest, still in the left hand, with the blade edge up and the tip pointing back. Place the left hand in the right hand. Keep looking forward. (image 1.2b)

Make a clear distinction between the weighted and unweighted legs. Form a natural circle with the arms when

1.2a   b

11

CHAQUAN, VOLUME III

carrying the sabre.

3. Raised Knee Framing Block   tíxī jià dāo   提膝架刀

Raise the left knee with the foot pointing down. Stand up on the right leg, almost straightening it. Take the grip in the right hand with the thumb web snug to the guard, pressing the blade's spine on top of the left forearm, cutting edge up. Support the right wrist with the left hand. Continue to look forward. (image 1.3)

Keep the one-legged stance stable. Grasp the grip firmly with the right hand.

4. Jump To Bow Stance Smear   tiào gōngbù mǒ dāo   跳弓步抹刀

Land the left foot forward, pressing it forward and raising the right heel with the knee slightly bent. Look forward. (image 1.4a) Push into the right foot to shift forward, lifting the right foot up behind with the knee bent. Press the blade down in front, and circle to pull it up behind with the tip down. Push forward with the left hand, fingers up. Look forward. (image 1.4b) Push off with the left foot to jump up. Laterally rotate the right arm to lift the blade up behind. Press down slightly with the left hand, palm down. Look forward. (image 1.4c) Land the right foot forward, then the left, and press the left knee forward. Straighten the right leg to take a left bow stance. Bring the right hand over from behind to circle down in front, pressing the blade down at the right side of the body, edge down, tip forward. Bring the left hand in, then push forward again, fingers up. Look forward. (image 1.4d)

Make the jump light, and land into a stable bow stance. Make sure to draw a full circle with the blade, and to coordinate the action of the hands with the sabre.

5. Bow Stance Stab   gōngbù zhā dāo   弓步扎刀

Without changing the stance, stab straight forward into the tip of the sabre, the arm and blade in a straight line, blade edge down, tip forward. Bring the left hand in to the right wrist. Look forward. (image 1.5)

CHA SABRE

Stab quickly and strongly.

6. Retreat, Coil The Head And Wrap The Brain

tuìbù chántóu guǒnǎo   退步缠头裹脑

Bring the blade spine to the outside of the left shoulder, circling the right hand up over the head to coil around it, tucking the blade onto the back. Hold the left hand out to the left side. Look forward. (image 1.6a) Retreat the left foot a half-step behind, touching down the ball of the foot and bending both legs. Circle the sabre around to the right, pulling it around to lay the blade spine on top of the left arm, edge up, tip back. Place the left hand on the right wrist. Look forward. (image 1.6b) Shift back, then retreat the right foot a full step. Pull the sabre back on the right side, up and around, to place the blade spine behind the head on the left side. Hold the left hand out to the left side. Look forward. (image 1.6c)

The blade coils on the left to the rear, then on the right to the front, and then on the right to the rear. Keep the blade spine close to the body throughout the coiling.

7. Empty Stance Smear   xūbù mǒ dāo   虚步抹刀

Shift back and withdraw the left foot a half-step, touching down the ball of the foot to take a left empty stance. Circle the blade forward, then down on the right, pulling it back to beside the right hip, edge down, tip forward. Bring the left hand in to the chest then push forward, fingers up. Look forward. (image 1.7)

Be sure to sit into a well-defined empty stance.

1.7

8. Raised Knee Framing Block   tíxī jià dāo   提膝架刀

Raise the left knee, turning the body slightly to the left and standing up on the right leg with the knee slightly bent. Raise the blade in front, to the left, edge up and tip back. Press the left hand on the right wrist. Look to the forward left. (image 1.8)

Stand firmly.

1.8

9. Jump To Bow Stance Stab   tiào gōngbù zhā dāo   跳弓步扎刀

Land the left foot to the forward left, touching down on the ball of the foot, and raising the right leg up behind. Circle the blade down and back, pulling it up with the edge down and tip pointing to the upper rear. Push the left hand to the forward left. Look to the forward left. (image 1.9a) Push off with the left leg to jump up, landing the right foot, then the left, to the forward left. Press into the left knee and straighten the right to take a left bow stance. Circle the blade over so that the tip circles up then stabs to the forward lower left, tip down, cutting edge forward. Press the left hand on the right wrist. Look past the tip. (image 1.9b)

1.9a   b

Jump lightly and stab strongly.

10. Turn Around, Bow Stance Chop

    zhuànshēn gōngbù pī dāo   转身弓步劈刀

Push into the left foot to turn around to the rear right, bending the right knee and straightening the left to take a right bow stance. Circle the blade up and over to the rear right to chop level with the edge down and tip

CHA SABRE

forward, the arm and blade forming a straight line. Hold the left hand out behind. Look forward. (image 1.10)

Turn quickly, set firmly into stance, and chop strongly.

1.10

11. Empty Stance Cradle The Sabre   xūbù bào dāo   虚步抱刀

Bring the right foot a half-step in, touching down the ball of the foot and bending both legs to take a right empty stance. Laterally rotate the right arm and place the hand in front of the chest, so that the blade edge is up, and the tip forward. Press the left hand on the right wrist. Look forward. (image 1.11)

Bring the foot in quickly, and sit into a distinctly weighted / unweighted empty stance.

1.11

12. Jump To Bow Stance Stab   tiào gōngbù zhā dāo   跳弓步扎刀

Raise the right knee, standing on the left leg. Cradle the sabre in both hands in front, at the left. (image 1.12a) Land the right foot forward, pushing off to jump up. Lower the sabre to the forward right with the edge down and tip forward. Lift the left hand out behind. (image 1.12b) Land on the left foot, then the right, setting forward into the right knee and straightening the left into a right bow stance. Stab directly forward with the edge down and tip forward, the blade and right arm forming a straight line. Hold the left arm out behind, fingers up. Look forward. (image 1.12c)

Jump lightly and land with good balance. Stab quickly and strongly.

1.12a   b   c

13. Drop Stance Press Down pūbù yā dāo 仆步压刀

Turn in the right foot and turn to the left, bending the right knee and squatting fully, extending the left leg out into a left drop stance. Circle the blade forward and up and over to the left to press down, edge out, tip pointing left. Press the left hand on the right wrist. Look to the forward left. (image 1.13)

Turn quickly and set firmly into the drop stance. Press down at the same time that you complete the drop stance.

1.13

14. Jump To Bow Stance Push tiào gōngbù tuī dāo 跳弓步推刀

Push into the right foot and bend the knee to lift up the foot behind. Circle the sabre forward and up to do a framing block above the head. Press the left hand on the right wrist. Look forward (image 1.14a) Push off with the left foot to jump up. Circle the sabre, still doing the framing block over the head, over to the rear right. Press the left hand into the right elbow crease. Look forward. (image 1.14b) Land forward on the right foot, then the left, bending the left knee and straightening the right to take a left bow stance. Circle the sabre over to press down in front, then push forward at face height with the edge forward and tip pointing right. Hook the left hand and hold it out to the rear left. Look to the forward left. (image 1.14c)

Jump lightly and land firmly. Push the sabre with power.

1.14a   b   c

15. Drop Stance Press Down pūbù yā dāo 仆步压刀

Push into the left foot and turn it in, shifting back and turning slightly rightward. Bend the right leg and extend the left to sit into a left drop stance. Circle the sabre up and to the left to press flat down in front, the edge facing

CHA SABRE

forward and the tip pointing left. Press the left hand on the right wrist. Look to the forward left. (image 1.15)

Change the stance quickly and stably. Complete the press down and the sit simultaneously.

1.15

16. Bow Stance Coil The Head gōngbù chántóu 弓步缠头

Push into the right foot and shift forward, bending the left knee and straightening the right to take a left bow stance. Circle the sabre up in front to do a flat framing block above the head, edge up, tip pointing left. Hold the left hand out to the side. Look forward. (image 1.16a) Without moving the feet, circle the sabre down and forward, then pull it across in front of the body, edge forward, tip to the left. Press the left hand on the right wrist. Look forward. (image 1.16b)

Draw the spine of the blade along the left arm and back whilst turning, then pull with force.

1.16a   b

17. Jumping Turn, Empty Stance Smear

tiàozhuàn xūbù mǒ dāo   跳转虚步抹刀

Push into the left leg and turn around to the right, standing up on the right leg with the left leg lifted behind. Smear across with the sabre to the rear right, blade lying flat. Hold the left hand out to the side. Look in the direction to which the sabre is smearing. (image 1.17a) Push off with the right foot to jump up and spin around to the right. Pull the sabre around with the turn until it lies behind and above the head. Hold the left hand out to the side. (image 1.17b) Land on the right foot and stand on it, holding the left knee up. Lift the sabre up at the rear right. Hold the left hand down at the side. Look forward. (image 1.17c) Land the left foot forward, just touching down the ball of the foot, sitting into a left empty stance. Circle the sabre forward and down, then pull it back to the outside of the right leg, edge down, tip forward. Bring the left hand to the belly then push forward with the fingers up. Look forward. (image 1.17d)

Jump lightly and land with good balance. Keep the blade tight to the body whilst rotating the body.

Section Two

18. Right Empty Stance Slice Up   yòu xūbù liāo dāo   右虚步撩刀

Stand up naturally on both legs. Circle the sabre forward then up to the rear right above the head, edge up, tip forward. Place the left hand inside the right upper arm. Look forward. (image 1.18a) Take a half-step forward with the left foot and turn slightly to the right. Circle the sabre back, holding it out to the rear right, edge down, tip back. Lower the left hand, circling it forward with a bent arm swing, fingers up. Look to the right side. (image 1.18b) Step the right foot a half-step forward and touch down the ball of the foot, bending both legs to sit into a right empty stance. Turn the body to the left and bend the torso slightly forward. Lower the sabre to slice forward and up, edge up, tip slanting down. Press the left hand on the right wrist. Look to the lower front. (image 1.18c)

Keep the blade close outside the right leg as it slices forward. Complete the slice as the step lands and the body turns.

19. Left Empty Stance Slice Up   zuǒ xūbù liāo dāo   左虚步撩刀

Stand up until the legs are almost straight, and turn slightly to the left. Circle the sabre up, back, and over to the upper rear left, edge facing the rear, tip up. Press the left hand on the right wrist. Look to the rear left. (image 1.19a) Step the right foot a half-step forward and press the knee forward, straightening the left leg. Circle the sabre down on the left side, edge down, tip back. Keep the left hand on the right wrist. Look down to the rear left. (image 1.19b) Turn right, turning the right foot out, and step the left foot forward, touching down the ball of the foot, then sit into a left empty stance. Circle the sabre forward and up, to slice up above the head on the right side, edge up, tip forward. Place the left hand inside the right forearm. Look forward. (image 1.19c)

Keep the blade tight to the outside of the left leg when slicing up. Be sure to step and turn the body to do the slice.

20. Right Empty Stance Slice Up   yòu xūbù liāo dāo   右虚步撩刀

Step the left foot a half-step forward, pressing the knee forward, extending the right leg, and turning slightly to the right. Circle the sabre down at the rear to the right side of the body, edge down, tip back. Keep the left hand on the right forearm. Look down to the rear right. (image 1.20a) Turn left and step the right foot forward, touching down the ball of the foot, then sit into both legs to take a right empty stance. Bring the sabre down and forward, to slice up with the edge up and tip slanting down in front. Press the left hand on the right wrist. Look forward. (image 1.20b)

Keep the blade close outside the right leg when slicing forward, and coordinate the slice with the step and turn.

21. Right Bow Stance Stab yòu gōngbù zhā dāo 右弓步扎刀

Without changing the stance, lower the sabre to in front of the belly, edge down, tip slanting up. Keep the left hand on the right wrist. Look forward. (image 1.21a) Step the right foot forward, pressing the knee forward and straightening the left leg to take a right bow stance. Stab directly forward with the sabre until the arm and blade form a straight line, edge down, tip forward. Hold the left hand out at the side to the rear. Look forward. (image 1.21b)

Step forward quickly and stab strongly.

22. Turn Around, Framing Block zhuànshēn jià dāo 转身架刀

Turn to the left, pressing forward into the left knee and straightening the right to take a left bow stance. Circle the sabre around with the leftward turn to swing it flat across to the rear left, placing the blade spine on top of the left arm, edge up, tip angled back. Place the left hand on the right wrist. Look forward [tr. note: in the new direction of the form]. (image 1.22)

Turn quickly, keeping a stable stance. Swing the sabre with power.

23. Jumping Turn, Empty Stance Smear

tiàozhuàn xūbù mǒ dāo 跳转虚步抹刀

Turn right and stride the right foot a half-step across to the right, turning the foot out and lifting the left heel. Swing and lift the sabre with the turn of the body flat across until the blade faces right and the tip points left. Hold the left hand out to the side. Look forward, to the right. (image 1.23a) Push off with the right foot to jump up, turning around two-seventy degrees whilst airborne. Land on the left foot, keeping the right knee raised. Swing the sabre flat around with the jump, holding the left hand out to the side. Look forward. (image 1.23b) Land the right foot behind, touching down the ball of the foot. Rotate the sabre to place it on the back, putting the spine of the blade tight to the upper back, tip down, edge facing the rear. Lower the

CHA SABRE

left hand, keeping it out to the side. Look forward. (image 1.23c) Settle into the right heel and shift back, lifting the left heel and sitting into the legs to take a left empty stance. Bring the sabre around the outside of the left arm to the front, then pull it back and down on the right side until it is outside the right thigh. The edge is down and the tip forward. Bring the left hand to the belly, then push forward, fingers up. Look forward. (image 1.23d)

Jump and turn lightly, and land firmly, keeping the empty stance distinctly weighted. Keep the blade tight to the back and shoulders whilst coiling.

Section Three

24. Hastening Step   qūbù   趋步

Without changing the positioning of the arms, sabre, and torso, step the left foot forward, shift forward, and push the ball of the right foot into the ground, lifting the heel. Look forward. (image 1.24a) Push off with the left foot to jump up, moving forward and hitting the right foot into the back of the left foot. Look forward and down. (image 1.24b)

Move quickly, go for distance, keep the body and footwork light.

25. Right Bow Stance Stab   yòu gōngbù zhā dāo   右弓步扎刀

Land the right foot, then the left, moving forward and lifting the right leg with a bent knee behind. Look forward. (image 1.25a) Land the right foot forward, bending the knee and straightening the left leg to take a right bow stance. Stab directly forward, until the sabre and right arm form a straight line, edge down, tip forward. Hold the left arm out level behind, to the side. Look forward. (image 1.25)

CHAQUAN, VOLUME III

Take a stable stance and stab strongly.

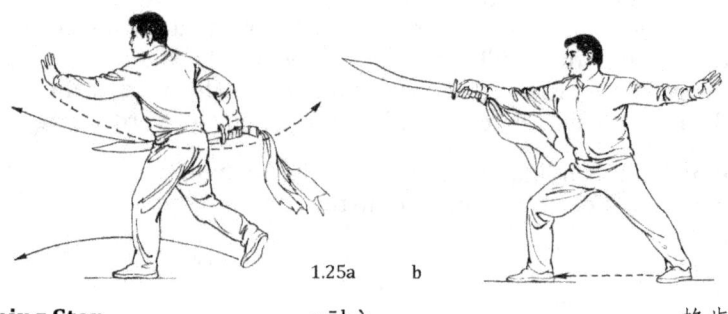

1.25a   b

26. Hastening Step   qūbù   趋步

Without changing the relative position of the torso, arms, and sabre, bring the left foot in to hit the right foot, landing on the ball of the foot. Look forward. (image 1.26a) Settle fully onto the left foot and stand up on it, bending and raising the right knee. Look forward. (image 1.26b)

Lift the right knee immediately and quickly upon the left foot striking the right foot. Stand firmly on the left leg.

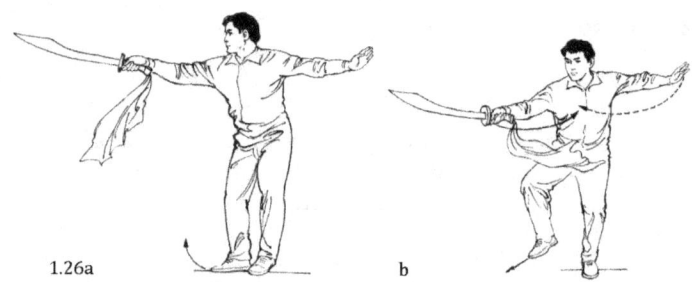

1.26a   b

27. Jumping Turn, Bow Stance Stab

tiàozhuàn gōngbù zhā dāo   跳转弓步扎刀

Land the right foot in front and shift forward, lifting the left heel. Bend the right arm to bring it in to the body, turning the blade edge up and keeping the tip forward. Place the left hand at the right wrist [tr. note: the image has the left hand pushing the end of the grip, where it remains throughout]. Look forward, to the right. (image 1.27a) Bend the left knee and swing it up in front, to the right, turning the body rightward. Turn the sabre to hook the tip flat across to the right. Keep the left hand on the right wrist. Look to the right side. (image 1.27b) Push into the right foot to jump up and turn around one-eighty degrees to the rear right, landing on the left leg and raising the right knee on landing. Bring the sabre in to cradle it in front of the chest, spine tight to the right upper arm, edge out, tip pointing right.

CHA SABRE

Keep the left hand on the right wrist. Look to the right side. (image 1.27c) Turn a further ninety degrees around to the right and land the right foot forward, pressing into the knee and straightening the left leg to take a left bow stance. Stab directly forward until the right arm and sabre form a straight line, with the cutting edge down and tip forward. Hold the left arm out to the rear. Look forward. (image 1.27d)

Keep light but stable whilst turning. Land firmly and stab strongly.

1.27a b c d

28. Turn Around, Bow Stance Framing Block

zhuànshēn gōngbù jià dāo   转身弓步架刀

Turn around to the rear left, pivoting on both feet, bending the left knee and straightening the right leg to take a left bow stance. Cut the sabre across with the turn of the body, keeping the edge out, then pull it flat across to the rear left, placing the spine on top of the left forearm. Place the left hand on the right wrist. Look forward. (image 1.28)

1.28

Turn quickly, keeping steady. Pull the sabre across with power.

29. Jumping Turn, Empty Stance Smear

tiàozhuàn xūbù mǒ dāo   跳转虚步抹刀

Turn around to the rear right and shift to the right leg, lifting the left heel. Pull the sabre around with the turn, to the rear right, with the edge forward and tip pointing left. Bend the left arm and hold it out to the side. Look forward, to the right. (image 1.29a) Swing the left leg forward and push off with the right foot, to jump up and spin to the right rear. Land on the left foot and lift the right knee. Spin the sabre and lift the grip up above the head, keeping the blade tight to the upper back. Hold the left arm out to the left. Look forward, to the right. (image 1.29b) Continuing to turn rightward, land the right foot behind and bend both legs, touching down the left foot, to take a left empty stance. Bring the sabre over to the front, then pull it back behind to place it outside the right leg, edge down, tip forward. Slide the left hand along the top of the sabre spine then push forward, fingers up. Look forward. (image 1.29c)

Jump and turn quickly and lightly. Land firmly.

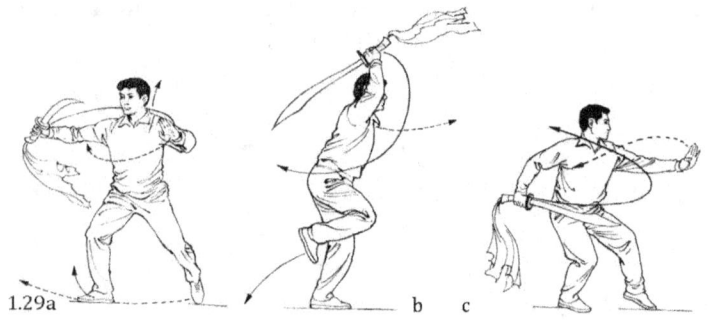

1.29a b c

Section Four

30. High Empty Stance Framing Block   gāoxūbù jià dāo   高虚步架刀

Stand up to a natural high empty stance. Circle the blade forward and up, to do a framing block above the head at the right, edge up, tip forward. Place the left hand inside the right arm. Look forward, to the left. (image 1.30)

Although in a higher stance, keep the usual empty stance distinction between weighted and unweighted legs.

1.30

31. Hastening Step   qūbù   趋步

Take a half-step forward with the left foot and shift forward, straightening the right leg. Circle the sabre back and down, edge down, tip back, turning the torso slightly to the right. Hold the left arm out to the side. Look down, back towards the sabre tip. (image 1.31a) Keep moving, tapping the right foot into the left foot whilst lifting the left foot and moving forward. Land on the right foot. Look forward and down. (image 1.31b) Land the left foot in front and bend the knee, straightening the right. Look down, back to the sabre tip. (image 1.31c)

Tap the feet together quickly and land firmly.

CHA SABRE

1.31a   b   c

32. Jumping Turn, Drop Stance Chop

tiàozhuàn pūbù pī dāo   跳转仆步劈刀

Push into the right foot and shift forward, turning left and raising the right knee, lifting up onto the left foot with the heel up. Slice the sabre down and forward in an arcing slice up, edge up, tip forward, slanting down. Lift the left hand up above the head at the left. Look forward, to the right. (image 1.32a) Push into the left foot to jump up, spinning around to the rear left. Land on the right foot, then the left, bending the left knee to squat fully, and extending the right leg to take a right drop stance. Circle the sabre up and around to the left to chop down, edge down, tip pointing right. Hold the left hand up at the left side, slightly bent. Look down, to the right. (image 1.32b)

Turn quickly and chop strongly. Land into a stable drop stance.

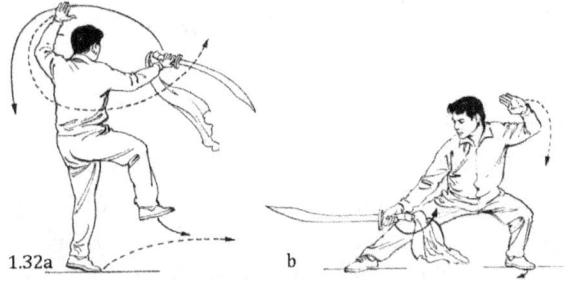

1.32a   b

33. Drop Stance Press Down   pūbù yā dāo   仆步压刀

Push into the left foot to shift to the right, turn leftward, and squat fully on the right leg, extending the left leg to take a left drop stance. Bring the sabre up, then circle it leftward, turning it over to press down, edge out, tip pointing left. Hold the left hand out, slanting downward. Look to the left side. (image 1.33)

Shift across quickly, keeping stable. Press down with power.

1.33

34. Jump To Bow Stance Framing Block And Push

tiào gōngbù jià tuī dāo   跳弓步架推刀

Push into the right foot and shift to the left, bending and raising the right knee. Circle the sabre forward and up to do a framing block above the head in front, edge up, tip pointing left. Slide the left hand along under the blade spine. Look forward. (image 1.34a) Push off with the left foot to jump up. Land the right foot, then the left, bending both legs. Draw the sabre back above the head, turning the blade to lie along the upper back. Lower the left hand at the left side. Look forward. (image 1.34b) Push into the left knee and straighten the right to take a left bow stance. Circle the sabre on the right side then push forward, edge forward, tip pointing right. Hook the left hand behind the body with the hook rolled under to point up. Look forward. (image 1.34c)

Jump lightly and land steadily. Push the sabre strongly.

35. Jumping Turn, Drop Stance Smear

tiàozhuàn pūbù mǒ dāo   跳转仆步抹刀

Turn right, bending both knees. Flip the sabre over towards the left, edge forward, tip pointing left. Place the left hand on the right wrist. Look forward. (image 1.35a) Push off with both legs to jump up, spinning around to the rear right. Land on the right foot, holding the left knee up. Circle the sabre around to the rear right with the jumping turn, pulling it to outside the left shoulder, edge out, tip down. Hold the left hand out to the side. Look forward [tr. note: in the new direction] and down. (image 1.35b) Continue to turn right and land the left foot forward. Squat fully on the right leg and extend the left leg along the ground to take a left drop stance. Circle the sabre

around the front and down then pull it to outside the right knee, edge down, tip pointing left. Hold the left hand out to the side, slanting down. Look to the left side. (image 1.35c)

Turn lightly and land firmly.

Section Five

36. Back-Cross Step, Cradle The Sabre   chābù bào dāo   叉步抱刀

Push into the right foot to stand up, shifting to the left. Step the right foot behind the left, touching down the ball of the foot to take a left back-cross step. The legs are now bent and crossed. Circle the sabre forward and up to the left side, cradling it in front of the chest, edge up, tip pointing to the right. Place the left hand at the right wrist. Look to the left side. (image 1.36)

1.36

Complete the cradling action with the completion of the cross step.

37. Side Thrust Kick   cèchuāituǐ   侧踹腿

Push into the left foot to shift to the right leg, bending and raising the left knee. Then do a side thrusting heel kick to the left. Both legs are almost straight. Lean the torso to the right side and open out the hands to either side. Look to the left side. (image 1.37)

Stand firmly on the right leg and kick strongly.

1.37

38. Step Forward, Chop   shàngbù pī dāo   上步劈刀

Land the left foot to the left side and turn left. Step the right foot forward, bending both knees. Bring the sabre over to the front to chop, edge angled forward and down, tip slanting up. Place the left hand inside the right forearm. Look forward. (image 1.38)

Step quickly and chop strongly.

1.38

39. Flowers, Horse Stance Tuck The Sabre At The Back

wǎnhuā mǎbù bēi dāo   腕花马步背刀

Without moving the feet, circle the sabre to chop further down in front, edge down, tip slanting down to the front. Lower the left hand, then circle it out to the rear to above the head at the left side. Look forward and down. (image 1.39a) Circle the sabre so that the tip lowers, then rises on the left side, edge forward, tip up. Hold the left hand out to the side. Look forward, to the right. (image 1.39b) Circle the sabre forward and down on the right side, edge up, tip back. Look forward, to the right. (image 1.39c) Circle the sabre forward and down until it is tucked onto the back. Place the left hand at the right shoulder. Look to the right side. (image 1.39d)

Keep the right hand in a fairly loose grip at the guard and keep the wrist relaxed throughout the flowers. The sabre completes a fully circle at the left and at the right.

40. Tornado Kick With The Sabre Tucked At The Back

bēi dāo xuànfēngjiǎo   背刀旋风脚

Push into the left foot to shift to the right foot, doing a rolling spin around to the left, lifting the left knee. Swing the left hand up to the left. Look up to the left. (image 1.40a) Push into the right foot to jump up, spinning around to the left. Land on the ball of the left foot. Simultaneously do an inside crescent kick with the right leg, slapping the sole of the foot with the left hand. Look forward. (image 1.40b)

Jump as high as you can, and spin quickly. Slap the foot with a sharp sound.

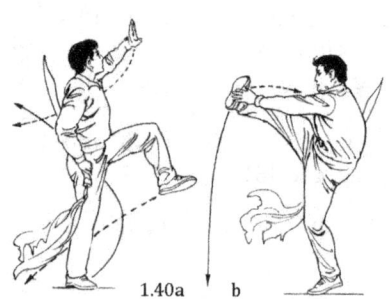

CHA SABRE

41. Horse Stance With The Sabre Tucked At The Back

mǎbù bēi dāo   马步背刀

Continuing to turn leftward, land the left foot, then the right, bending both legs to sit into a horse stance. Place the left hand at the right shoulder. Look to the right side. (image 1.41)

Land into a stable stance.

42. Turn Around, Bow Stance Framing Block

zhuànshēn gōngbù jià dāo   转身弓步架刀

Turn left, pivoting on both feet, bending the left knee and straightening the right, to take a left bow stance. Bring the sabre around to the left with the turn, circling it and raising it behind the left shoulder. Look forward. (image 1.42a) Pull the sabre over across the back and to the left, pulling it flat in front of the body, placing the blade on the left forearm, edge up, tip pointing left. Place the left hand on the right wrist. Look forward. (image 1.42b)

Turn quickly and take a firm stance.

43. Jumping Turn, Empty Stance Smear

tiàozhuàn xūbù mǒ dāo   跳转虚步抹刀

Push into the left foot to lift it up, turning around to the rear right. Pull the sabre flat around to the right, edge out, tip pointing left. Hold the left hand out in front. Look forward. (image 1.43a) Push into the right foot to jump up and spin around to the rear right. Pull the sabre flat around to the rear right with the jump, edge out, tip back. Hold the left hand out to the side. Look forward, to the right. (image 1.43b) Land the left foot, then the right. Lift the sabre up behind. Look forward. (image 1.43c) Shift back and sit into both legs, touching the ball of the left foot down in front to take a left empty stance. Bring the sabre around the outside of the left shoulder, then pull it back beside the right thigh, completing the head wrapping action, edge down, tip pointing forward. Bring the left hand in to the belly, then push forward. Look forward. (image 1.43d)

Turn quickly and lightly and land firmly. Take a well-defined empty stance, weighting the rear leg and keeping the front leg empty. Keep the blade tight to the upper back when doing the head wrap.

44. Bow Stance Stab gōngbù zhā dāo 弓步扎刀

Step the left foot a half-step forward and push the right leg straight to set into a bow stance. Stab directly forward until the sabre and arm form a straight line, edge down, tip forward. Place the left hand on the right wrist. Look forward. (image 1.44)

Compete the stab with the completion of the bow stance. Stab with power.

45. Bow Stance, Coil And Wrap The Head, Framing Block

gōngbù chánguǒtóu jià dāo 弓步缠裹头架刀

Without changing the stance, circle the sabre to the left and up, raising the grip above the head at the back, the blade sticking tightly to the left shoulder, and circling to the upper back. Push the left hand forward. Look forward. (image 1.45a) Pull the sabre to the right and around to the front, the blade spine sticking on top of the left forearm, edge forward, tip pointing left. Place the left hand

on the right wrist. Look forward. (image 1.45b)

Pull the sabre around quickly and strongly.

46. Turn Around, Bow Stance Carry

zhuànshēn gōngbù tuō dāo 转身弓步托刀

Push into the left foot and turn around to the right, pivoting on both feet, Bend the right leg and straighten the left to take a right bow stance. Pull the sabre around in front of the body to the rear right, then raise the grip above the head behind, sticking the blade spine to the upper back. Hold the left hand out to the left side. Look to the left side. (image 1.46a) Without moving the feet, circle the sabre outside the left arm, pulling it to the front right and pulling the grip up. Lay the blade spine along the top of the left arm, edge up, tip back. Place the left hand on the grip. Look forward, to the right. (image 1.46b)

Turn quickly, keeping the blade tight to the upper back to coil and wrap the head.

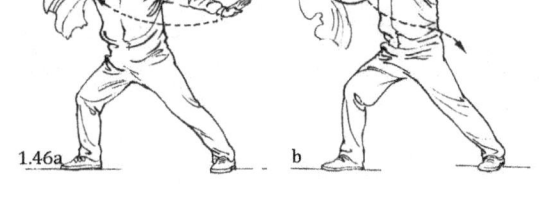

47. High Empty Stance Flash Palm   gāoxūbù liàngzhǎng   高虚步亮掌

Push into the left foot and shift to the right leg, shifting the left foot forward a half-step, touching down the ball of the foot. Take the guard in the left hand and bring the sabre to stand at the left side, spine tight to the left arm, edge forward, and tip up. Raise the right hand up above the head at the right. Look to the left side. (image 1.47)

Take a distinctly weighted empty stance.

48. Withdraw And Cradle The Sabre   chèbù bào dāo   撤步抱刀

Withdraw the left foot a half-step. Swing the right hand forward, to the right, and down. Look to the left. (image 1.48a) Withdraw the right foot a half-step. Circle the right hand at the right until it is out to the side. Look to the left. (image 1.48b) Bring the left foot to meet the right foot and stand up. Circle the right hand forward and down, to press down at the right side, palm down. Look to the left. (image 1.48c)

Step lightly, taking agile and steady steps.

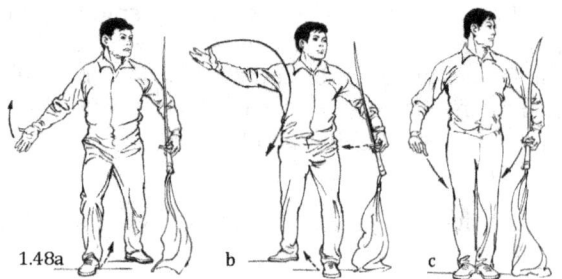

49. Closing Posture   shōu shì   收势

Stand to attention, lowering the hands at the sides. Look forward. (image 1.44)

KUNWU SWORD

昆吾剑

ABOUT THE CHA SYSTEM SWORD: KUNWU SWORD

The sword is made up of a grip, a guard, and a straight, double-edged blade. The parts of the blade are the edges, the spine, the peak, and the tip. The whole blade can be differentiated into the fore-section – the half nearest the tip – and aft-section – the half nearest the guard.

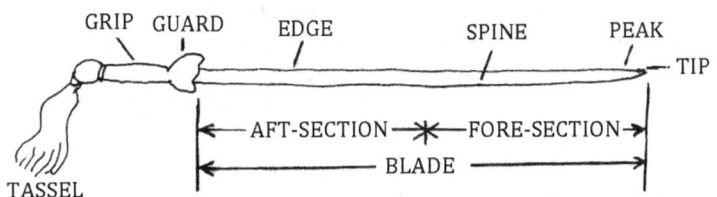

The length of the sword that an individual will use is determined by cradling the sword by the guard, upright at the side with the arm straight. The tip should reach at least the top of the ear. The tassel is usually a short one, or it may be left off. The blade is straight and double-edged, and may be made of metal, wood, or bamboo. There is no weight restriction.

Cradling means to place the palm at the guard, curling the thumb around the guard, extending the forefinger along the grip, with the other fingers curled on the grip side of the guard. The wrist is held straight so that the flat of the blade is tight to the forearm.

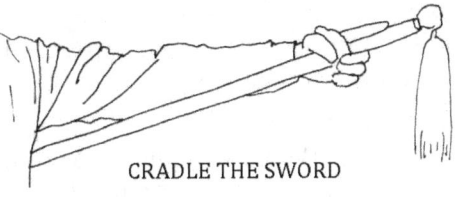
CRADLE THE SWORD

Holding or grasping, means to hold the grip with the thumb web close to the guard and aligned with the edge of the blade.

The hand not holding the sword (usually the left hand) holds the 'sword fingers' shape. The palm is held with the thumb bent and tucked onto the bent ring and little fingers (the thumb may also be straight and opened out, and the two fingers tucked in on their own). The index and middle fingers are held together, straight, and pulled back.

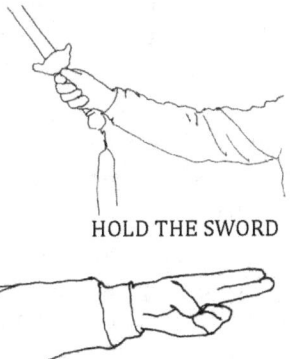
HOLD THE SWORD

SWORD FINGERS HAND

The Main Techniques of the Kunwu Sword

Chop: With a standing blade (edges on top and bottom), chop down from above, putting power to the body of the blade, and extending the blade and arm to form one line. A swinging chop brings the blade around in a vertical circle on one side or the other, then chops down horizontally in front. A rear swinging chop comes around with a turn of the body to chop behind.

Pierce: With a standing (blade turned with the edges above and below) or flat blade (blade turned with the edges lying flat, left to right), stab directly forward, power going to the tip, extending the blade and arm along one line. When the edges are on top and bottom, it is called a standing pierce. When the edges are on the left and right, it is called a flat pierce. A level pierce is at shoulder height. A high pierce is at head height. A low pierce is at knee height. A diving pierce is close to the ground, but not touching. A rear pierce goes behind, and is coordinated with a backwards lean, a prone lean, or a rearward turn. A reaching pierce is done with a medially rotated forearm so that the palm is turned out, and is done by bringing the blade past above the shoulder to the front, stabbing either high or low with a standing blade, with the torso and arm aligned to reach forward.

Slice up: A slice up brings the standing blade forward and up from below, putting power to the fore-section. A normal slice up has the forearm laterally rotated to turn the palm up, and the blade circles through close to the body. A reverse slice up has the forearm medially rotated to turn the palm to the right, and the blade circles though close to the body.

Dab: With a standing blade, lift the wrist to strongly dab the tip forward and down, putting power to the tip and extending the arm.

Snap: With a standing blade, settle the wrist to strongly pop the sword tip up, power reaching the tip. The arm is fully extended, and the tip is higher than the head.

Parry, hook: With a standing blade, from a starting place in front, hook the sword tip up then back, or down then back, keeping the blade close to the body. An upper parry goes up and over to the rear, staying close to the body. A lower parry goes down, then back, staying close to the body. A swinging parry does a complete vertical circle.

Intercept: With the blade angled, move it either upwards or downwards at that angle, power reaching the fore-section. An upper intercept is angled upwards. A lower intercept is angled downwards. A rear intercept is angled down to the rear right.

Flowers: Forward wrist flowers pivot around the wrist, using a standing blade, drawing a full vertical circle forward and down on either side of the arm, circling close to the body and chopping forward and down. Power goes to the tip. Slicing wrist flowers pivot around the wrist, using a standing blade, drawing a full vertical circle forward and up on either side of the arm, circling close to the body, transmitting power to the tip.

NAMES OF THE MOVEMENTS OF THE KUNWU SWORD FORM

Position Of Preparation
Section One
1. Step Forward Cradle The Sword
2. Closed Stance Press Down
3. Jump To Empty Stance Trap
4. Closed Stance Dab
5. Empty Stance Lift The Sword, Point The Hand
6. Raised Knee Point
7. Turn Around, Bow Stance Pierce
8. Raised Knee Smear (White Crane Flashes Its Wings)
9. Jumping Turn To Bow Stance Pierce
10. Resting Stance Carry
11. Turn Around, Level Smear

Section Two
12. Jump To Stab (Golden Needle Enters The Earth)
13. Turn Around, Chop (Forcefully Split Mount Hua)
14. Turn Around, Empty Stance Low Intercept
15. Jump To Empty Stance Low Intercept
16. Turn Around, Pare
17. Empty Stance Dab
18. Jumping Turn, Level Dab
19. Side Balance (Reach Into The Sea)
20. Basin Stance Press Down
21. Jumping Turn, Level Smear
22. Closed Stance Dab
23. Empty Stance Lift The Sword And Point The Hand

Section Three
24. Raised Knee Present The Sword
25. Left And Right Hooking Parries To The Side
26. Step Forward With An Insertion Step, Press Down
27. Roll Over, Bow Stance Chop
28. Empty Stance Press Down
29. Step Forward And Pierce Thrice
30. Turn Around, Left And Right Hooking Parries
31. Rear-Bent-Leg Balance, Point The Hand

Section Four
32. Bow Stance Pierce

CHAQUAN, VOLUME III

33. Retreat, Left And Right Traps
34. Raised Knee Smear
35. Prone Low Pierce (Leopard Cat Pounces On A Rat)
36. Raised Knee Smear
37. Step Forward Scoop
38. Closed Stance Dab
39. Empty Stance, Lift The Sword And Point The Hand

Section Five

40. Jump To Insertion Stance Reverse Slice Up
41. Roll Over, Hook And Chop
42. Turn Around, Hook And Dab
43. Withdraw And Carry
44. Empty Stance Separate
45. Step Forward Dabs (Phoenix Nods Its Head Thrice)
46. T Stance Diving Stab (Golden Needle Enters The Ground)
47. Turn Around, Raised Knee High Dab

Section Six

48. Turn Around, Smear (Swallow Skims The Water)
49. Step Forward With Right And Left Smears (Push Aside The Clouds To Look At The Sun)
50. Turn Around, Raised Knee Hooking Parry
51. Jump To Low Pierce
52. Take The Sword In The Left Hand
53. Left Sweep Kick
54. Flying Kick
55. High Empty Stance Flash The Hand
56. Withdraw, Press Down With The Palm
57. Closing Posture (Stand To Attention Holding The Sword)

0. Position Of Preparation　　　yùbèi shì　　　预备势

Stand to attention with the feet together, the toes turned out. Hold the grip in the left hand, cradling the guard, with the flat of the blade tight to the back side of the left forearm, tip up. Keep both arms almost straight. Look forward. (image 2.0a) Medially rotate the arms and hold the elbows out to the sides. Extend the index and middle fingers of the right hand and bend the ring and little fingers, pressing the thumb onto them. Look to the left. (image 2.0b)

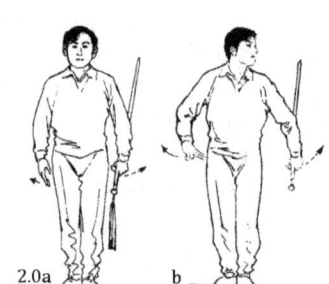

KUNWU SWORD

Section One

1. Step Forward Cradle The Sword   shàngbù bào jiàn   上步抱剑

Step the left foot forward and shift forward, keeping the ball of the right foot on the ground, lifting the heel so that both legs are almost straight. With the arms naturally extended, open them down and out to either side. Look to the left. (image 2.1a) Step the right foot forward and shift forward, touching down the ball of the left foot with the heel lifted so that both legs are almost straight. Lift the arms up at the sides, palms down. Look forward. (image 2.1b) Bring the left foot up to meet the right and stand up, reaching forward into the chest. Circle the hands forward, bending the elbows to bring the hands flat across to meet in front of the chest, left palm out, right palm in, placing the grip into the right hand. Look forward. (image 2.1c)

Step lightly and take the closed stance with quick but agile steps. Keep the arms rounded as they separate then come together. Time the cradling of the sword grip to finish as the feet complete the closed stance.

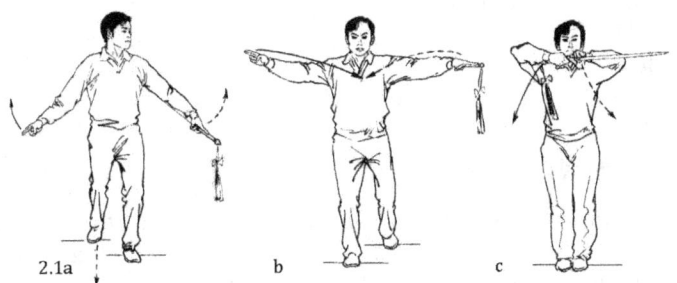

2. Closed Stance Press Down   bìngbù àn jiàn   并步按剑

Take the grip in the right hand with the thumb web snug to the guard. Put the left hand into the 'sword fingers' shape – the index and middle fingers straight and the other fingers tucked, pressing the thumb onto them. Press down with both hands in front of the body until the arms are almost straight. The sword points to the left. Look to the left. (image 2.2)

Look to the left as you complete the press down. Reach the chest forward slightly.

3. Jump To Empty Stance Trap   tiào xūbù lán jiàn   跳虚步拦剑

Push into the left foot to raise the knee, standing up on the right leg. Circle the hands up to raise them at either side above the head. The tip still points left. Look forward. (image 2.3a) Push into the right foot, jump up, and spin around to the right. Land on the left foot, bending the knee slightly and raising the right knee. Press the left hand on the right wrist. Lift the sword towards the right to do a trapping lift, turning the tip up. Look forward, to the right side. (image 2.3b) Land the right foot, touching down the toes and sitting into the legs to take a right empty stance. Lift the sword to trap to the right with the tip up, the edges to the sides. Press the left hand on the right wrist. Look to the right side. (image 2.3c)

Jump lightly and land into a well-defined empty stance. Circle the blade to do a clear trapping action towards the right side.

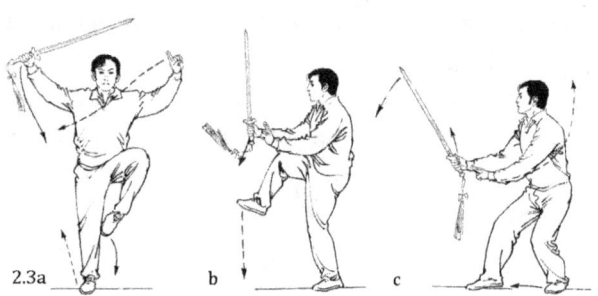

2.3a   b   c

4. Closed Stance Dab   bìngbù diǎn jiàn   并步点剑

Push into the left foot and stand up, turning left, then bring the left foot up to meet the right foot in a closed stance. Do a dabbing action with the sword, completing a level dab on the right side with the peak of the blade. The right arm is almost straight, with the wrist cocked. Lower the left hand to circle it up on the left, raising it above the head. Look to the right side. (image 2.4)

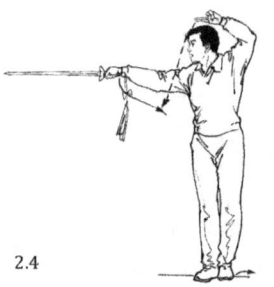

Step up quickly and firmly. Press the thumb web down into the grip and simultaneously tuck in the ring and little finger strongly to do the dabbing action.

2.4

5. Empty Stance Lift The Sword, Point The Hand

xūbù tí jiàn zhǐshǒu   虚步提剑指手

Turn left and shift the left foot a half-step to the left, touching down the toes, sitting down to take a left empty stance. Bring the right arm back, turning the sword tip down and placing the blade close inside the right leg. Press the left hand on the right wrist. Look back, to the lower right. (image 2.5a) Without changing the stance, turn slightly to the left. Point with the left hand flat out to the left, extending the arm at shoulder height, palm down.

Look to the left side. (image 2.5b)

Do not change the stance with the action. Point quickly with the left hand.

6. **Raised Knee Point**   tíxī zhǐshǒu   提膝指手

Turn slightly to the right and stand up slightly, lifting the left heel and turning it out. Turn the blade to standing, placing it in front of the belly, tip pointing forward to the right. Lower the left hand and hold it down at the right side. Look forward, to the right side. (image 2.6a) Push into the left foot to raise the knee, standing up on the right leg. Pull the blade to press down outside the right hip, arm slightly bent. Lift the left hand to scoop forward to shoulder height on the right side, fingers up, arm almost straight. Look forward, to the right side. (image 2.6b)

Raise the knee as high as possible and stand firmly. Press the blade down, extend the left hand, and complete the stance all at the same time.

7. **Turn Around, Bow Stance Pierce**

    zhuànshēn gōngbù cì jiàn   转身弓步刺剑

Turn left and land the left foot back to the left side, touching down the ball of the foot and bending both legs. Lower the left hand, then circle it out to hold it out to the left. Look forward, to the left. (image 2.7a) Settle into the left foot and turn left, bending into the left knee and straightening the right to take a left bow stance. Pierce with the sword directly forward to the left with a standing blade, right arm straight at shoulder height. Press the left hand on the right wrist. Look forward, to the left. (image 2.7b)

Turn quickly and land firmly. Pierce strongly.

8. Raised Knee Smear (White Crane Flashes Its Wings)

tíxī mǒ jiàn (báihé liàngchì)   提膝抹剑（白鹤亮翅）

Push into the left foot and shift to the right, turning right, bending the right knee and almost straightening the left. Flip the right hand over so that the palm faces down, and smear the blade flat around to the front, then across to the right in an arc, holding the arm out and down, so that the sword tip slants slightly upwards. Hold the left arm out, slanting down, at the left side, palm down. Look forward, to the right. (image 2.8a) Push into the left foot and shift to the right, raising the left knee, supporting on the right leg. Do not change the relative position of the arms. Look forward, to the right. (image 2.8b)

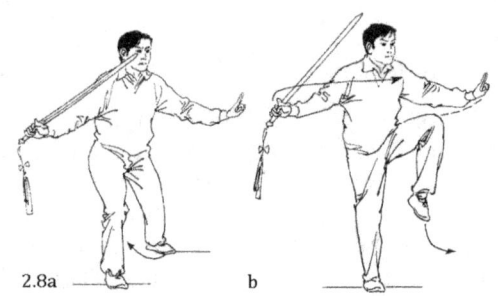

2.8a   b

Turn quickly and stand firmly.

9. Jumping Turn To Bow Stance Pierce

tiàozhuàn gōngbù cì jiàn   跳转弓步刺剑

Land the left foot forward to the right with the foot turned out and knee bent, almost straightening the right leg and lifting the heel. Turn slightly to the left and reach the torso slightly forward. Look back, to the left. (image 2.9a) Push into the left foot to jump up, spinning around to the left. Land the right foot, then the left. Bend the right knee forward and straighten the left to take a right bow stance. Pierce to the rear left with the arm straight at shoulder height. Press the left hand on the right wrist. Look forward [tr. note: in the direction of the pierce]. (image 2.9b)

2.9a   b

Jump and spin quickly and land firmly. Pierce strongly.

10. Resting Stance Carry   xiēbù tuō jiàn   歇步托剑

Withdraw the right foot a half-step, turning out the foot, and sit down into a crossed leg resting stance. Circle the hands to the left and down, separating them. Then bring them together to cradle in front of the body, right palm up, left palm pressing on the right wrist. Reach the torso forward slightly. Look down to the front. (image 2.10)

KUNWU SWORD

2.10

11. Turn Around, Level Smear   zhuànshēn píngmǒ   转身平抹

Push into both feet to stand up, turning right. Withdraw the right foot to the rear right, with legs bent. Smear with the sword flat around to the right with the tip pointing left. Hold the left hand out to the left side. Look to the right side. (image 2.11a) Push into the left foot and shift right, turning around to the right. Bring the left foot in to beside the right foot. Smear with the sword flat around to the forward right, right palm up, sword tip pointing to the forward right. Circle the left hand out to above the head. Look to the forward right. (image 2.11b)

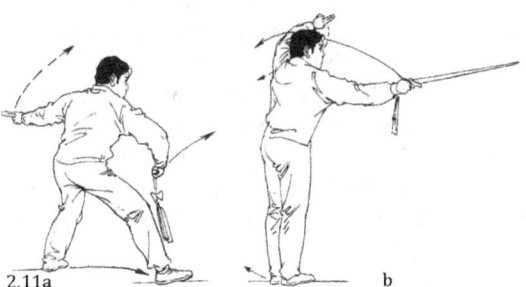

Turn quickly, step cleanly. Use a soft power for the smearing.

Section Two

12. Jump To Stab (Golden Needle Enters The Earth)

tiàobù zhā jiàn (jīnzhēn rùdì)   跳步扎剑（金针入地）

Turn left, stepping the left foot forward to the left, bending the knee. Circle the sword up, then to the left to finish at the forward left, tip up. Press the left hand on the right wrist. Look forward, to the left. (image 2.12a) Push into the right foot and shift forward, then step the right foot forward to the left, foot turned out. Lift the left heel and bend both legs. Circle the sword down, then pull back, holding the arm and sword slanting with the tip down. Point the left hand flat out to the forward left, arm slightly bent. Look forward to the left. (image 2.12b) Push into the left foot, then the right, to jump up and forward to the left. Land forward on the left foot, then the right, bending both legs and raising the right heel. Circle the sword up from the rear right, then stab down to the forward left, tip down, right arm bent, palm out. Press the left hand on the right wrist. Look down to the forward left. (image 2.12c)

41

CHAQUAN, VOLUME III

Jump lightly and land firmly. Draw a nicely rounded circle with the sword.

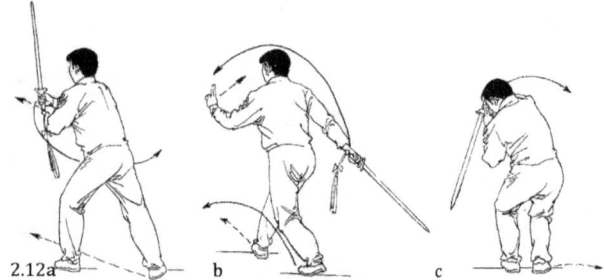

13. Turn Around, Chop (Forcefully Split Mount Hua)

zhuànshēn pī jiàn (lìpī huáshān)　　　　　　转身劈剑（力劈华山）

Push into the left foot, stand up, and turn around to the right. Step the right foot forward to the right, bending the knee. Bring the sword up, circling around to the right with a swinging lift, blade horizontal and tip pointing to the rear left. Keep the left hand on the right wrist. Look forward to the right. (image 2.13a) Push into the left foot to shift forward, then step the left foot forward to the right, foot turned out. Lift the right heel and bend both legs. Lift the sword slightly up to the front right side, tip slanting up. Hold the left hand out to the side. Look forward to the right. (image 2.13b) Push into the right foot and shift forward towards the right. Step the right foot forward to the right, then bring the left foot up to meet it, standing up. Circle the sword out towards the forward right to chop at shoulder height. Hold the left hand out above the head at the left side, arm bent. Look forward to the right. (image 2.13c)

Step quickly. Chop strongly.

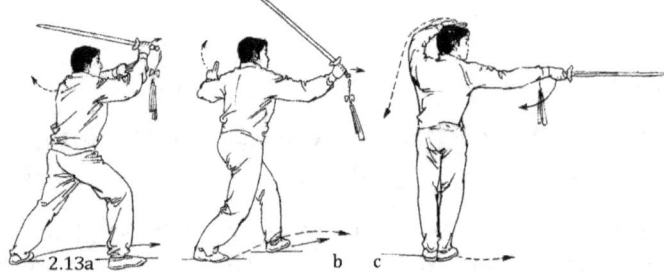

14. Turn Around, Empty Stance Low Intercept

zhuànshēn xūbù xiàjié　　　　　　转身虚步下截

Turn to the left and step the right foot across to the right, bending the left leg and straightening the right. Smear with the sword across to the left and down, right palm up. Hold the left hand out to the left side. Look to the left side. (image 2.14a) Push into the left foot and shift back, then withdraw the left foot, touching down the toes. Bend the right leg and sit into a left empty stance. Circle the sword across to the left with a low intercept, the sword and right arm making a line, tip pointing forward and down, palm up. Press the left hand on the right wrist. Reach the torso forward slightly. Look forward and down. (image 2.14c)

Turn and retreat the foot quickly. Take a well-defined empty stance. Circle the sword with a strong low interception.

15. Jump To Empty Stance Low Intercept

tiào xūbù xiàjié   跳虚步下截

Retreat the left foot, touching down the ball of the foot and bending both legs. Flip the sword over, turning the right palm down. Hold the hands out to their respective sides, keeping the sword tip slanting down. Look to the lower front. (image 2.15a) Push into the right foot and shift back, standing on the left leg and raising the right knee. Lift both hands in front, lifting the sword up in front, across in front of the head. Look forward and up. (image 2.15b) Push into the left foot to jump up. Land on the right foot, then the left, touching just the toes of the left foot down and bending the right leg to take a left empty stance. Circle the sword out to the right, then down in front to do a low intercept, right palm up, sword tip forward, slanting down. Press the left hand on the right wrist. Look forward and down. (image 2.15c)

Jump lightly and land firmly. Take a well-defined empty stance. Intercept with power.

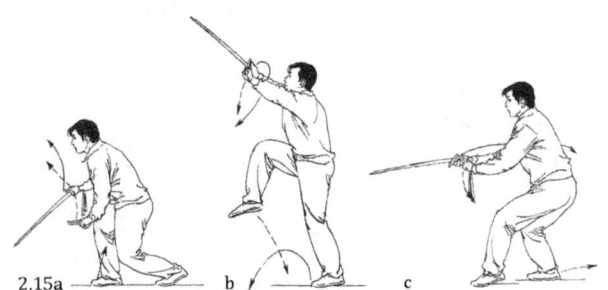

16. Turn Around, Pare   zhuànshēn xiāo jiàn   转身削剑

Pivot on both feet to turn around to the right, then retreat the right foot to the rear right. Bend the right foot towards the right side and straighten the left leg to take a right bow stance. Start to pare a bit with the sword across flat to the right. Hold the left hand down to the rear left. Look forward, to the right. (image 2.16a) Without moving the feet, turn slightly to the right. Pare across to the front, palm up. The sword and right arm form a flat line, tip to the right. Hold the left hand up over the head at the left. Look to the right side. (image 2.16b)

Turn quickly, step firmly. Pare with power.

17. Empty Stance Dab   xūbù diǎn jiàn   虚步点剑

Push into the right foot to shift and turn to the left. Step the right foot across to the left side, touching the toes down. Sit onto the left leg to take a right empty stance. Dab with the sword, bringing it across from the right side to dab down on the left. The right arm and sword are slanting down, the tip down. Press the left hand on the right wrist. Look to the lower front. (image 2.17)

Turn quickly and take a well-defined empty stance. Dab with power.

18.   Jumping Turn, Level Dab   tiàozhuàn píngdiǎn   跳转平点

Shift back and raise the right knee, standing up on the left leg then pushing off to jump around to the right. Land on the right foot and raise the left knee. Circle the sword up on the right to parry upwards, tip pointing to the rear upper right. Both legs are bent, and the hands are in front of the belly. Look forward. (image 2.18a) Land the left foot forward and bend the knee, straightening the right leg to take a left bow stance. Circle the sword flat across on the right and forward, to dab horizontally. The right arm straightens slightly, with the palm up. The blade is flat. The left hand presses on the right wrist. Look forward. (image 2.18b)

Jump and turn quickly and lightly, and land firmly. Use a short, sharp, power for the horizontal dab.

KUNWU SWORD

19. **Side Balance (Reach Into The Sea)**

    cèshēn pínghéng (tànhǎi shì)　　　　　　侧身平衡（探海式）

Push into the right foot to shift forward, turning right. Bring the right foot up to meet the left foot and stand up in a closed stance. Bend both arms to bring the hands to the chest, keeping the sword blade flat. Look to the left side. (image 2.19a) Circle the sword so that the tip rises in front, then lowers, drawing a full circle until the tip points up again. Look to the left side. (image 2.19b) Circle the sword in front until the tip points down. Bend the body so that the torso leans forward to the left. Bend both legs. Look down. (image 2.19c) Stand on the left leg and raise the right knee out to the side behind the body. Lean the torso to the left side, bending at the hip. Lift the sword up with the tip pointing down. Point the left hand down, extending the arm straight. Look down. (image 2.19d)

Keep a supple grip with the right hand to draw the circles with the sword. Stand firmly on the left leg.

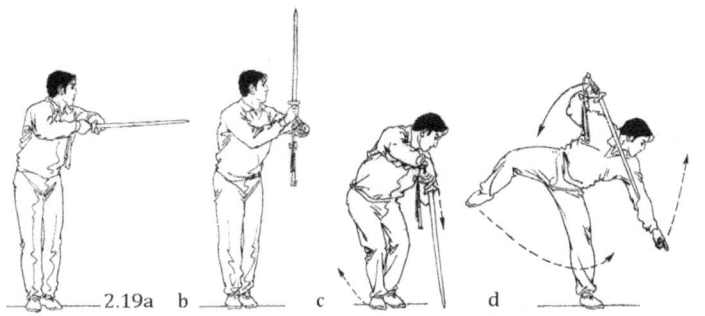

20. **Basin Stance Press Down**　　　　pǎntuǐ yā jiàn　　　　盘腿压剑

Staying on the left leg, straighten the body, then lean to the right side. Raise the right knee and foot up in front without touching down. Press down with the sword flat, the right palm facing down and the blade flat, tip pointing left. Hold the left arm level out to the left side, palm down. Look to the left side. (image 2.20)

21. **Jumping Turn, Level Smear**　　　tiàozhuàn píngmǒ　　　跳转平抹

Turn right and land the right foot to the right side. Step forward with the left foot, then the right, bending the right knee and straightening the left. Look forward, to the right. (images 2.21a, b, c)

CHAQUAN, VOLUME III

Push off with the left foot, then the right, to jump up and spin around to the right. Land on the left foot, keeping the right knee up. Press the left hand on the right wrist. Look forward, to the right. (image 2.21d) Pivot on the ball of the left foot to turn around to the right, then land the right foot forward, to the right. Bend the right knee forward and straighten the left leg to take a right bow stance. Circle the sword around to the right as you turn back, with a flat smear, right palm down. Bring the arm and sword around flat with the tip pointing forward. Place the left hand on the right wrist. Look forward, to the right.
(image 2.21e)

Keep the steps continuous, jump lightly, and land firmly. Do the smearing action with a supple power.

| 22. | **Closed Stance Dab** | bìngbù diǎn jiàn | 并步点剑 |

Withdraw the right foot a half-step, touching down the ball of the foot. Parry down to the left, turning the tip down and turning the body slightly to the left. Look to the right side. (image 2.22a) Bring the left foot in to beside the right foot and stand up, turning further to the left. With a straight arm and cocked wrist, circle the sword tip up on the left, up and forward, then dab out on the right side. The tip points forward to the right. Press the left hand inside the right forearm.
Look to the right side. (image 2.22b)

Step quickly. As the body and sword rotate, keep a supple grip with the right hand. Put a short, sharp power into the sword when dabbing.

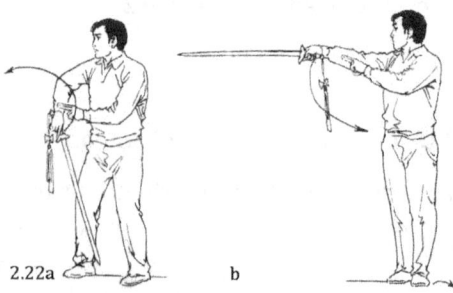

KUNWU SWORD

23. Empty Stance Lift The Sword And Point The Hand

xūbù tí jiàn zhǐshǒu   虚步提剑指手

Turn left and bend the right leg, moving the left foot a half-step to the left, touching down the toes to take a left empty stance. Bend the right arm to hold the sword grip in front of the right chest, tip hanging down. Press the left hand on the right wrist. Look at the hands. (image 2.23a) Without changing the stance, hold the left arm out straight at shoulder height to point to the left with the 'sword fingers', palm down. Look past the left hand. (image 2.23b)

Make the weighting distinct in the empty stance. Coordinate the finger point with the turn of the head.

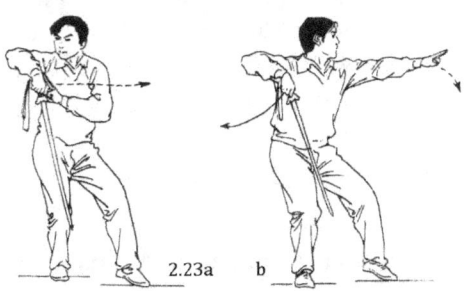

2.23a   b

Section Three

24. Raised Knee Present The Sword   tíxī jǔ jiàn   提膝举剑

Stand up on both legs, keeping the left heel lifted. Pull the right hand back on the right, pulling and holding out the sword with the arm and blade angled down in a straight line. Lower the left hand slightly. Look forward. (image 2.24a) Raise the left knee, standing up straight on the right leg. Circle the sword up to the right and back, then over, pulling it to lift over the head at the right, blade horizontal, tip pointing forward. Place the left hand inside the right arm. Look forward. (image 2.24b)

Stand firmly on one leg. Be sure to first circle the blade, and then pull and lift.

2.24a   b

25. Left And Right Hooking Parries To The Side

zuǒyòu cèguà jiàn   左右侧挂剑

Land the left foot forward, turning out the foot and lifting the right heel, bending both legs and turning to the left. Circle the sword tip forward and down on the left side to parry, holding it out at the left side with the blade horizontal, tip pointing back on the left. Place the left hand on the right wrist. Look to the left side. (image 2.25a) Take a step forward with the right foot and stand up in a relaxed manner on both legs. Circle the sword so that the tip goes up and forward, parrying up above the head on the left side, in front, tip pointing up. Turn the body slightly right, keeping the left hand pressed on the right wrist. Look forward. (image 2.25b) Turn further right and lean forward, turning the right foot out and lifting the left heel. The legs are now crossed and bent. Circle the sword so that the tip parries down on the right, to the lower rear on the right side, tip pointing down and back on the right side. Keep the left hand on the right wrist. Look past the sword tip. (image 2.25c)

When parrying to the left and then the right, draw full vertical circles very close to the legs.

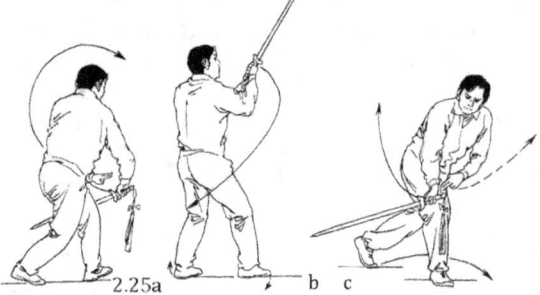

26. Step Forward With An Insertion Step, Press Down
shàng chābù àn jiàn 上叉步按剑

Step the left foot forward, turning right and standing up. Circle the sword to parry upwards towards the rear right, arm straight, blade tip pointing back. Hold the left arm out to the side. Look to the left side. (image 2.26a) Step the right foot behind the left leg towards the front, to the left, taking a back-cross step, touching down the ball of the foot. The legs are crossed and bent. Circle the sword up and to the left, then press down in front of the legs, tip slanting down. Circle the left hand up, then right, to press onto the right wrist. Lean the torso slightly forward. Look down to the left. (image 2.26b)

Cross the legs quickly and settle into a stable stance. Press down with power.

27. Roll Over, Bow Stance Chop   fānshēn gōngbù pī jiàn 翻身弓步劈剑

Stand up on both legs and roll the body over, turning right. Circle the sword to the right and up, holding it above and in front of the head. Keep the left hand pressed on the right wrist. Look at the sword. (image 2.27a) Continue to turn right and step the right foot out to the right side, bending the knee and straightening the left leg to take a right bow stance. Chop down to horizontal at the right, aligning the arm and blade at shoulder height, tip forward. Hold the left hand up above the head at the left. Look forward. (image 2.27b)

Roll over quickly, take a firm step, and chop strongly.

28. Empty Stance Press Down   xūbù yā jiàn   虚步压剑

Push into the right foot to shift back, bending both legs. Parry downwards, sword tip pointing down. Place the left hand inside the right forearm. Look forward. (image 2.28a) Shift the right foot back, touching down the toes, and sit into a right empty stance. Circle the sword back and up to parry then move forward to press down, the tip pointing to the upper front. Press the left hand on the right wrist. Keep the hands close to the belly. Look forward. (image 2.28b)

Sit into a well-defined empty stance. Circle, parry, and press down with power.

29. Step Forward And Pierce Thrice   shàngbù sāncì jiàn   上步三刺剑

Take a half-step forward with the right foot and bend the knee. Pierce directly forward. Press the left hand inside the right forearm. (image 2.29a) Push into the left foot to step forward, lifting the right foot and bending both legs. Bring the sword grip in to the chest with the blade horizontal, then pierce directly forward, tip forward. Keep the left hand inside the right forearm. (image 2.29b) Push into the right foot to step forward, bending the knee and straightening the left leg to take a right bow stance. Pierce forward again with the tip forward and the left hand on the right forearm. Look forward. (image 2.29c)

Take three steps and pierce three times in a coordinated and connected manner. Step quickly and firmly, piercing strongly.

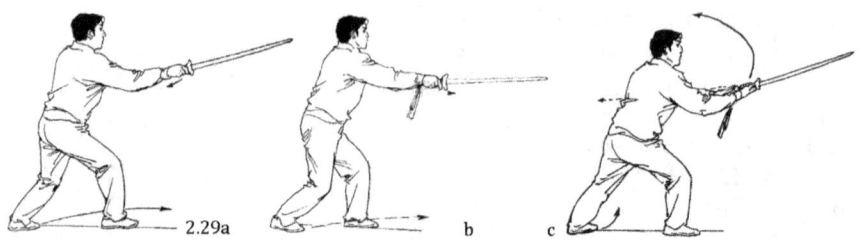

30. Turn Around, Left And Right Hooking Parries

zhuànshēn zuǒyòu guà jiàn   转身左右掛剑

Push into the right foot and shift back, turning around to the left. Shift onto the right leg and raise the left knee. Circle the sword up and to the left to parry to the left with the tip slanting down. Hold the left hand out in front. Look forward, to the left. (image 2.30a) Land the left foot forward with the foot turned out, crossing the legs and bending them, lifting the right heel. Circle the sword down and to the left to parry in front of the legs, tip pointing to the rear left. Place the left hand on the right wrist. Turn to the left and bend forward at the hip. Look to the rear left. (image 2.30b) Step the right foot forward and stand up on both legs, turn to the right. Circle the sword up and right to parry on the right side, tip pointing right. Keep the left hand on the right wrist. Look forward to the right. (image 2.30c) Turn further to the right and turn out the right foot, lifting the left heel and bending both legs. Circle the sword down and to the rear right to parry outside the right leg, tip pointing to the lower rear right. Keep the left hand on the right wrist. Look to the lower rear right. (image 2.30d)

Follow an arcing line to complete both parries to the left and right. The right hand uses a fairly loose grip in order to do this.

31. Rear-Bent-Leg Balance, Point With The Hand

hòuqūtuǐ zhǐshǒu pínghéng   后屈腿指手平衡

Settle the left foot and shift forward slightly, turning right. Parry upwards with the tip pointing up. Place the left hand in front of the right chest. Look to the rear right. (image 2.31a) Shift forward and lift the left foot and knee up behind. Point straight forward with the left hand. Look forward. (image 2.31b)

Stand firmly on the right leg.

Section Four

32. Bow Stance Pierce gōngbù cì jiàn 弓步刺剑

Land the left foot behind, straightening the left leg and bending the right, to take a right bow stance. Lower the sword to in front of the belly, then pierce directly forward, the arm and blade aligned at shoulder height, tip forward. Place the left hand on the right wrist. Look forward. (image 2.32)

Take a stable bow stance and pierce with power.

33. Retreat, Left And Right Traps tuìbù zuǒyòu lán jiàn 退步左右拦剑

Push into the right foot and shift back. Retreat the right foot and bend both legs. Take the sword flat across out to the left and turn slightly to the left. The tip points forward and the right palm is turned up. Place the left hand on the right wrist. Look forward. (image 2.33a) Retreat the left foot and bend both legs, turning slightly to the right. Take the sword flat across to the right side and turn right. The tip slants up and the right palm is turned down. Hold the left hand out to the left side. Look forward. (image 2.33b)

The right and left retreating steps are quick, and the trapping actions are powerful.

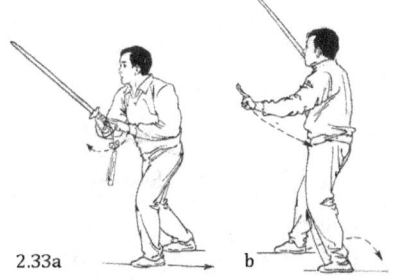

34. Raised Knee Smear tíxī mǒ jiàn 提膝抹剑

Push into the right foot to shift back, then retreat a step behind. Raise the left knee and stand up on the right leg. Smear the sword down to the right with the tip slanting up and the right palm down. Hold the left hand out to the left side. Look forward. (image 2.34)

Stand firmly on the right leg.

2.34

35. Prone Low Pierce (Leopard Cat Pounces On A Rat)

fúshēn xiàcì (límáo pūshǔ)　　　　　　伏身下刺（狸猫扑鼠）

Sit down, squatting fully on the right leg. Land the left foot in front and straighten the leg. Bring the sword in beside the right waist, then lean forward and pierce forward and down, the arm and blade aligned and the tip pointing forward and down, the right palm down. Place the left hand on the right wrist. Look past the tip. (image 2.35)

Stay stable when leaning forward. Pierce with power.

2.35

36. Raised Knee Smear　　　　tíxī mǒ jiàn　　　　提膝抹剑

Push into the right leg to stand up on it, raising the left knee. Bring both hands out to either side, palms down. Point the sword tip and the 'sword fingers' up. The torso leans forward slightly. Look forward. (image 2.36)

Stand firmly on the right leg.

2.36

37. Step Forward Scoop　　　　shàngbù tiǎo jiàn　　　　上步挑剑

Land the left foot forward and bend both legs. Lower both hands slightly. (image 2.37a) Step the right foot, then the left, moving forward one step each. Look forward. (images 2.37b, 2.37c) Shift forward and push into the left foot to jump forward, raising the right knee. Open and lift the hands out to the sides, keeping the sword tip pointing forward. Look forward and down. (image 2.37d)

KUNWU SWORD

2.37a b c d

Land the right foot forward and bend both legs, turning slightly leftward. Circle the sword tip down past the torso then scoop up so that the blade slants up. Hold the left hand up out to the side. Look forward. (image 2.37e)

Step and jump smoothly and in a well coordinated manner. Scoop up strongly.

2.37e

38. Closed Stance Dab   bìngbù diǎn jiàn   并步点剑

Bring the left foot up to meet the right and stand into a closed stance, turning left. Circle the sword tip around to dab horizontally to the front. The right arm is fully extended and the sword tip is just below wrist height. Hold the left hand up above and behind the head. Look forward, to the right. (image 2.38)

Step up quickly into stance. Dab strongly.

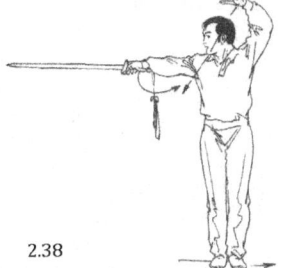
2.38

39. Empty Stance, Lift The Sword And Point With The Hand

xūbù tí jiàn zhǐshǒu   虚步提剑指手

Sit down into both legs, then move the left foot a step to the left, touching down the ball of the foot. Lift the sword grip at the right side, tip slanting down. Place the left hand on the right wrist. Look to the right side. (image 2.39a) Shift to the right, bending the legs further to take a left empty stance. Point with the left hand directly out to the left side, palm down. Look forward. (image 2.9b)

Keep a clear distinction between weighted and unweighted legs in the stance.

2.39a b

53

CHAQUAN, VOLUME III

Section Five

40. Jump To Insertion Stance Reverse Slice Up

tiao chābù fǎnliǎo   跳叉步反撩

Move the left foot forward, settling the foot down and turning it out. Lift the right heel and bend both legs, shifting to the left leg. Circle the sword forward from below, then to the left, lifting it above the head to the forward left. Turn the body left. The tip points to the upper front on the left. Place the left hand on the right wrist. Look forward, to the right. (image 2.40a) Push into the left foot to jump up, moving the right foot forward whilst airborne. Land on the right foot, holding the left foot up behind with the knee bent. Turn the body slightly leftward. Hold the sword up on the left side, tip pointing to the upper left. Keep the left hand on the right wrist. Look forward, to the right. (image 2.40b) Step the left foot behind the right leg with an insertion step, touching down the ball of the foot. Straighten the left leg and bend the right, to take a back-cross stance. Circle the sword from above, to the left, down, and across to the lower right to slice up. The arm and sword form an angled line with the tip pointing down. Lean slightly to angle the body to the left. Hold the left hand out to the left side. Look to the lower right. (image 2.40c)

Take and hold a stable cross-step. Do the reverse slice up strongly.

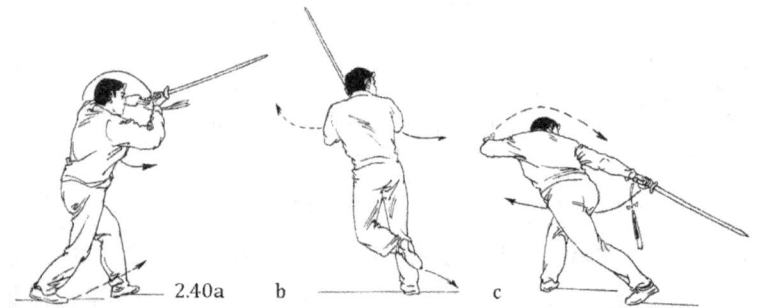

2.40a   b   c

41. Roll Over, Hook And Chop   fānshēn guà pī jiàn   翻身挂劈剑

Roll over to the left, pivoting around on the spot to stand up whilst twisting and leaning back, keeping the legs slightly bent. Circle the sword around with the turn to parry up to the left, the tip slanting up. Hold the left hand angled out to the left side. Look at the blade. (image 2.41a) Turn left, pivoting to the left foot on the spot, then bend the left leg and straight the right. Circle the sword to parry down to the left, tip down. Hold the left hand under the right forearm. Look down to the front. (image 2.41b) Shift forward. Step the right foot forward, straightening both legs in a relaxed manner. Circle the sword to parry to the left and up, tip pointing back, blade at the height of the left shoulder. Hold the left hand out to the left side. Look forward. (image 2.41c) Shift to the right and raise the left knee. Chop out to the front, tip forward. Hold the left hand above the head at the left. Look forward. (image 2.41d)

Keep balance when doing the rolling over and stepping. Chop strongly.

2.41a b c d

42. Turn Around, Hook And Dab

zhuànshēn guà diǎn jiàn   转身挂点剑

Turn left and land the left foot forward to the left, turning the foot slightly out. Bend both legs. Lift the sword above the head, tip pointing to the upper left. Hold the left hand out, slanting down. Look forward, to the left. (image 2.42a) Twist to the left, turning the left foot out and lifting the right heel, with both legs bent. Circle the sword to parry down to the left, tip down. Place the left hand on the right wrist. Look forward, to the right. (image 2.42b) Shift forward and step the right foot forward, keeping both legs bent. Circle the sword up on the left to the rear to finish above the head in front, tip up. Hold the left hand out to the left side. Look forward, to the right. (image 2.42c) Bring the left foot up to meet the right, touching down the ball of the foot and sitting down into a T stance. Do a horizontal dab forward. Hold the left hand above and in front of the head. Look forward, to the right. (image 2.42d)

Turn and step quickly. Parry and dab with power.

2.42a b c d

43. Withdraw And Carry   chèbù tuō jiàn   撤步托剑

Withdraw the left foot to the rear left, bending the knee, extending the right leg almost straight, and shifting the weight mostly to the left leg. Bend the right arm and lift the sword grip in front of the right shoulder, tip pointing to the upper right. Press the left hand on the right wrist. Look forward, to the right. (image 2.43)

CHAQUAN, VOLUME III

Withdraw the foot quickly. Carry the sword up with power.

2.43

44. Empty Stance Separate   xūbù fēn jiàn   虚步分剑

Push into the left leg and shift to the right. Step the left foot forward in front of the right foot, touching down the ball of the foot. Bend both legs to sit into a left empty stance. Circle the sword so that the tip goes up, then left, and then turns in front of the body to the right, to open out to the right side with the tip pointing up. Hold the left hand out to the side with the 'sword fingers' pointing up. Look forward. (image 2.44)

Sit into a distinctly weighted / unweighted empty stance.

2.44

45. Step Forward Dabs (Phoenix Nods Its Head Thrice)
shàngbù diǎn jiàn (fènghuáng sān diǎntóu) 上步点剑（凤凰三点头）

Step the left foot a half-step forward, then bring the right foot up a half-step with a follow step, touching down the ball of the foot. Do a horizontal dab to the front at the right. Hold the left hand out level at the left side. Look forward. (image 2.45a) Shift forward and raise the right knee. Scoop up with the sword tip. Scoop up also with the left hand. Look forward. (image 2.45b) Land the right foot forward, bending the knee. Lift the left heel, almost straightening the leg. Do a horizontal dab to the front at the right with the sword tip. Hold the left hand out to the left side. Look forward. (image 2.45c)

2.45a   b   c

Shift forward, raising the left knee. Scoop up with the sword tip, also scooping up with the left hand. Look forward. (image 2.45d) Land the left foot forward, bending both legs. Do a horizontal dab forward on the right, and hold the left hand out to the left side. Look forward. (image 2.45e)

Connect the steps and dabs and keep the action continuous. When dabbing, cock the wrist. When scooping, settle the wrist down.

46. T Stance Diving Stab (Golden Needle Enters The Ground)

dīngbù xiàzhā jiàn (jīnzhēn rùdì)　　　　丁步下扎剑（金针入地）

Shift forward and bring the right foot up to meet the left, touching down the ball of the foot and bending both legs to take a T stance. Stab downwards in front, leaning slightly to the forward leg. Place the left hand on the right wrist. Look down in front. (image 2.46)

Complete the T stance at the same time as the downward stab.

47. Turn Around, Raised Knee High Dab

zhuànshēn tíxī shàngdiǎn jiàn　　　　转身提膝上点剑

Pivot on the left foot to turn back around to the right, then withdraw the right foot to the rear right. Straighten the right leg in a relaxed manner and bend the left. Circle the sword across so that the tip goes to the outside of the left leg, keeping the left hand on the right wrist. Look back to the right. (image 2.47a) Shift to the right and turn further to the right, raising the left knee. Bring the sword up, circling it then dabbing upwards with the tip slanting up and the arm straight. Hold the left hand up above the head at the left. Look up to the right. (image 2.47b)

Turn quickly, stand firmly, dab with power.

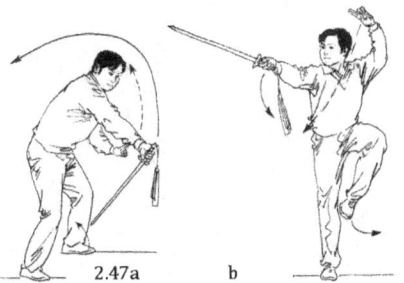

Section Six

48. Turn Around, Smear (Swallow Skims The Water)

zhuànshēn mǒ jiàn (yànzi chāoshuǐ)　　转身抹剑（燕子抄水）

Land the left foot to the rear left, bending both legs. Circle the sword down, right palm up, sword tip pointing to the rear right. Hold the left hand palm down in front of the belly. Look to the rear right. (image 2.48a) Turn left, bending into the left knee and straightening the right to take a left bow stance. Circle the sword down from the lower right, then left and up with a smearing action, tip slanting up. Lift the left hand above the head. Look forward, to the left. (image 2.48b)

Land, turn, and smear in one coordinated move.

2.48a　　　　　　　　　　　b

49. Step Forward Right And Left Smears (Push Aside The Clouds To Look At The Sun)

shàngbù yòuzuǒ mǒ jiàn (bōyún wàngrì)　　上步右左抹剑（拨云望日）

Shift to the left. Bring the right foot up to meet the left, touching the ball of the foot down and keeping both legs bent. Lower both hands slightly. Look forward, to the left. (image 2.49a) Step the right foot forward, to the right, bending the right knee and straightening the left to take a right bow stance. Turn the sword blade over, palm down, and smear flat across to the right, tip forward. Place the left hand on the right wrist. Look forward, to the right. (image 2.49b) Shift forward. Bring the left foot up to meet the right foot, touching down the ball of the foot and bending both legs. Look forward, to the left. (image 2.49c) Step the left foot forward, to the left, bending the knee and straightening the right leg to take a left bow stance. Turn the sword blade over, right palm up, and smear flat across to the forward left. The tip still points forward. Keep the left hand on the right wrist. Look forward, to the left. (image 2.49d)

2.49a　b　　　　　　c　　　　　　d

KUNWU SWORD

Step forward and smear with continuous, coordinated, well rounded movements.

50. Turn Around, Raised Knee Hooking Parry

zhuànshēn tíxī guà jiàn　　　　　　　　转身提膝挂剑

Shift forward. Step the right foot forward, turning it inwards. Turn around to the left. Bring the sword around with the turn, holding it in front of the body, tip up. Hold the left hand out in front of the belly. Look forward. (image 2.50a) Shift to the right. Retreat the left foot and turn left, bending both legs and sitting towards the left leg. Chop down in front until the arm and blade are aligned horizontally. Hold the left hand out behind at the left side. Look forward. (image 2.50b) Shift back and raise the right knee. Circle the sword tip down and back, doing a parry with the inside of the blade, drawing a full vertical circle in front of the body until the tip is up. Hold the left hand over the head. Look forward. (image 2.50c)

Stay steady when you turn and raise the knee. Hold the grip firmly to do the parry, but keep the wrist supple, to draw a full vertical circle.

51. Jump To Low Pierce

tiàobù xiàcì jiàn　　　　　　　　跳步下刺剑

Land the right foot forward and push into the left foot, lifting the foot and knee up behind and leaning the torso slightly forward. Lower the sword down to horizontal in front of the body, tip still forward. Place the left hand on the right wrist. Look forward and down. (images 2.51a, 2.51b) Push into the right foot to jump up. Land on the left foot, then the right, bending both legs. Pierce forward and down, the right arm and blade forming a line. Hold the left hand out behind at the left. Look forward and down. (images 2.51c, 2.51d)

CHAQUAN, VOLUME III

Jump lightly and pierce strongly.

52. Take The Sword In The Left Hand   zuǒ shǒu chí jiàn   左手持剑

Shift back without moving the feet, and bring the right hand in to in front of the chest, turning the sword tip up. Place the left hand on the right wrist. Look forward, to the right. (image 2.52a) Still not moving the feet, push into the right knee and almost straighten the left leg. Hold the sword horizontal in front of the chest, tip back. Take the guard in the left hand, keeping the right hand on the grip. Look forward, to the right. (image 2.52b)

Take the guard into the left hand quickly and accurately.

53. Left Sweep Kick   zuǒ sǎo tāng tuǐ   左扫蹚腿

Still not moving the feet, hold the sword in a reverse grip with the left hand and lower it to the left side. Point the right hand flat out in front, in 'sword fingers' shape. Look forward, to the right leg. (image 2.53a) Shift to the right. Half-squat on the right leg, then pivot on the ball of the foot to sweep the sole of the left foot around to the right, turning around one-eighty degrees rightward. Keep the left hand in a reverse grip on the sword and hold the flat of the blade tight behind the left forearm. Hold the right hand out to the right side. Look to the left side. (image 2.53b) Continue to turn around to the right, turning around another one-eighty degrees, finishing with the feet open and the legs almost straight. Keep holding the sword in a reverse grip in the left hand, tucking the flat of the blade under the left arm. Lift the right hand over in front. Look forward. (image 2.53c)

Stay stable when turning around. Sweep the flat of the left foot along the ground.

KUNWU SWORD

54. Flying Kick   fēijiǎo   飞脚

Shift forward, lifting the left heel. Swing the sword, still in reverse grip in the left hand, up in front to level. Hold the right hand out to the right side. Look forward. (image 2.54a) Push into the left foot, bend the knee, and swing it up in front. Bring the right hand up to level in front. Look forward. (image 2.54b) Push into the right foot to jump up, swinging the right leg up. Slap the right foot with the right hand. Look forward. (image 2.54c)

Jump lightly and slap with a clear, crisp, sound.

55. High Empty Stance Flash The Hand   gāo xūbù liàngzhǐ   高虚步亮指

Land on the left foot, then the right, bending both legs. Hold the sword out to the forward right, still in the left hand, palm down. Bring the right hand to the right side of the waist, palm up. Look forward, to the right. (image 2.55a) Turn left and shift to the right. Lift the left heel and hold the sword upright on the left side, still in reverse grip. Hold the right hand out to the right side. Look forward, to the left. (image 2.55b) Shift to the right. Move the left foot forward, touching down the ball of the foot. Bend the right leg slightly to take a left high empty stance. Hold the right hand above the head with the palm up and the 'sword fingers' angled up. Place the left arm at the left side with the arm bent, keeping the sword upright at the side. Look to the left. (image 2.55c)

Stand in a well-defined empty stance, weighted on the right leg.

CHAQUAN, VOLUME III

56. Withdraw, Press Down With The Palm   chèbù ànzhǎng   撤步按掌

Retreat the left foot. Lower the right hand. Look forward. (image 2.56a) Shift back. Retreat the right foot. Open the hands out to either side. Look forward. (image 2.56b) Shift back. Bring the left foot in to beside the right and stand up. Lower the arms to the sides. Look to the left. (image 2.56b)

Lower the arms while retreating, to complete the movement as the stance is taken.

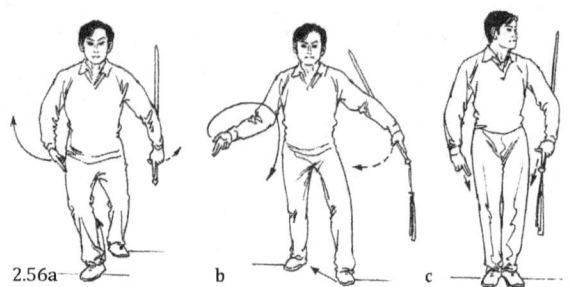

57. Closing Posture (Stand To Attention Holding The Sword)
     shōu shì (lìzhēng chí jiàn)   收式（立正持剑）

Stand to attention. Let the arms hang in a relaxed manner. Look forward. (image 2.57)

LOCKING SPEAR

锁口枪

About the Locking Spear

The spear is made up of wooden shaft – usually a trimmed white waxwood tree – and a metal head. The shaft can be differentiated into the fore-section – the third nearest the tip, the mid-section - the middle third, and the aft-section – the third nearest the butt. The thicker end of the shaft, near the butt, is called the grip. The slenderer end, called the thin end, has the head fitted into it. The blade part of the head is flat with diagonal edges and a tip. A tassel is attached where the head meets the shaft.

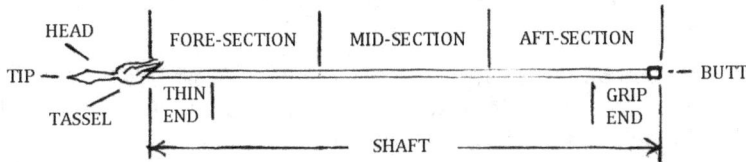

The length of the spear that an individual will use is determined by standing with the butt on the floor and the shaft vertical beside the body. The tip should be to the top of a fully upstretched arm and hand. The circumference of the shaft is measured at the midline of the shaft, and must be 2.29 cm for men and 2.13 cm for women. There is no circumference restriction for children. There is no weight restriction for either shaft or head.

Smooth grip means to hold the shaft with both hands, the thumb webs both facing the spear head.

SMOOTH GRIP

Single grip means to hold the spear in one hand, on any part of the shaft. You may also hold with both hands with the thumb webs facing each other.

The hand shape when not holding the spear is with the thumb and palm tucked and the four fingers straight and pulled back.

The Main techniques of the Locking Spear

Stab: Holding the shaft in both hands, stab straight forward, transmitting power to the tip, the rear hand at the butt touching the front hand that the shaft has slid through. [tr. note: A stab may be done in other ways, as long as the shaft is stabilized.] A high stab angles upwards between shoulder and head height. A low stab angles downwards below the knees but does not touch the ground. A level stab is horizontal. A high level stab is at chest height. A middle level stab is between waist and chest height. A low level stab is at knee height. A bottom level stance is about twenty centimeters from the ground.

Outer Trap: The spear tip circles anti-clockwise left, outside, and downwards. The left forearm laterally rotates. Power goes to the thin end of the shaft. The tip travels no higher than the shoulders and no lower than the knees.

Inner Trap: The spear tip circles clockwise from the left, inside, and downwards. The left forearm medially rotates. The power goes to the thin end of the shaft. The tip travels no higher than the shoulders and no lower than the knees.

Dab: The spear tip dips down from above with a short power. The power reaches the tip. A high dab is between head and shoulder height. A level dab is between shoulder and hip height. A low dab is between knee and ground height.

Snap: The spear tip snaps upwards or to either side with a short power, the force making the tip shake. A high snap finishes with the tip no higher than the head. A level snap finishes with the tip no higher than the chest. A low snap finishes with the tip between knee and ground height.

Chop: With both hands on the shaft, chop down quickly and forcefully from above. The power goes to the tip. In a reverse chop, the forward hand is underneath the shaft with the palm up. In a swinging chop, the shaft first draws a fast, full, vertical circle, and continues immediately to chop.

Grip Strike: With both hands on the spear, chop down forcefully with the grip end. Power goes to the grip end. A crossing grip strike is horizontal to either side, also strong, and with power going to the grip end.

Flowers: With the hands in the mid-section of the shaft, circle the spear in circles so that it 'dances'. Vertical flowers draw a vertical circle close to the body at either side. Level flowers draw a flat circle above the head. The flowers must be quick and the movement must be well connected.

NAMES OF THE MOVEMENTS OF THE LOCKING SPEAR FORM

Position Of Preparation (Stand To Attention Holding The Spear)
Section One
1. Step Forward, Lash The Hand
2. Closed Stance Level Stab
3. Jumping Turn To Chop

LOCKING SPEAR

4. Closed Stance Inner Trap And Stab
5. Bow Stance Outer Trap And Stab
6. Bow Stance Inner Trap And Stab
7. Raised Knee Present The Spear

Section Two

8. Walking Presenting The Spear
9. Jumping Turn To Stab
10. Half Horse Stance Hold The Spear
11. Jump To Bow Stance Push
12. Raised Knee Crossing Grip-Strike
13. Drop Stance Thread The Spear
14. Raised Knee Cradle The Spear
15. Jump To Bow Stance Press Down

Section Three

16. Half Horse Stance Inner Trap
17. Closed Stance Stab
18. Closed Stance Inner Trap And Stab
19. Bow Stance Outer Trap And Stab
20. Bow Stance Inner Trap And Stab
21. Turn Around, Bow Stance Stab
22. Closed Stance Stand The Spear

Section Four

23. Flowers On The Left
24. Jumping Turn, Bow Stance Lay The Spear On The Back
25. Turn Around, Horse Stance Lift
26. Jump To The Side, Press Down
27. Bow Stance Stab
28. Roll Over And Chop
29. Bow Stance Stab
30. Tuck The Wrist And Stab
31. Thread The Spear Behind The Back
32. Turn Around Thread The Spear (Lock The Opening or Mouth)
33. Bow Stance Inner Trap And Stab

Section Five

34. Turn Around, Parry On The Right (Surging Current)
35. Parry On The Left (Surging Current)
36. Parry And Press Down
37. Roll Over And Stab
38. Jump To Back-Cross Stance Low Stab
39. Jump To Leaning Dab (Go Fishing)
40. Bow Stance Outer Trap, Inner Trap, Stab

CHAQUAN, VOLUME III

Section Six
41. Turn Around, Bow Stance Stab
42. Flowers On Left And Right
43. Jumping Turn To Low Stab
44. Hastening Step, Pull The Spear, Tornado Kick
45. Bow Stance Pull The Spear And Flash The Palm
46. Bow Stance Inner Trap And Stab
47. Bow Stance Chop With The Grip End
48. Raised Knee Lay The Spear On The Back

Section Seven
49. Single Handed Grip, Leap Over A Sweeping Spear
50. Turn Around To Bow Stance, Swinging Chop With The Grip End
51. Toss The Spear And Catch The Grip
52. Empty Stance Scoop Up
53. Closed Stance Hold The Spear And Lash The Hand
54. Withdraw, Hold The Spear And Lash The Hand
55. Closing (Stand To Attention Holding The Spear)

0. Position Of Preparation (Stand To Attention Holding The Spear)

yùbèi shì (lìzhèng chí qiāng)　　　预备势（立正持枪）

Stand to attention with the right hand holding the mid-section of the spear, which is standing upright with the butt on the ground at the right side of the body. Look forward. (image 3.0a) Without moving the body, bend the left arm slightly and medially rotate the hand to turn the palm down, fingers pointing in. Look to the left. (image 3.0b)

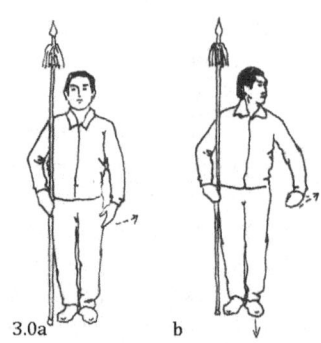

Section One

1. Step Forward, Lash The Hand　　shàngbù bǎizhǎng　　上步摆掌

Step the left foot a half-step forward, lifting the right heel. Lift the spear slightly with the right hand. Hold the left hand low out to the side. Look forward. (image 3.1a) Shift forward, then step the right foot forward, lifting the left heel. Hold the left hand out level to the side. Lift the spear, still vertical, at the right side. Look forward. (image 3.1b) Shift forward, bringing the left foot up to meet the right in a closed stance, then stand up. Lift the spear slightly. Circle the left hand up, then across to the right, to stop in front of the right side of the chest. Look to the left. (image 3.1c)

LOCKING SPEAR

Lash the left hand across in coordination with the stepping.

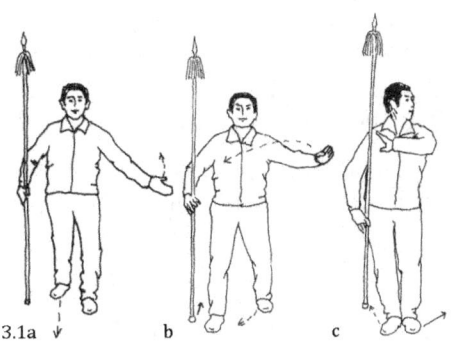

3.1a　　b　　c

2. Closed Stance Level Stab　　bìngbù píngzhā qiāng　　并步平扎枪

Turn left and bend the right knee to swing and lift the spear butt up to the rear, at the right. Hold the spear out with the tip slanting up. Bring the left hand to the belly. Look forward. (image 3.2a) Step the right foot forward and turn further left, almost straightening both legs. Still holding the spear just in the right hand, move the spear to the right with the tip pointing forward and up. Look forward, to the right. (image 3.2b) Shift to the right, then bring the left foot up to meet the right foot, turning further to the left. Stab level out to the right side, the spear still in the right hand. Hold the left arm out level to the side. Look to the right. (image 3.2c)

Stand firmly, turning and stabbing as one action.

3.2a　　b　　c

3. Jumping Turn To Chop　　tiàozhuàn pī qiāng　　跳转劈枪

Step the left foot across to the left. Bend the right arm to circle the spear tip downwards, parrying to in front of the right knee with the tip slanting down. Bend the left arm to bring the hand to the belly. Look to the right side. (image 3.3a) Shift to the left and raise the right knee. Laterally rotate the right forearm and raise the hand to circle the spear tip to the left, up, and out to the upper right, tip pointing up. Place the left hand on the grip end. Look forward, to the right. (image 3.3b) Push into the left leg to jump up, turning right. Land the right foot, holding the left knee up. Circle the spear in the right hand so that the tip goes to the right then down, drawing a full circle, ending with the tip up. Switch the left hand to the shaft mid-section.

67

Look forward. (image 3.3c) Turn right and land the left foot forward, standing up on both legs with the knees slightly bent. Slide the right hand to the grip and use both hands to forcefully chop the spear level forward to the left, tip pointing left. Look forward, to the left. (image 3.3d)

Jump lightly and chop with power. When circling the spear, keep the right hand at the mid-section in a loose grip.

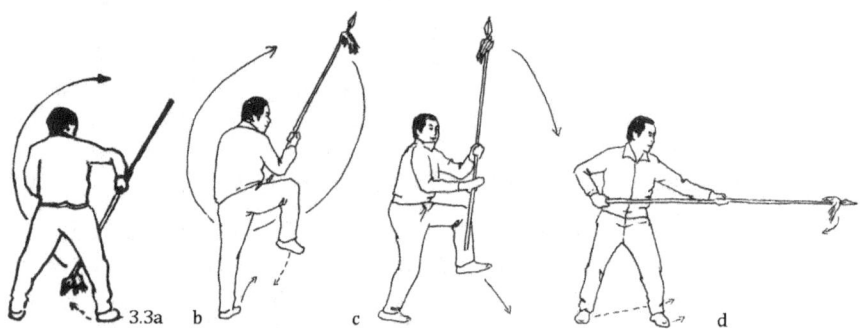

3.3a b c d

4. **Closed Stance Inner Trap And Stab**

    bìngbù názhā qiāng   并步拿扎枪

Shift to the left, then step the right foot through behind the left knee with an insertion step, touching down the ball of the foot in a back-cross stance. With both hands on the spear, laterally rotate the left hand to circle the tip to the left, so that the tip goes to the left, forward, and down. Look forward, to the left. (image 3.4a) Step the left foot forward, bending both legs. With both hands on the spear, medially rotate the left hand to circle the spear tip up and to the right. The shaft presses flat on the belly, the tip pointing forward, to the left. Look forward. (image 3.4b) Shift forward, then bring the right foot up to meet the left foot, standing up in a closed stance. With both hands on the spear, drive the right hand forward, sliding the spear through the left hand until the right hand meets the left hand to stab flat forward. The spear tip points forward. Reach the torso slightly forward. Look forward. (image 3.4c)

Do the back-cross stance and closed stance quickly. The inner trap must be round (a half-circle). Stab with strong power transmitting to the spear tip.

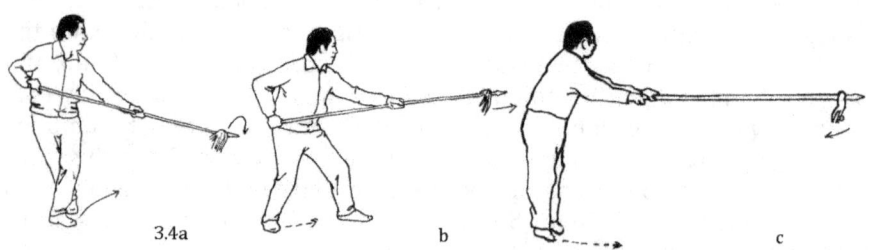

3.4a b c

LOCKING SPEAR

5. Bow Stance Outer Trap And Stab

gōngbù lánzhā qiāng   弓步拦扎枪

Step the right foot forward, bending the knee forward. Pull the grip with the right hand back to the right hip joint, sliding the left hand along the shaft until it is at the mid-section. The shaft is flat, the tip forward. Look forward. (image 3.5a) Shift to the right and take an arcing step with the left foot, moving forward, landing with the foot turned out. With the spear in both hands, laterally rotate the left hand so that the spear tip circles up and left. The shaft remains flat, with the tip forward. Look forward. (image 3.5b) Shift forward and step the right foot forward, bending the knee forward and almost straightening the left leg to take a right bow stance. Drive the right hand forward to meet the left hand to stab forward. The shaft is still at the left, the tip forward. Look forward. (image 3.5c)

Step forward quickly, be sure to circle to complete the outer trap, and to stab with power.

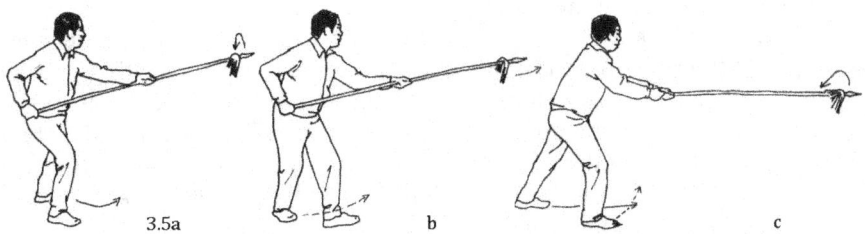

6. Bow Stance Inner Trap And Stab   gōngbù názhā qiāng   弓步拿扎枪

Shift forward and step the left foot forward to the left. Step the right foot behind the left leg with an insertion step, touching down the ball of the foot. Turn slightly to the right to take a back-cross stance. Bring the spear grip back to the right flank with the right hand and laterally rotate the left hand to circle the tip to the left, sliding the left hand to the mid-section. The tip slants down. Look forward, to the left. (image 3.6a) Step the left foot forward to the left, bending both knees slightly. With both hands on the spear, medially rotate the left hand to circle the tip to the left and up with an inner trap. The shaft is flat and the tip points forward, to the left. Look to the left. (image 3.6b) Push into the right foot to shift to the left, bending the left knee and straightening the right to take a left bow stance. Drive the right hand forward to meet the left hand, stabbing directly forward with the shaft level and the tip forward. Look forward. (image 3.6c)

Step quickly, do a circular trap, and stab strongly.

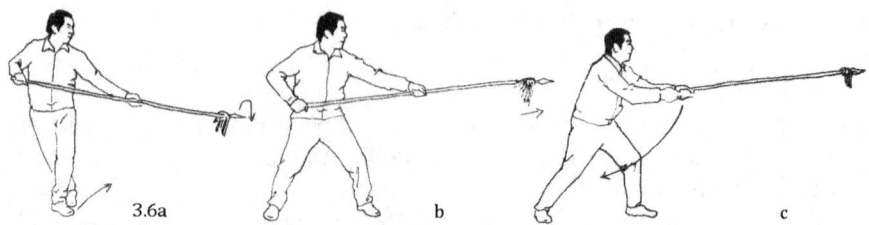

7. Raised Knee Present The Spear   tíxī jǔ qiāng   提膝举枪

Shift back and bend both knees to squat, turning slightly to the right. Pull the right hand back to bring the grip to between the legs, sliding the left hand to the midsection. The tip slants up. Look to the left side. (image 3.7a)

Turn right, pushing forward into the right knee and straightening the left leg to take a bow stance. Pull the grip in the right hand up to the head. The shaft is level and the tip points back [tr. note: behind the body, but still pointing in the same direction as before]. Release the left hand and bring it to the right forearm. Look forward, to the right. (image 3.7b) Push into the right foot and shift to the left, raising the right knee. Circle the left hand down then to the left, to hold it out on the left side with the arm straight, fingers up. Look to the left. (image 3.7c)

Follow an arc to pull the spear back, holding it level. Keep the action soft. Keep stable on the raised knee balance.

Section Two

8. Walking Presenting The Spear   jǔ qiāng xíngbù   举枪行步

Land the right foot forward to the right. Take a step in the same direction with the left foot, then the right. Turn gradually to the right as you walk. Hold the left hand out to the left side. Look forward [tr. note: look in the direction of travel, the spear still pointing in the same direction, which is now behind]. (images 3.8a, 3.8b, 3.8c)

9. Jumping Turn To Stab   tiàozhuàn zhā qiāng   跳转扎枪

Turn right and raise the left knee. Bring the right hand, bending the elbow, to hold the spear up in front of the chest. Place the left hand on the right wrist. The shaft is level at shoulder height, the tip pointing back [tr. note: the tip has not changed its direction, the body has turned around]. Look to the right. (image 3.9a) Push off with the right foot to jump up, spinning around to the right. With the right hand holding the grip, stab the spear directly out to the right after the body turns [tr. note: the tip has not changed its direction]. The arm and shaft form a straight line, the tip points right. Hold the left hand out to the side. Look to the right. (image 3.9c)

Jump and turn quickly, stab strongly.

10. Half Horse Stance Hold The Spear bànmǎbù chí qiāng 半马步持枪

Land on the left foot and turn right, landing the right foot behind the left foot, bending both legs to take a left half horse stance. Bring the right hand with the grip back to the right side of the belly. The shaft is level, at belly height, the tip pointing forward, to the left [tr. note: the tip has not changed its direction, the concept of front and rear, right and left, has changed]. Place the left hand on the mid-section. Look to the left. (image 3.10)

Land and take a firm stance.

3.10

11. Jump To Bow Stance Push   tiào gōngbù tuī qiāng   跳弓步推枪

Step the right foot forward and bend the knee to the side. Bring the spear, in both hands, to circle the tip left and down, then hold it up, forward to the left with the tip slanting up. Look forward, to the left. (image 3.11a) Push into the right foot to jump up. Land on the left foot then the right, to the right side. Bend the right knee to the side and straighten the left leg to take a right bow stance. Using both hands, circle the tip up, left, then push out to the right with the tip slanting down. Look forward, to the lower left. (image 3.11b)

Jump lightly and land firmly. Push into the fore-section of the shaft.

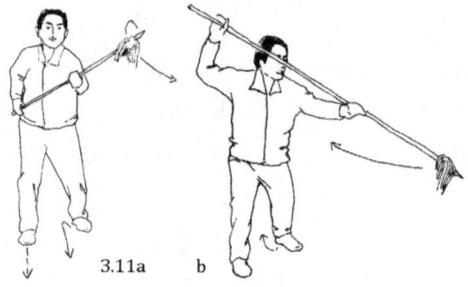

3.11a b

12. Raised Knee Crossing Grip-Strike   tíxī héngbà   提膝横把

Shift to the right and raise the left knee. Bring the left hand in underneath the left ribs and lash the spear forward with the right hand, to strike across to the right side with the butt. Slide the right hand to the shaft mid-section. Look at the spear butt. (image 3.12 and from the side)

Do the one-legged stance with good balance. Strike strongly.

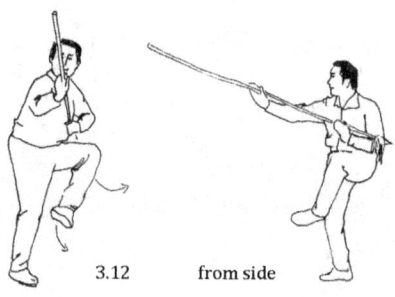

3.12   from side

LOCKING SPEAR

13. Drop Stance Thread The Spear   pūbù chuān qiāng   仆步穿枪

Land the left foot behind to the left and turn left, squatting on the right leg and extending the left leg to take a left drop stance. Using both hands, thread the spear down to the rear left, holding it out inside the left leg with the tip slanting down to the left. Lean the torso forward slightly. Look down to the left. (image 3.13 and from the side)

Turn quickly and drop into a solid stance.

3.13   from side

14. Raised Knee Cradle The Spear   tíxī bào qiāng   提膝抱枪

Push into the right foot to shift to the left and stand up, turning left, bending into the left knee and straightening the right leg. Thread the spear forward and up using both hands, sliding the hands along to the aft-section, spear tip moving forward and up. Look forward. (image 3.14a) Shift forward and step the right foot forward with the foot turned out and knee bent, lifting the left heel. Grip the shaft fore-section in the right hand and stand the spear vertically at the right side with the tip up. Look forward. (image 3.14b) Shift forward and raise the left knee. Circle the spear tip to the right, down, then left, using both hands, to complete the circle at the upper left with the tip up and aft-section tight to the left chest. Look to the right. (image 3.14c)

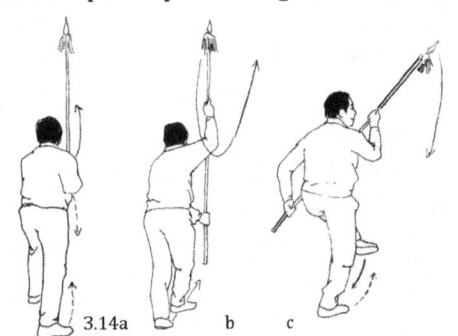

Step forward quickly and raise the knee with good balance. Circle to the cradle with a soft action.

3.14a   b   c

15. Jump To Bow Stance Press Down
tiào gōngbù yā qiāng   跳弓步压枪

Land the left foot forward and shift forward, raising the right knee. Circle the spear with both hands to bring the tip down and to the right to parry out to the lower right side, tip slanting down. Look forward and down. (image 3.15a) Push into the left leg to jump up. Land forward on the right foot, then the left. Bend the left knee forward and straighten the right leg. Circle the spear with both hands so that the tip goes back and up, then

73

forward and down, to press down in front at the left. The shaft is at waist height and the tip points forward, to the left. Look forward, to the left. (image 3.15b)

Jump lightly. Press down with power, focussing on the shaft fore-section.

Section Three

16. Half Horse Stance Inner Trap   bànmǎbù ná qiāng   半马步拿枪

Step the right foot to the right, bending both legs and shifting to the left leg to take a right half horse stance. Turn to the right and bring the spear tip down, then circle up to the right until the spear is level and the spear tip points right. Look to the right. (image 3.16)

Complete the step and the inner trap at the same time.

17. Closed Stance Stab   bìngbù zhā qiāng   并步扎枪

Shift to the right and bring the left foot up to meet the right foot, standing up. Turn to the right and stab the spear forward to the right to a level stab. The right hand switches to the end of the grip. Look forward, to the right. (image 3.17)

Complete the closed stance simultaneously with the stab.

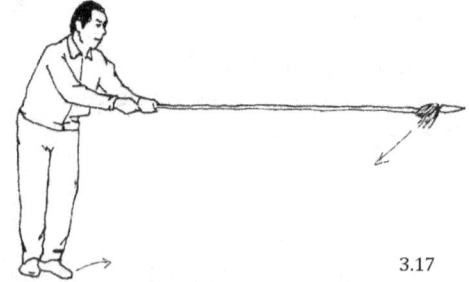

18. Closed Stance Inner Trap And Stab

bìngbù názhā qiāng   并步拿扎枪

Step the left foot forward and turn right. Bring the right hand, on the grip, to the belly and slide the left hand to the shaft mid-section. The tip slants down. Look forward, to the left. (image 3.18a) Shift to the left and step the

LOCKING SPEAR

right foot behind the left leg, touching the ball of the foot down and bending both legs. Laterally rotate the left hand, holding the grip in the right, to circle the spear tip to the left, the tip still slanting downwards. Look forward, to the right. (image 3.18b) Step the left foot forward, bending both legs. Medially rotate the left hand, holding the grip in the right, to circle the spear tip to the left and up. The shaft is level, and the tip points forward. Look forward, to the right. (image 3.18c)

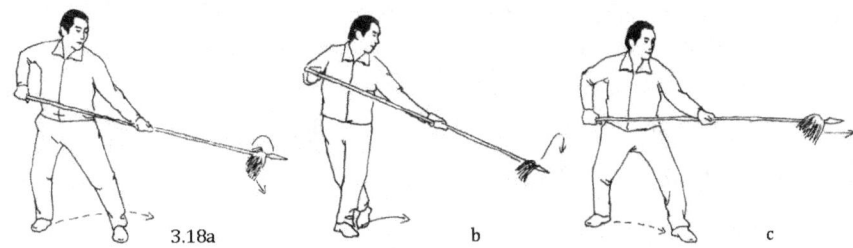

Shift to the left and bring the left foot in to meet the right foot, standing up. Stab the spear directly forward, to the right, sliding the shaft through the left hand, so the hands come together at the grip. Look forward, to the right. (image 3.18d)

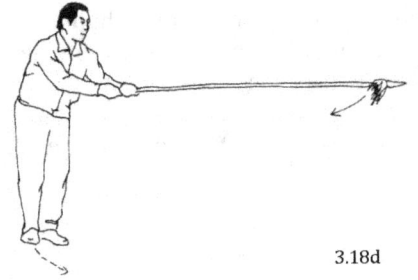

Do a full circle for the trap, and stab strongly.

19. Bow Stance Outer Trap And Stab
gōngbù lánzhā qiāng 弓步拦扎枪

Step the right foot forward to the right, bending the knee. Bring the spear grip to the right side of the belly with the right hand. Slide the left hand to the mid-section, keeping the shaft level. Look forward, to the right. (image 3.19a) Shift to the right and take an arcing step to the forward right with the left foot, turning the foot out and bending the knee. Working the spear in both hands, laterally rotate the left hand to circle the spear tip to the left, drawing a half circle with the shaft level.

75

Look forward, to the right. (image 3.19b)

Shift forward and take an arcing step forward with the right foot, bending the knee. Working with both hands, stab the spear directly forward, to the right, sliding the shaft through the left hand so that the hands meet at the grip. Look forward, to the right. (image 3.19c)

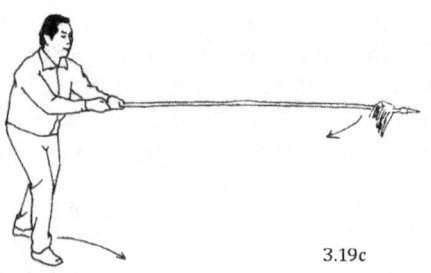

Draw a circle for the outer trap, and stab strongly.

20. Bow Stance Inner Trap And Stab

gōngbù názhā qiāng   弓步拿扎枪

Shift forward and step the left foot forward, to the right, turning right. Circle the spear tip to the left in a half-circle, working with both hands and sliding the left hand to the mid-section. The tip slants downwards. Look forward, to the right. (image 3.20a) Shift to the left and step the right foot forward behind the left leg, touching the ball of the foot down and bending both legs. Look forward, to the right. (image 3.20b)

Step the left foot forward, to the right, bending both legs. Working with both hands, medially rotate the left hand to circle the spear tip to the right a half-circle. The shaft is level at the waist. Look forward, to the right. (image 3.20c) Shift forward and bend the left knee. Stab the spear forward to the right, using both hands, and sliding the shaft through the left hand so that the hands meet at the grip. Look forward, to the right. (image 3.20d)

Step quickly, trap with a well defined circle, and stab strongly.

LOCKING SPEAR

21. Turn Around, Bow Stance Stab

zhuànshēn gōngbù zhā qiāng   转身弓步扎枪

Shift back, raising the left knee and turning around to the left. Slide the hands and lift the spear grip so that the tip moves to the rear left. Look back, to the left. (image 3.21a) Land the left foot to the left side, bending the knee. Stab the spear level to the left, sliding the shaft through the left hand, so that the hands meet at the grip. Look forward, to the left. (image 3.21b)

Turn quickly, land firmly, and stab powerfully.

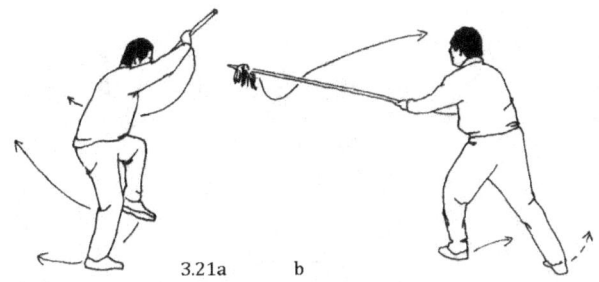

22. Closed Stance Stand The Spear   bìngbù lì qiāng   并步立枪

Turn right and step the right foot forward, to the right. Bring the left foot up to meet the right and stand up into a closed stance. Using both hands, lift the spear to stand vertically at the right side of the body, tip up. Look to the left. (image 3.22)

Take quick and firm steps.

CHAQUAN, VOLUME III

Section Four

23. Flowers On The Left   zuǒcè wǔhuā qiāng   左侧舞花枪

Step the left foot to the left side, turning the foot to the left and turning the body leftward. Separate the hands on the spear shaft and circle the tip down on the left, lifting the grip up on the right., so that the shaft is in front of the chest. Look to the left. (image 3.23a) Shift to the left and turn leftward, then step the right foot forward, almost straightening both legs. With both hands, circle the spear tip up and to the left, tucking the shaft under the right arm with the tip slanting up. Look forward and down to the right. (image 3.23b) Without moving the legs, circle the spear with both hands so that the butt goes left and up, around a full circle, until the shaft is in front of the chest and the tip points to the upper left. Look forward. (image 3.23c) Shift to the right and step the left foot back behind the right leg, touching the ball of the foot down, bending and crossing the legs. Lean forward. Circle the spear in both hands so that the tip goes up and to the right until the shaft is angled in front of the chest, tip slanting down. Look to the lower right. (image 3.23d)

Step through quickly. Move the spear through a full smooth circle.

3.23a   b   c   d

24. Jumping Turn, Bow Stance Lay The Spear On The Back

tiàozhuàn gōngbù bēi qiāng   跳转弓步背枪

Push into the right foot and raise the left knee, rolling over into the back to the left. Circle the spear in both hands to bring the tip down and to the left until the tip is up. Look up. (image 3.24a) Push into the right foot to jump up, spinning around to the left. Land the left foot, then the right, pressing into the right knee and straightening the left leg to take a right bow stance. Circle the spear in both hands

3.24a   b

LOCKING SPEAR

to bring the tip to the left and down until the aft-section lies behind the left arm at the side, the tip slanting down, and the right hand is above the head at the right. Look to the left. (image 3.24b)

Jump and spin around lightly. Land and tuck the spear onto the back as one coordinated action.

25. Turn Around, Horse Stance Lift

    zhuànshēn mǎbù tí qiāng　　　　　　　　　转身马步提枪

Without moving the feet, bring the spear in the left hand to the left side behind the body at belly height, and grasp the grip with the right hand. Look at the right hand. (image 3.25a) Shift to the right and turn back to the right. Step the left foot to the right and bend both legs to sit into a horse stance. Slide the right hand along the spear shaft to the mid-section until the spear is level, across the belly, tip pointing right. Hold the left hand up above the head at the left. Look to the right side. (image 3.25b)

Slide the right hand accurately to the mid-section. Turn quickly.

26. Jump To The Side, Press Down　　cètiàobù yā qiāng　　侧跳步压枪

Without moving the feet, bring the spear in the right hand to lay the shaft on the belly and take the grip in the left hand. Look to the right side. (image 3.26a) Shift to the left and raise the right knee. Hold the spear up in front of the chest in both hands, tip slanting down. Look down to the right. (image 3.26b) Push into the left foot to jump up. Land the right foot, then the left, opening the feet out to their respective sides with the knees bent. Circle the spear in both hands so that the tip moves back and up, drawing a full circle until the shaft is level across the belly, tip pointing right. Look to the right side. (image 3.26c)

Jump to the side quickly and lightly. Draw a full circle with the spear tip, pressing down strongly.

27. Bow Stance Stab   gōngbù zhā qiāng   弓步扎枪

Shift to the right and turn right, bending the right knee and straightening the left to take a right bow stance. Stab level out to the right, sliding the shaft through the right hand, so that it goes to the grip. The shaft is level and the tip points right. Look to the right. (image 3.27)

Turn quickly and stab strongly.

28. Roll Over And Chop   fānshēn pī qiāng   翻身劈枪

Shift to the right and step the left foot forward, turning rightward. Pull the spear grip back to the belly in the right hand, tip slanting down. Slide the left hand along to the shaft mid-line. Look down to the left. (image 3.28a) Push into the left foot to jump up, rolling around to the right. Land on the right foot, holding the left knee up. Circle the spear up over the head, tip slanting down. Look down to the left. (image 3.28b) Pivot on the ball of the right foot to turn back around to the right, then land the left foot forward, to the left, bending both legs. Circle the spear up and around to the right until it chops down, shaft level with the waist, tip pointing left. Look to the left. (image 3.28c)

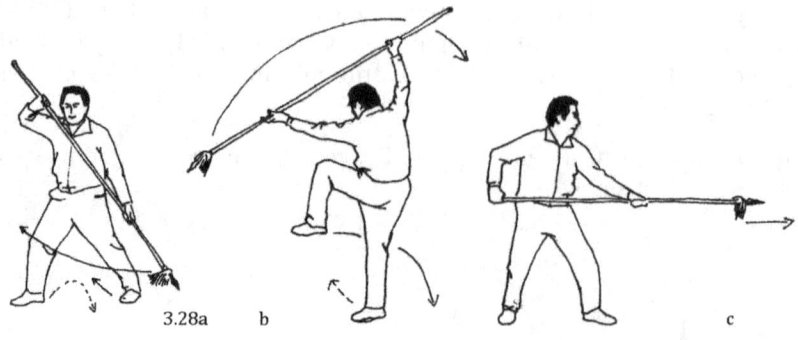

LOCKING SPEAR

Roll around quickly and land with good balance. Chop strongly.

29. Bow Stance Stab   gōngbù zhā qiāng   弓步扎枪

Shift to the left, bending the left leg and straightening the right to take a left bow stance. Do a level stab directly forward, sliding the shaft through the left hand back to meet the right hand at the grip. Look to the left. (image 3.29)

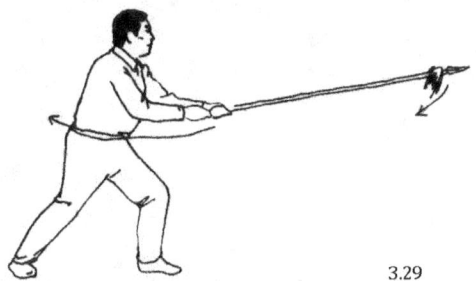

3.29

Stab with power.

30. Tuck The Wrist And Stab   kòuwàn zhā qiāng   扣腕扎枪

Without moving the feet, switch the grasp of the right hand and draw the spear grip to the rear, now with the palm up. Slide the left hand along to the mid-section. Turn slightly to the right. Look forward. (image 3.30a) Stab the spear forward with the right hand holding the grip with the wrist tucked under. Turn slightly to the left. Slide the spear through the left hand to grasp at the aft-section. Look forward. (image 3.30b)

Roll the right hand under and stab with the wrist tucked in one smooth action. The spear will be slanting slightly upwards for the stab.

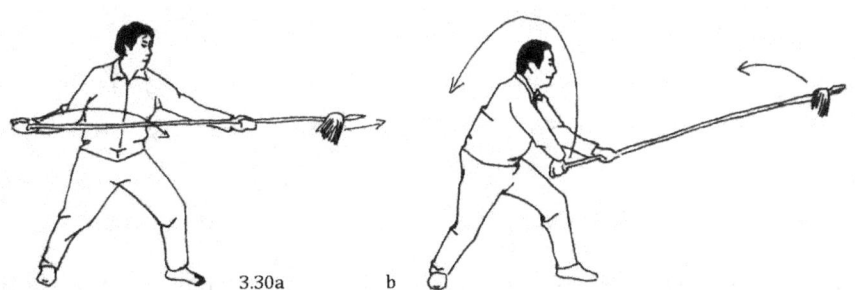

3.30a   b

31. Thread The Spear Behind The Back

bèihòu chuān qiāng   背后穿枪

Without moving the feet, lift both hands up over the head, then pull back with the right hand and roll the shoulder under until the shaft is laid on the back. Lean forward slightly. Slide the left hand along to the forward end of the mid-section. Look forward. (image 3.31a) Still without moving the feet, bend the right arm and push the spear butt strongly forward with the right hand [tr. note: push with a snap of the right wrist and release the spear] so that the spear travels forward along the back. Let the spear slide through the left hand, then catch it in the aft-section. Look forward. (image 3.31b)

Lean forward slightly to enable the placement of the spear on the back and facilitate the threading throw. Thread the spear quickly.

3.31a b

32. Turn Around Thread The Spear (Lock The Opening or Mouth)

zhuànshēn chuān qiāng (suǒkǒu)　　　　　　　　转身穿枪（锁口）

Without moving the feet, swing the right hand forward to grasp the spear grip, palm up. Look forward. (image 3.32a) Pull the grip back with the right hand, sliding towards the mouth to draw flat to the right. Slide the spear through the left hand until the right hand grasps at the fore-section, keeping the shaft at shoulder height. Hold the left hand out to the left side. Turn to the right, standing up with the legs almost straight in an open position. Look to the right. (image 3.32b)

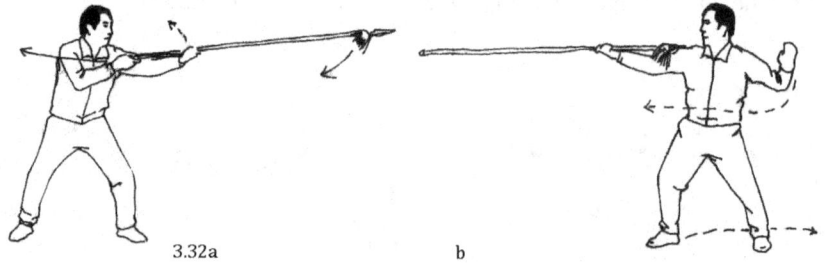

3.32a b

Shift to the left and retreat the right foot, turning around to the right. Thread the spear in towards the mouth, keeping it flat and pulling it to the right side. Take the aft-section in the left hand. The shaft is now at chest height. Look to the left. (image 3.32c) Hold the spear in the left hand and thread to stab it flat out to the right. Slide the spear through the right hand along to the grip. The spear remains at chest height, tip pointing right. Bring the left hand to the belly. Look to the right. (image 3.32d)

Turn quickly. Thread the spear in a smooth manner past the mouth area, keeping it level at all times.

LOCKING SPEAR

3.32c   d

33. Bow Stance Inner Trap And Stab
gōngbù názhā qiāng   弓步拿扎枪

Shift to the right and step the left foot forward, turning right. Step the right foot back behind the left leg towards the left, touching the ball of the foot down. Pull the spear grip back on the right side with the right hand, taking the mid-section in the left hand, to circle the tip to the left and down. The tip slants downwards. Look to the left side. (image 3.33a) Step the left foot across to the left, standing up naturally on both legs. Using both hands, circle the spear tip down, to the left, and up with an inner trap, the shaft at waist height. Look forward. (image 3.33b)

3.33a   b

Shift forward, bending the left knee and straightening the right, to take a left bow stance. Stab straight forward, sliding the spear through the left hand along to the grip. Look forward. (image 3.33c)

3.33c

Take quick steps, draw a full circle for the trap, and stab strongly.

CHAQUAN, VOLUME III

Section Five

34. Turn Around, Parry On The Right (Surging Current)

zhuànshēn yòucè guà qiāng (lìshuǐ qiāng)　转身右侧挂枪（立水枪）

Shift back, turning right, and bend the right knee to the side. Pull the spear grip back on the right side with the right hand, sliding the left hand along to the mid-section, angling the tip down. Look to the left. (image 3.34a) Shift to the right, turning around to the right, then circle the left foot around to step forward, to the right, bending the knee forward slightly. Circle the spear with both hands so that the tip goes across low and finishes angled down in front. Look forward and down. (image 3.34b) Shift forward and step the right foot, then the left, forward to the right. Lift the spear in both hands to the forward right, tip slanting up. Look forward, to the right. (image 3.34c)

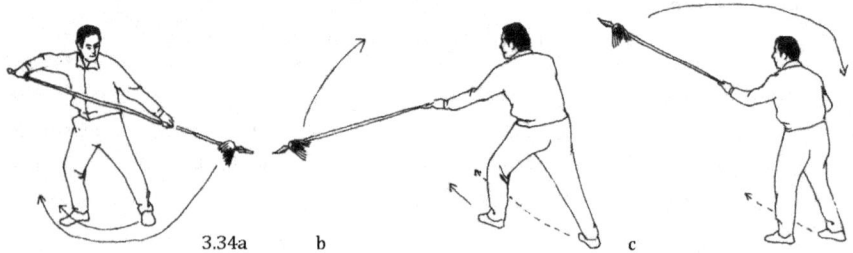

Step the right foot forward, to the right, and turn left. Circle the spear in both hands so that the tip goes across above towards the rear, holding the shaft up behind at the left, tip slanting down. Look back, to the left. (image 3.34d) Shift to the right and turn right, then step the left foot in an arcing step forward, to the right, touching the ball of the foot down and bending both legs to take a left empty stance. Circle the spear with both hands to do a parry towards the right in front, finishing with the shaft vertical and the tip down. Look forward. (image 3.34e)

Turn and step quickly and lightly. Tuck the left wrist in to parry down to the right.

35. Parry On The Left (Surging Current)

zuǒcè guà qiāng (lìshuǐ qiāng)　　　　　　　左侧挂枪（立水枪）

Step the left foot across to the left and turn left. Circle and lift the spear up with both hands so that the tip goes left then up to finish in front at the upper left. Slide the left hand along to the shaft mid-section. Look forward, to the left. (image 3.35a) Shift to the left and step the right foot forward to the left, touching down the ball of the foot with the toes turned out. Shift the

LOCKING SPEAR

right hand from the grip towards the mid-section. Look forward. (image 3.35b) Step the left foot forward to the left. Circle the spear in both hands so that the tip goes right and down, finishing with the tip pointing down to the right. Look down to the right. (image 3.35c) Shift to the left and turn left. Circle the right foot across to the left and stand up naturally on both legs. Circle the spear in both hands so that the tip goes forward, then left to parry inside the right leg. Look forward and down. (image 3.35d)

Move the feet lightly. Tuck the right wrist to parry with the spear.

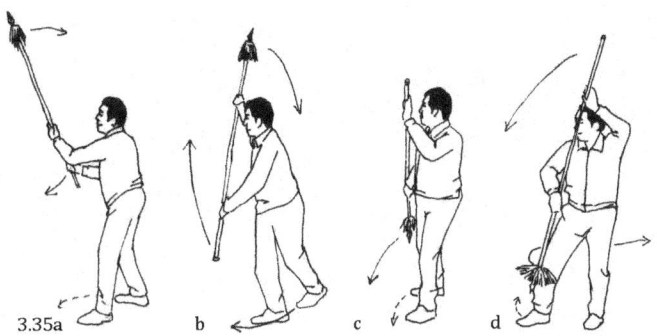

36. Parry And Press Down   guà yā qiāng   挂压枪

Move the right foot forward to the right, turning the foot out and bending both legs, turning to the right. Circle the spear in both hands so that the tip goes forward, then right to parry to the right side, tip angled to the rear. Look forward. (image 3.36a) Shift forward and turn further to the right. Step the left foot to the right behind the right leg in a cross-step. The left foot is turned out, the right heel is lifted, and the legs are crossed and bent. Circle the spear in both hands so that the tip goes up, then forward, finishing by pressing down at the left side, slanting down. Switch the right hand to the spear grip. Look down to the left. (image 3.36b)

Step quickly. Switch the grasp quickly. Press down strongly.

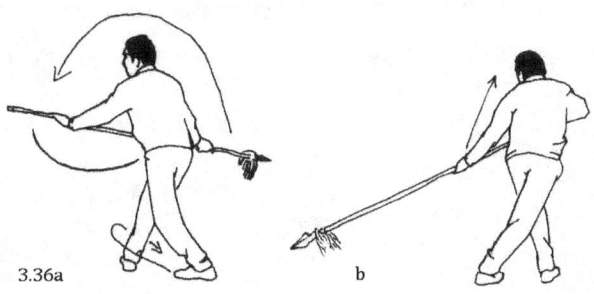

37. Roll Over And Stab   fānshēn zhā qiāng   翻身扎枪

Pivot around on both feet to do a rolling turn around to the right. Lift the spear above the head with both hands, sliding the left hand along to the grip.

Look upwards in front. (image 3.37a) Without moving the feet, turn further to the right. Hold the spear in front of the chest with the hands crossed, spear tip pointing right. Look forward. (image 3.37b) Continue to turn to the right, turning the right foot out. Hold the spear level at belly height, tip pointing forward. Look forward. (image 3.37c)

Roll over quickly, pivoting with stability.

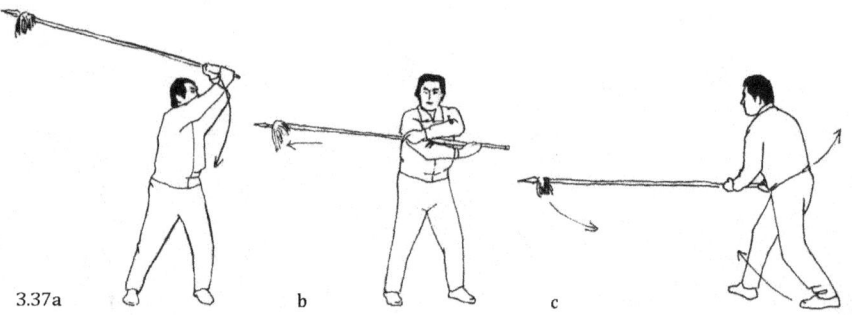

38. Jump To Back-Cross Stance Low Stab

tiào chābù xiàzhā qiāng　　　　　　　　　　跳插步下扎枪

Shift forward and bend the left knee, lifting the foot behind. Turn slightly to the right. Pull the spear grip back and up with the right hand, sliding the left hand to the mid-section. The spear tip slants down. Look forward. (image 3.38a) Push off with the right foot to jump up. Pull the spear forward and up above the head with both hands. Look to the left. (image 3.38b) Land the left foot, then the right, crossing it through behind the left leg, touching down the ball of the foot. Lean to the left. Stab down to the left, sliding the left hand towards the aft-section. Look down to the left. (image 3.38c)

Jump to the cross-step landing with good balance. Stab down strongly.

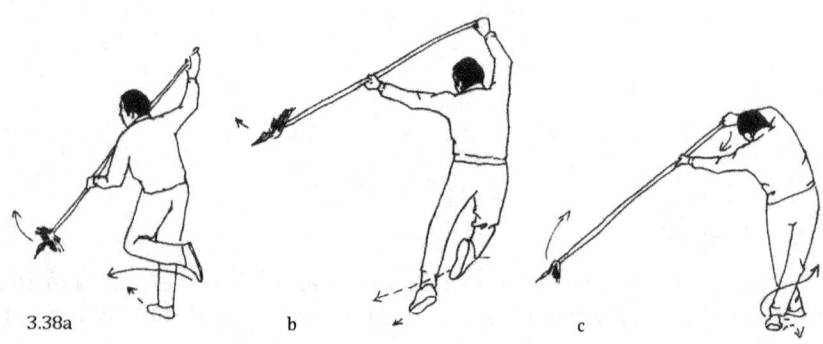

LOCKING SPEAR

39. Jump To Leaning Dab (Go Fishing)

tiàobù cèshēn diǎn qiāng (diàoyú)   跳步侧身点枪（钓鱼）

Push into the left foot to jump up. Land on the right foot, holding the left foot with bent knee up behind. Turn to the left. Do a level dab towards the right, using both hands. Look forward and down. (image 3.39a) Land the left foot behind and turn slightly to the left. Look forward and down. (image 3.39b)

Jump with stability. Do the curving dab with power.

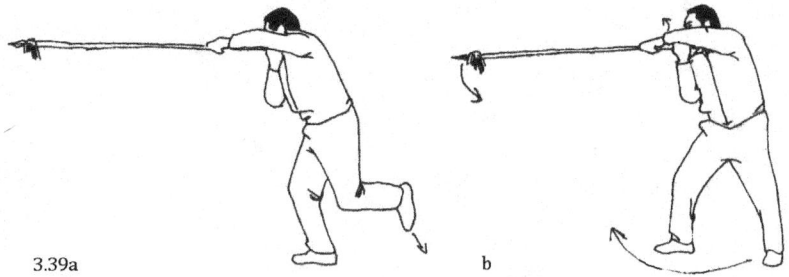

40. Bow Stance Outer Trap, Inner Trap, Stab

gōngbù lánnázhā qiāng   弓步拦拿扎枪

Shift forward and step the left foot forward, straightening the leg. Bend the right leg and turn right. Circle the spear in both hands to bring the tip to the left and down with an outer trapping action, ending with the tip slanting down. Look to the left. (image 3.40a) Shift forward, bending both legs and turning left. Circle the spear in both hands to do an inner trapping action to the left, up, and right, finishing with the shaft at waist height, tip forward. Look forward. (image 3.40b) Shift forward, bend the left knee and straighten the right, to take a left bow stance. Stab forward with the spear level. Look forward. (image 3.40c)

Make sure that both the outer and inner traps are circular. Stab with power.

CHAQUAN, VOLUME III

Section Six

41. Turn Around, Bow Stance Stab
zhuànshēn gōngbù zhā qiāng 转身弓步扎枪

Shift back and raise the left knee. Turn around to the left, pulling the spear across and down to the left side of the body, tip down. Slide the left hand towards the shaft fore-section. Look down to the left. (image 3.41a) Swivel on the right foot to turn left, then land the left foot forward, bending the knee and straightening the right to take a left bow stance. Turn further left and do a level stab, sliding the left hand towards the aft-section. Look forward. (image 3.41b)

Turn quickly, land firmly, and stab strongly.

42. Flowers On Left And Right   zuǒyòu wǔhuā qiāng   左右舞花枪

Shift back and withdraw the left foot, standing up with the feet open front and back. Pull the spear in to in front of the chest, tip slanting down. Slide the left hand along to the fore-section. Look forward, to the left. (image 3.42a) Shift forward and take a half-step forward with the left foot. Step the right foot forward and turn left. Circle the spear butt around to level in front, tucking the shaft into the right armpit, so that the tip points back. Look forward. (image 3.42b) Without moving the feet, turn slightly to the left. Circle the shaft with both hands so that the butt goes down, to the left, and up to the left side. Look forward. (image 3.42c) Swivel both feet and shift to the right, turning right. Circle the spear in both hands so that the butt goes right and down, completing a full circle with the tip slanting down. Look forward and down. (image 3.42d)

Keep the shaft close to the body whilst doing the vertical full-circle flowers. Slide the hands naturally along the shaft so that they coordinate well with the spear and enable the circles to be smooth.

LOCKING SPEAR

43. Jumping Turn To Low Stab   tiàozhuàn xiàzhā qiāng   跳转下扎枪

Shift forward and turn right, stepping the left foot forward. Circle the spear back, up, then forward, using both hands. Finish with the right hand raised above the head and the left hand slid to the fore-section at shoulder height. Look forward. (image 3.43a) Push into the right foot, then the left, to jump up and spin around in the air. Hold the spear with the tip down, spinning around behind at the lower left of the body. Look down to the left. (image 3.42b)

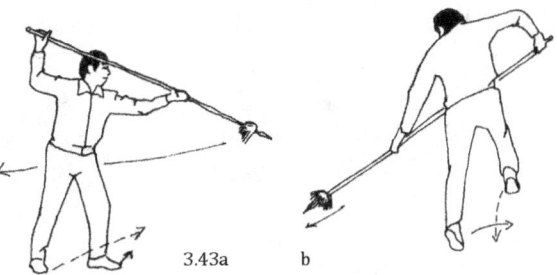

Turn left and land on the right foot. Hold the left foot up inside the right leg. Stab down to the front until the tip touches the ground. Release the left hand from the spear and lift it in front of the chest. Look to the right side. (image 3.42c) Land the left foot to the left and bend the knee. Circle the left hand down and out to the left, straightening the arm at shoulder height. Look down to the right. (image 3.42d)

Jump and spin quickly, land firmly, and stab strongly.

44. Hastening Step, Pull The Spear, Tornado Kick

    qūbù lā qiāng xuànfēngjiǎo   趋步拉枪旋风脚

Pull the spear back with the right hand without changing the relative position of the left hand. Push off with the right foot to jump up, doing a hastening step to move leftward – the right foot tapping the back of the left foot whist airborne. (images 3.44a and 3.44b) Land the right foot and step the left foot to the left, bending the knee and straightening the right leg to take a left bow stance. Look to the right. (image 3.44c)

Shift to the left and step the right foot forward to the left, hooking the foot in and turning around to the left. Lean forward slightly. Bend the left elbow to place the hand in front of the right chest. Look forward and down. (image 3.44d) Spin around up and to the left, swinging the left leg up around to the left. Swing the left hand up in front. Look at the left hand. (image 3.44e) Push off with the right foot to jump up. Swing the left leg to circle around to the left over the spear shaft. Do an inside crescent kick up and forward with the right foot. Slap the sole of the right foot with the left palm. Look forward. (image 3.44f)

Do not hit the spear with either leg. Do a crisp, loud slap with the inside crescent kick.

45. Bow Stance Pull The Spear And Flash The Palm

gōngbù lā qiāng liàngzhng　　　　　　　　　　　　　弓步拉枪亮掌

Turn left. Land on the left foot, then complete the right leg's circling kick over the spear shaft, keeping the knee up after the kick. Look down to the right. (image 3.45a) Settle the right foot then move the left foot across to the left, bending the knee. Lower the left hand, circling down then over to the left to shoulder height. Look down to the right. (image 3.45b)

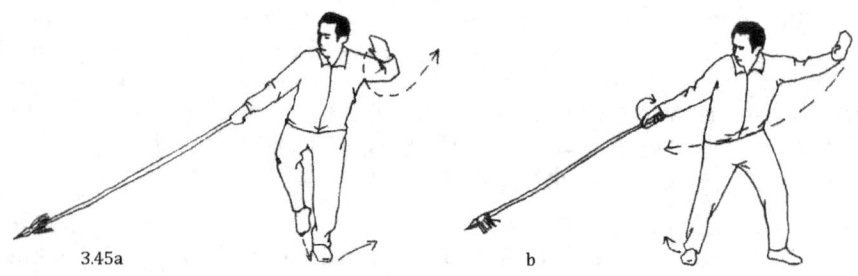

LOCKING SPEAR

Be sure not to touch the spear with the right leg.

46. Bow Stance Inner Trap And Stab   gōngbù názhā qiāng   弓步拿扎枪

Turn around to the right, turning the right foot out and bending both legs. Grasp the spear with the left hand at the mid-section. Hold the spear up in front of the chest with both hands. Look forward. (image 3.46a) Shift forward and step the left foot forward. Circle the spear tip to trap left and up, then stab forward. Look forward. (image 3.46b)

Coordinate the step and trap, and stab strongly.

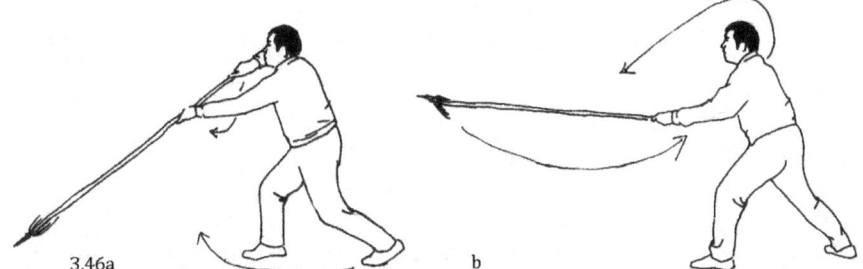

47. Bow Stance Chop With The Grip End   gōngbù pī qiāng   弓步劈把

Pull the spear back to the right side with both hands, switching them to the shaft fore-section. Bring the butt back, then up, then forward, to slap down on the ground. Lean the torso forward. Look forward and down. (image 3.47) [tr. note: the drawing must be a transitional move. The text definitely says that the hands switch to do a grip end slap on the ground]

Pull the spear back and switch the grip quickly. Chop the butt down strongly.

48. Raised Knee Lay The Spear On The Back   tíxī bēi qiāng   提膝背枪

Shift back and raise the left knee. Hold the spear up over the head and pull it back to lie on the upper back, reversing the grip of the left hand. Look forward. (image 3.48)

Place the spear onto the back quickly and stand firmly.

CHAQUAN, VOLUME III

Section Seven

49. Single Handed Grip, Leap Over A Sweeping Spear
dānshǒu wò qiāng sǎotuǐ téngyuè   单手握枪扫腿疼钺

Land forward on the left foot, step the right foot forward, then the left again. Look forward. (images 3.49a, 3.49b, 3.49c)

Shift forward and take an arcing step forward to the right with the right foot. Hold the left hand up over the head. Grasp the spear near its head in the right hand and sweep the shaft under the right leg. Look forward and down. (image 3.49d) Land the right foot, after jumping over the spear, lifting the left leg up behind. Swing the spear flat around to the left and back, leaning forward. Look forward and down. (image 3.49e)

Take three quick steps, keeping the centre of gravity stable and level. When jumping over the sweeping spear, neither leg may touch the shaft.

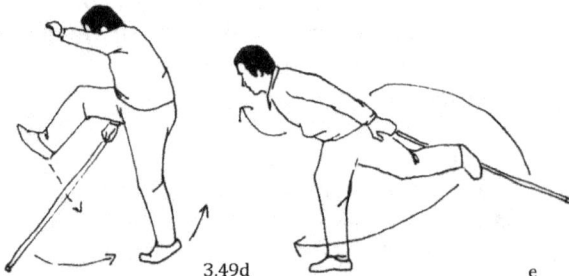

50. Turn Around To Bow Stance, Swinging Chop With The Grip End
zhuànshēn gōngbù lúnpī bà   转身弓步抡劈把

Land the left foot forward, turn right, and stand up. With the right hand, swing the spear up and over to the right, drawing a circle up over the head, with the butt following on the left. Look forward and up. (image 3.50a) Push into both legs and turn, shifting to the right and turning right. Bend the right leg and straighten the left to take a right bow stance. With the right hand, swing the spear over so that the butt circles up and to the right, then chops down on the ground. Lean the torso forward. Hold the left hand out to the side. Look down to the front. (image 3.50b)

Turn quickly. Chop forcefully with the spear butt.

LOCKING SPEAR

3.50a b

51. Toss The Spear And Catch The Grip   pāo qiāng wòbà   抛枪握把

Without moving the feet, pop the spear up and over with the right hand, so that it spins on itself, drawing a full circle in front of the body and the grip comes to the hand. Hold the left hand out to the side. Look forward. (image 3.51)

Lift the right hand to bring the spear shaft level, then toss it. Catch the grip quickly and accurately.

3.51

52. Empty Stance Scoop Up   xūbù tiǎo qiāng   虚步挑枪

Shift back and retreat the right leg, turning right. Withdraw the right hand up to the rear to shoulder height at the right side, holding the grip, bringing the spear up until the tip points to the upper left. Place the left hand standing at the right shoulder. Look forward. (image 3.52a) Shift to the right and move the left foot over to in front of the right foot, touching down the ball of the foot. Bend both knees to sit into a left empty stance. Push with the left hand, still standing, out in front to the left. Look forward, to the left. (image 3.52b)

3.52a b

Sit in a clear-cut empty stance.

53. Closed Stance Hold The Spear And Lash The Hand

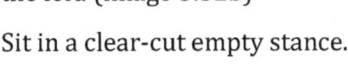

bìngbù chí qiāng bǎizhǎng   并步持枪摆掌

Without moving the feet, bring the right hand, still on the grip, across to the left ribs so that the shaft is upright at the left side of the body. Grasp the shaft mid-section in the left hand. Look forward, to the left. (image 3.53a) Still without moving the feet, stand up, straightening the legs in a relaxed manner. With both hands, circle the spear tip back, down, then forward to stand the spear up vertically at the right side of the body, tip up. Look forward. (image 3.53b) Bring the left foot in beside the right foot in a closed stance and place the spear butt on the ground. Slide the right hand down to the shaft mid-section. Place the left hand standing to press down in front of the right chest. Look to the left. (image 3.53c)

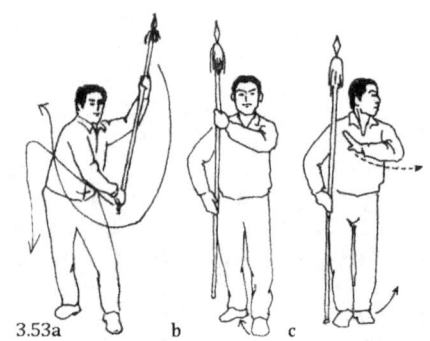

Keep the spear close to the body when moving it in a vertical circle.

54. Withdraw, Hold The Spear And Lash The Hand

chèbù chí qiāng bǎizhǎng　　　　　　　　撤步持枪摆掌

Lift the spear slightly with the right hand and retreat the left foot, touching down the ball of the foot. Lash the left hand out to the left, slanting down. Look forward. (image 3.54a) Shift back and retreat the right foot. (image 3.54b) Bring the left foot back to beside the right foot in a closed stance. With the right hand, replace the spear butt on the ground. Circle the left hand to lash in to in front of the right chest. Look forward. (image 3.54c)

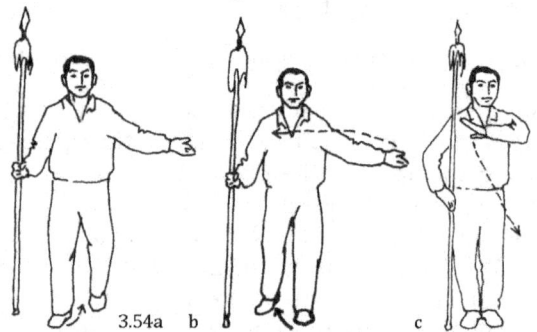

Coordinate the stepping with the action of the left hand.

55. Closing (Stand To Attention Holding The Spear)

shōu shì (lìzhèng chí qiāng)　　　　　　　收势（立正持枪）

Lower the left hand to hang at the side and stand to attention. Look forward. (image 3.55)

SHEPHERD'S STAFF

群羊棍

About the 'Flock of Sheep' Staff

The staff is a wooden shaft with a thick end, called the butt, and a thin end, called the tip. The shaft can be differentiated into the fore-section or tip-section – the third nearest the tip, the mid-section, and the aft-section or grip-section – the third nearest the butt. The length of the staff that an individual will use should equal his or her height standing with the butt on the floor and the shaft vertical beside the body. The circumference of the shaft is measured at the midline of the shaft, and should be 6.4 to 6.7 centimetres for men, and 6.0 to 6.4 centimetres for women. There is no circumference restriction for children. The staff is usually made of a prepared white waxwood tree, but may be made from any wood, or bamboo. There is no weight restriction.

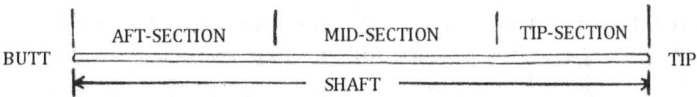

Smooth grip means to hold the shaft with both hands, the thumb webs both facing the tip.

SMOOTH GRIP

Facing grip means to hold the shaft with both hands, the thumb webs facing each other.

FACING GRIP

Single grip means to hold the staff in one hand, on any part of the shaft.

The hands may grip together or be separated on the shaft, depending on the needs of the various techniques.

The Main Techniques Of The Shepherd's Staff

Chop: With either a two-handed or single-handed grip, chop down quickly and forcefully from above. The power goes to the tip-section. In a swinging chop, the shaft first draws a fast, full, vertical circle, and goes immediately to a smoothly linked chop.

Swing: With either a two-handed or single-handed grip, swing the staff level to either side in a half-circle or more, at least chest height. The power goes to the tip-section.

Poke: With a two-handed grip, stab the tip or the butt directly in a straight line, going forward, to the side, or to the rear. The power goes directly into the end that is striking.

Snap: With a two-handed grip, snap the tip up or to either side, with a short, powerful, snapping strike. The power goes to the tip. A high snap finishes with the tip above the chest but no higher than the head. A level snap finishes with the tip between waist and chest height. A low snap finishes with the tip between knee and ground height, not touching the ground.

Dab: With a two-handed grip, the tip dips down from above with a short power. The power reaches the tip. A high dab is between head and shoulder height. A level dab is between shoulder and hip height. A low dab is between knee and ground height, not touching the ground.

Slice Up: In a two-handed grip, swing the shaft quickly at either side of the body in. a vertical circle forward or backward, to slice up in the direction of travel. Power reaches the tip-section.

Sweep: With a single-handed grip, sweep the staff tip below waist height in a level swing. May also swing the staff with the tip on the ground and the shaft slanting downwards. It must be quick and forceful. Power reaches the fore-section.

Flowers: With the hands in the mid-section of the shaft, circle the staff in vertical circles close to the body, alternating at each side. The flowers must be quick and the movement must be smooth.

Names Of The Movements Of The Shepherd's Staff Form

0. Position Of Preparation (Stand To Attention Holding The Staff)

Section One
1. Step Forward, Stand The Staff
2. Empty Stance Poke
3. Stamp And Raise The Staff
4. Jump To Bow Stance Poke
5. Left And Right Parry And Chop
6. Jumping Turn To Empty Stance Cradle The Staff

7. Right Drop Stance Chop
8. Left Drop Stance Chop
9. Right Drop Stance Chop
10. Empty Stance Cradle The Staff
11. Bow Stance Poke
12. Turn Around, Poke

Section Two

13. Jumping Turn With A Swing
14. Empty Stance Cradle The Staff
15. Left And Right Flowers
16. Jumping Turn, Scoop Up With The Butt
17. Turn Around, Flowers, And Chop
18. Closed Stance Poke
19. Empty Stance Cradle The Staff

Section Three

20. Right Handed Left Side Flowers
21. Left Handed Right Side Flowers
22. Right Handed Left Side Flowers
23. Turn Around, Back-Cross Stance Cover
24. Roll Over, Jump To Drop Stance Chop
25. Turn Around To Bow Stance Chop

Section Four

26. Left Side Lifting Slice Up
27. Right Side Lifting Slice Up
28. Left Side Lifting Slice Up
29. Right Side Lifting Slice Up
30. Left Side Lifting Slice Up
31. Jumping Turn To Drop Stance Chop
32. Bow Stance Snap
33. Jump To Bow Stance Cradle The Staff

Section Five

34. Step Forward, Uppercut
35. Left Jumping Turn With A Swing
36. Bow Stance, Shoulder The Staff
37. Right Jumping Turn With A Swing
38. Bow Stance, Shoulder The Staff
39. Left Rear Jumping Turn With A Swing
40. Bow Stance, Shoulder The Staff
41. Right Rear Jumping Turn With A Swing
42. Bow Stance, Shoulder The Staff
43. Left Jumping Turn With A Swing

CHAQUAN, VOLUME III

44. Horse Stance Carry The Staff Level
45. Turn Around, Thread The Staff Like A Shuttle
46. Jump To Drop Stance Chop
47. Turn Around To Bow Stance Chop

Section Six

48. Raised Knee, Shoulder The Staff
49. Step Forward, Sweep
50. Turn Around, Shoulder The Staff
51. Step Forward, Sweep
52. Turn Around, Shoulder The Staff
53. Step Forward Sweep
54. Bow Stance, Shoulder The Staff
55. Step Forward, Scoop
56. Bow Stance Press Down
57. Turn Around, Stand The Staff
58. Withdraw Standing The Staff
59. Closing Posture (Stand To Attention Holding The Staff)

0. Position Of Preparation (Stand To Attention Holding The Staff)

yùbèi shì (lìzhèng chí gùn)　　　　　预备势（立正持棍）

Stand up straight, holding the staff in the right hand with the staff vertical at the right side of the body. (image 4.0a) Lift the staff slightly in the right hand and brace the left hand out to the left side, palm down, fingers turned inwards. Look to the left. (image 4.0b)

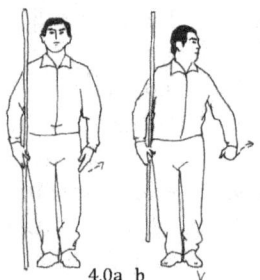

4.0a b

Section One

1. Step Forward, Stand The Staff　　shàngbù lì gùn　　上步立棍

Step the left foot forward and shift forward. Raise the left arm at the left side, palm forward. Lift the staff in the right hand at the right side. Look forward. (image 4.1a) Shift forward and step the right foot forward. Look to the left. (image 4.1b) Shift forward and bring the left foot up beside the right foot in a closed stance. Circle the left hand up and to the right, swinging it to in front to the right side of the chest. Place the staff vertical at the right side with the butt on the

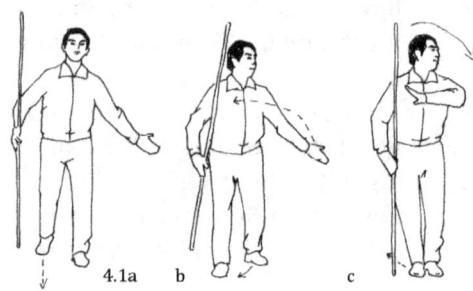

4.1a b c

SHEPHERD'S STAFF

ground. Look to the left. (image 4.1c)

Step quickly and lightly.

2. Empty Stance Poke   xūbù chuō gùn   虚步戳棍

Lift the staff butt across to the right by kicking it with the outside of the right foot, bending the knee and lifting the foot behind. Bend the left leg slightly. Turn to the left. Hold the staff angled out to the right side. Slide the left hand to touch the fore-section of the staff. Look to the left. (image 4.2a) Land the right foot to the rear right and shift back. Withdraw the left foot a half-step, touching the ball of the foot down and bending both legs to take a left empty stance. Poke levelly forward, using the right hand, tucking the shaft aft-section into the right armpit. Press the left hand on the right hand, fingers up. Look forward. (image 4.2b)

Bend both legs to sit into an empty stance.

3. Stamp And Raise The Staff   zhènbù jǔ gùn   震步举棍

Shift forward, bending into the left knee and raising the right knee in front. Raise the staff in the right hand, keeping it level at waist height at the right side. Look forward. (image 4.3a) Settle onto the right foot with a stamp and raise the left knee in front. Raise the staff in the right hand above the head. Lift the left hand to inside the right hand. Look forward. (image 4.3b)

Land the right foot with an audible stamp. Keep good balance.

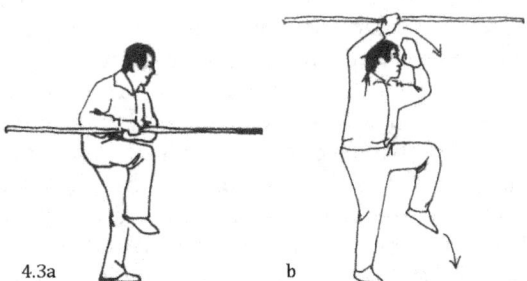

4. Jump To Bow Stance Poke   tiào gōngbù chuō gùn   跳弓步戳棍

Land the left foot forward and shift slightly forward. Send the staff levelly forward with the right hand, pressing the left hand on the right wrist. Look forward. (image 4.4a) Push into the right foot and shift forward, lifting the right foot up behind with the knee bent. Lower the staff in the right hand at the right side, following a curving line. Slide the left hand along the staff shaft. Look forward. (image 4.4b) Push into the left foot to jump up. Lift the

99

staff in the right hand, going back and up in an arcing line to above the head. Lift the left hand under the staff. Look forward. (image 4.4c)

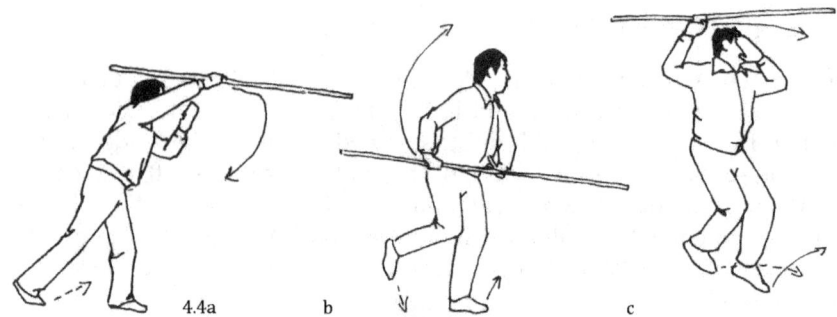

Land the right foot forward, then the left, bending the left knee and straightening the right to take a left bow stance. Poke the staff directly forward to shoulder height with the right hand, aligned with the right shoulder. Hold the left hand out to the rear left. Look forward. (image 4.4d)

Jump lightly and quickly. Poke strongly.

5. Left And Right Parry And Chop   zuǒyòu guàpī gùn   左右挂劈棍

Shift forward and raise the right knee. With the right hand, circle the tip of the staff down then to the left, holding it out on the left side. Hold the left hand out to the left side. Look forward. (image 4.5a) Raise the right knee some more. With the right hand, continue to circle the staff tip at the left to go back then up and forward to in front of the body. Bring the left hand to the staff mid-section. Look forward. (image 4.5b) Land the right foot behind. With both hands, circle the staff tip forward and down on the right so that the tip points down in front on the right side. Switch the grip of the left hand to one-third along from the aft-section. Look forward. (image 4.5c) Turn right, bending the right knee and straightening the left to take a right bow stance. With the staff in both hands, circle it on the right to the rear, up, then forward with a swinging chop. Then pull the staff in front of the chest, switching the left hand towards the grip-section. Look to the rear left. (image 4.5d)

Do the parry and chop to left and right with full circles that stay close to the body at the left side, then the right side. Complete the withdrawing step and the pull back in one smooth action.

SHEPHERD'S STAFF

4.5a b   c   d

6. Jumping Turn To Empty Stance Cradle The Staff

tiàozhuàn xūbù bào gùn　　　　　　　　　　跳转虚步抱棍

Shift to the right and lift the left leg straight out to the rear. Turn around to the right. Swing the staff in the right hand, level across to the right to the rear. Hold the left hand out to the left side. Look forward, to the right. (image 4.6a) Push into the right foot to jump up and spin around to the right rear. Land on the left foot, holding the right leg up behind. Continue to swing the staff in the right hand flat around to the right, to the rear, holding the right hand up above the head. Hold the left hand up at the left side. Look forward. (image 4.6.b) Land the right foot behind, then withdraw the left foot a half-step, touching down the ball of the foot. Bend both legs to take a left empty stance. Continue to circle the staff flat around to the right until it is in front of the body. Catch the tip-section of the staff in the left hand. The staff tip points forward and up. The staff shaft is touching the right side of the body. Look forward. (image 4.6c)

Jump quickly and lightly. Land with stability.

4.6a   b   c

7. Right Drop Stance Chop　　　yòu pūbù pī gùn　　　右仆步劈棍

Shift forward and move the left foot forward. Pull the staff up and back, switching the left hand's grasp so that the thumb web faces in. Look forward. (image 4.7a) Push into the right foot and shift forward, turning

101

around to the left and stepping the right foot forward. Squat fully on the left leg and extend the right leg along the ground to take a right drop stance. Circle the staff up in both hands so that the grip end goes up then forward to chop down in front. Slide the right hand along to the shaft mid-section. Hit the staff tip on the ground, leaning forward. Look forward, to the right. (image 4.7b)

Step and turn quickly. Drop into a stable stance. Chop strongly.

8. Left Drop Stance Chop   zuǒ pūbù pī gùn   左仆步劈棍

Push into the left leg to stand up, shifting to the right leg. Pull the staff back with both hands, to hold it back on the left. Slide the left hand along to the fore-section. Look forward, to the right. (image 4.8a) Push into the left foot and shift to the right, turning around to the right. Step the left foot forward and squat onto the right leg, extending the left leg to take a left drop stance. Circle the staff over with both hands, from the rear left, up, and forward, to chop down in front. Slide the left hand along to the right hand and strike the ground with the butt. Lean forward. Look forward, to the lower left. (image 4.8b)

Step forward and turn quickly. Drop into a stable stance. Chop with power.

9. Right Drop Stance Chop   yòu pūbù pī gùn   右仆步劈棍

Push into the right foot to stand up, shifting to the left leg. Lift the staff in both hands to the rear right. Slide the right hand along to the fore-section, turning the hands to a thumb web facing grip. Look forward. (image 4.9a) Push into the right leg and shift forward, turning around to the left. Step the right foot forward and squat fully on the left leg, extending the right leg to take a right drop stance. Circle the staff in both hands up from behind, then forward to chop down in front. Slide the right hand towards the shaft fore-section. Hit the ground with the staff butt. Look forward, to the right. (image 4.9)

SHEPHERD'S STAFF

Step and turn quickly. Drop into a solid stance. Chop strongly.

4.9a b

10. Empty Stance Cradle The Staff   xūbù bào gùn   虚步抱棍

Push into the left foot and stand up. Bring the right foot in a half-step, touching down the foot with the heel up. Bend both knees to take a right empty stance. Pull the staff tip to the left and back, pulling the butt in front of the body, the right hand sliding towards the aft-section. The staff butt slants up. Look forward, to the right. (image 4.10)

Sit in a well-defined empty stance.

4.10

11. Bow Stance Poke   gōngbù chuō gùn   弓步戳棍

Step the right foot forward, bending the knee forward and straightening the left knee to take a right bow stance. Poke the staff butt levelly forward with both hands, sliding the right hand along to the mid-section. Look forward, to the right. (image 4.11)

Poke strongly, focussing on the butt.

4.11

12. Turn Around, Poke   zhuànshēn chuō gùn   转身戳棍

Push into the right foot to turn around to the left., pivoting around to the left on both feet. Bend the left knee and straighten the right, to take a left bow stance. Poke directly with the staff tip to the rear left with both hands, sliding the left hand to the aft-section. Look forward. (image 4.12)

Turn quickly, stand firmly, poke strongly.

CHAQUAN, VOLUME III

4.12

Section Two

13. Jumping Turn With A Swing   tiàozhuàn lūn gùn   跳转抡棍

Shift forward and step the right foot forward and across to the right side, bending the knee out to the side and almost straightening the left knee, turning to the right. Pull the staff to the right with the right hand. Look forward, to the right. (image 4.13a) Push into the left foot, then the right to jump up, spinning around to the right. Swing the staff flat around to the right with the right hand, following behind the body. Hold the left hand out to the left side. Look forward, to the right. (image 4.13b) Continue to spin around to the right, lifting the staff in the right hand up over the head so that the staff passes overhead behind at the right, to the left side of the body. Land the left foot, then the right, bending both legs. Grasp the mid-section of the staff in the left hand. Look forward, to the left. (image 4.13c)

Jump and spin quickly. Land with good balance. Swing the staff around with power. Pass the shaft overhead with a flat swing.

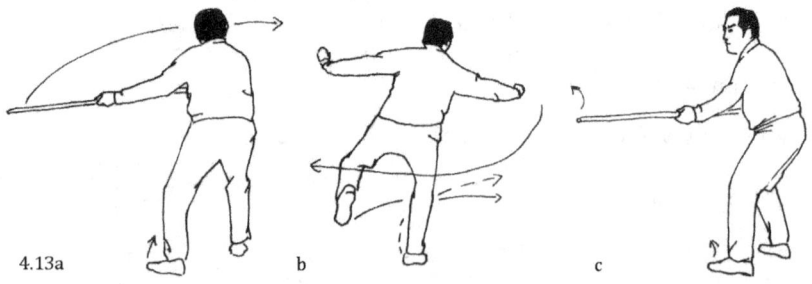

4.13a   b   c

14. Empty Stance Cradle The Staff   xūbù bào gùn   虚步抱棍

Shift to the right and move the left foot to the right, touching down the ball of the foot. Sit into a left empty stance. Lift the staff with both hands in front of the chest, tip slanting up. Look forward. (image 4.14)

SHEPHERD'S STAFF

Sit into a distinctly weighted/unweighted empty stance. Hold the staff firmly.

4.14

15. Left And Right Flowers   zuǒyòu wǔhuā gùn   左右舞花棍

Move the left foot forward and straighten the legs a bit. Hook down to the lower right with the staff tip to in between the legs. Use both hands and switch the left hand's grip so that the thumb webs face each other. Look forward. (image 4.15a) Turn left and pivot to the left on both feet to cross the legs. Circle the staff so that the butt moves forward then to the left and down to parry at the left side of the left leg. Cross the arms in front to hold the staff in front of the body. Look forward and down. (image 4.15b) Shift forward and step the right foot forward, almost straightening the legs. Do a full circle with the staff using both hands, so that the staff butt goes left, then up, continuing until it points to the lower front. The tip then points to the upper left. The thumb web of the left hand faces the staff tip. Look forward, to the right. (image 4.15c) Turn right and lean forward slightly. Circle to parry with both hands so that the staff tip goes forward then down to the right to outside the right leg. The arms are now crossed in front of the body. Look forward and down. (image 4.15d) Shift to the right and step the left foot forward, bending both legs. Circle the staff so that the tip goes back, then up to the front to do a swinging chop with the tip pointing to the upper front. Look forward. (image 4.15e)

Coordinate the flowers with the stepping. Keep the flowers to the left and right sides close to the body – but be careful to not accidentally hit yourself.

4.15a   b   c   d   e

16. Jumping Turn, Scoop Up With The Butt
tiàozhuàn tiǎobà 跳转挑把

Shift forward, lifting the right leg up behind with the knee bent. Circle the staff butt back then up until it arrives above the head in front of the body. Settle the staff with the left hand tucked in at the right flank. Lean forward slightly. Look forward and down. (image 4.16a) Push into the left leg to jump up, turning around to the left. Land on the right foot, then the left, bending the right knee and straightening the left to take a right bow stance. Circle the staff butt down in front, and around at the left side until it scoops up behind, which is now the front. Place the left hand snug to the right flank. Look forward. (image 4.16b)

Jump and turn quickly, landing firmly. Scoop up strongly.

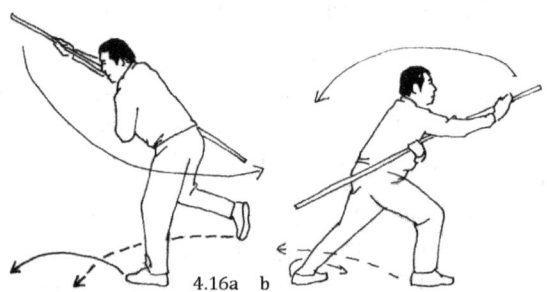

17. Turn Around, Flowers, And Chop
zhuànshēn wǔhuā pī gùn 转身舞花劈棍

Shift back and turn around to the right. Step the right foot forward and naturally straighten both legs. Hold the staff in both hands in front of the body, moving the butt upwards and the tip downwards. Look forward and down. (image 4.17a) Without moving the feet, circle the staff so that the tip moves back and up, then forward and down, finishing at the right side. Both hands hold the staff above the head. Look forward. (image 4.17b) Shift to the right and turn right, then step the left foot forward, bending both legs. Circle the staff in both hands so that the fore-section goes back, then up, then forward to chop in front of the body. The tip is now forward. Look forward, to the left. (image 4.17c)

SHEPHERD'S STAFF

Turn quickly. Complete fully rounded flowers. Chop strongly.

18. Closed Stance Poke   bìngbù chuō gùn   并步戳棍

Shift forward and step the right foot to the left behind the left foot, touching down the foot with the heel lifted, with an insertion step. Lower the staff tip slightly. Look forward. (image 4.18a) Step the left foot forward, bending both legs. Use both hands to circle the staff tip to hold it level in front of the body. Look forward. (image 4.18b) Shift forward and bring the right foot up to meet the left in a closed stance. Poke directly forward, using both hands. Slide the left hand along the shaft to meet the right. Look forward. (image 4.18c)

Step quickly. Poke strongly.

4.18a   b   c

19. Empty Stance Cradle The Staff   xūbù bào gùn   虚步抱棍

Withdraw the right foot, bending the right knee and straightening the left. Turn right and pull the staff back to in front of the belly with the right hand, sliding the left hand along to the staff mid-section. Look back, to the left. (image 4.19a) Shift to the right and step the left foot forward, turning right. Circle the staff tip down and across in front to the right to finish in front of the body to the right. Look forward. (image 4.19b) Shift forward and step the right foot forward to the right side, standing up with an open stance, both legs relatively straight. Circle the staff in both hands so that the tip circles left and lowers. Look forward. (image 4.19c)

4.19a   b   c

Move the left foot towards the right foot, touching down the ball of the foot and bending both legs to take a left empty stance. Cradle the staff in both hands in front of the body, the tip up. Look forward. (image 4.19d)

Turn and step in a continuous, coordinated manner. Take a well-defined empty stance.

4.19d

Section Three

20. Right Handed Left Side Flowers

yòushǒu zuǒcè wǔhuā gùn   右手左侧舞花棍

Push into the right foot and move the left foot forward, shifting to the left leg. Bring the staff butt up, circling it over the head. Switch the grasp of the left hand so that the thumbs are facing. Look forward. (image 4.20a) Shift forward, turning left and settling the right foot into the ball of the foot, lifting the heel. Circle the staff so that the butt moves forward to parry down at the left side of the left leg. Tuck the left hand into the right armpit. Look forward, to the right. (image 4.20b) Shift forward, turning left. Step the right foot forward and stand up in an open stance. Circle the staff in the right hand so that the butt goes left, then up, drawing a full circle and a half until the staff is standing in front of the body, butt up. Clench the left hand and set it at the elbow. Look forward. (image 4.20c)

Step and turn as one action. Do fully rounded flowers.

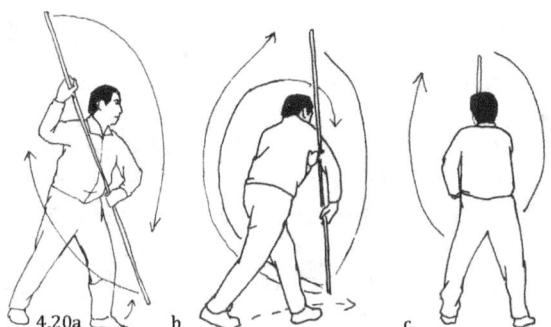

4.20a   b   c

21. Left Handed Right Side Flowers

zuǒshǒu yòucè wǔhuā gùn   左手右侧舞花棍

Without moving the feet, turn the left hand's thumb web over to face out and grasp the staff stuck close to the back of the right hand. Turn the palm up so that the staff tip moves left and the shaft is level with the throat. Look forward. (image 4.21a) Shift to the right and circle the staff in the left hand so that the butt goes down then to the left, coming up above the head at the right. The staff mid-section is tucked into the left armpit. Hold the right hand up in front of the chest. Look forward, to the right. (image 4.21b) Shift right and turn right, crossing and straightening the legs, and lifting the left heel. Circle the staff in the left hand so that the butt goes right and down to in front of the belly, shaft level. Place the right hand inside the left arm. Look forward and down. (image 4.21c) Shift forward and step the left foot forward to an open stance. Circle the staff in a full circle with the left hand, the butt going right and up, finishing with the tip slanting up. Hold the right hand in front of the belly. Look forward and up. (image 4.21d)

Step and turn smoothly. Draw full, vertical circles during the flowers.

4.21a   b   c   d

22. Right Handed Left Side Flowers

yòushǒu zuǒcè wǔhuā gùn 　　　　　　　　　　右手左侧舞花棍

Without moving the feet, turn the right palm up and slide it along to the back of the left hand to grasp the staff, thumbs facing. Both arms are bent in front of the chest. Look forward and up. (image 4.22a) Still without moving the feet, lean slightly to the left. With the staff in the right hand, circle the tip down, then right, until it is above the head. Hold the left hand out to the left side. Look forward, to the left. (image 4.22b) Push into the right foot, staying on the spot, and shift to the left, turning left and leaning slightly forward. With the staff in the right hand, circle the tip to the left and down until it is behind the body at the right side. The staff shaft is tucked into the right armpit with the tip pointing back. Grip the staff mid-section in the left hand. Look forward, to the left. (image 4.22c) Shift forward, turning left. Step the right foot forward. With both hands, circle the staff butt down and to the left until it is at the lower left side of the body. Look down to the left. (image 4.22d)

Step and turn in a coordinated way. Keep the flowers vertical and rounded.

CHAQUAN, VOLUME III

23. **Turn Around, Back-Cross Stance Cover**

zhuànshēn chābù gàibà   转身插步盖把

Without moving the feet, turn right. Holding the staff with the right hand, circle the butt to the left and up so that the staff comes up in front of the body, tip up. Place the left hand at the left side of the waist. Look forward. (image 4.23a) Shift to the right, turn the right foot out, and turn to the right. Circle the staff in the right hand, bring the tip to the right and down, holding the staff at the right side of the body with the tip down. Look forward and down to the right. (image 4.23b) Shift to the right and continue to turn right. Step the left foot forward and stand up in an open stance. Continue to circle the staff in the right hand so that the tip goes back then up and over to chop level at the left. Grasp the left hand mid-section in the left hand to chop. Look to the left. (image 4.23c) Shift to the left and step the right foot behind the left leg in a back-cross step, touching down the ball of the foot and bending both legs. With both hands, circle the staff so that the butt goes up, left, and over to cover down at the left side. The arms are crossed in front of the belly. Look to the left. (image 4.23d)

Step, turn, and back-cross to an insertion stance all quickly. Coordinate the right-handed flower with the step forward and turn.

SHEPHERD'S STAFF

24. Roll Over, Jump To Drop Stance Chop

fānshēn tiào pūbù pī gùn   翻身跳仆步劈棍

Push into the right foot to spin around to the right, rolling over, raising the right knee. Lift the staff in both hands to circle it to the right and up and over the head. Look up. (image 4.24a) Push into the left foot to jump up, continuing to turn to the right. Move the staff, continuing to turn so that tip goes up. Look up. (image 4.24b) Spin to the right whilst airborne, then land on the right foot, then the left. Squat fully on the right leg and extend the left leg along the ground to sit into a left drop stance. Bring the staff forward to chop down, sliding the left hand along to meet the right hand. Hit the ground with the staff tip-section. Look forward and down. (image 4.24c)

Roll and spin quickly. Land into a solid drop stance. Chop strongly.

25. Turn Around To Bow Stance Chop

zhuànshēn gōngbù pī gùn   转身弓步劈棍

Push into both legs to stand up. Lift the staff in both hands above the head, sliding the left hand along to the mid-section. Look up. (image 4.25a) Push into the left foot and turn right, bending the right knee and straightening the left to take a right bow stance. Circle the staff, holding the grip in the right hand, up and over to the right to chop down, hitting the tip on the ground. Hold the left hand above the head. Look down to the right. (image 4.25b)

Turn and chop strongly.

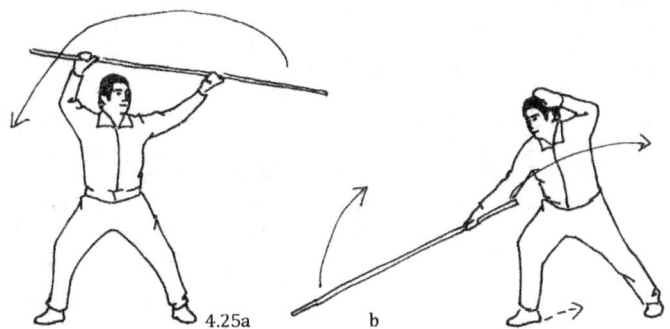

CHAQUAN, VOLUME III

Section Four

26. Left Side Lifting Slice Up   zuǒcè tíliāo gùn   左侧提撩棍

Shift back and move the right foot back, turning to the left. With the right hand, circle the staff tip up to hold the staff over the head. Bring the left hand to the right hand and hold the staff in both hands with the elbows bent, in front of the left side of the chest. Look forward, to the right. (image 4.26a) Shift forward, raising the left heel. With both hands, swing the staff so that the tip goes up and over to the rear, then down and forward, to slice up towards the right. Turn right. The tip finishes forward, slanting down. The arms are bent and in front of the chest. Look forward. (image 4.26b)

The lifting slice up completes a vertical circle. Keep the whole action coordinated with the movement of the body.

4.26a   b

27. Right Side Lifting Slice Up   yòucè tíliāo gùn   右侧提撩棍

Shift forward, raising the left knee. Circle the staff, using both hands, so that the tip rises and does a full circle, completing with a lifting slice up on the right side. The hands finish in front of the chest with the elbows bent. The staff tip points to the lower front. Look to the lower front. (image 4.27)

Turn slightly to the right to aid the hands do the circle up and to the rear to take the staff back. Turn slightly to the left to aid the hands swing the staff down then forward with the lifting slice up. Make sure that the staff moves vertically during all circling.

4.27

28. Left Side Lifting Slice Up   zuǒcè tíliāo gùn   左侧提撩棍

Land the left foot and raise the right knee. With both hands, swing the staff so that the tip goes up on the right, beside the body, then around and completes a lifting slice forward on the left side. The hands finish in front of the chest with the elbows bent. The staff tip points forward. Look forward. (image 4.28)

SHEPHERD'S STAFF

Turn slightly to the left to aid the hands do the circle up and to the rear to take the staff back. Turn slightly to the right to aid the hands swing the staff down then forward with the lifting slice up. Make sure to keep the whole circling action vertical.

4.28

29. Right Side Lifting Slice Up   yòucè tíliāo gùn   右侧提撩棍

Land the right foot and raise the left knee. Swing the staff in both hands to bring the tip up and back, then circle by the right side of the body to complete a lifting slice up in front. The hands are in front of the body with the elbows bent. The staff tip points forward and down. Look forward and down. (image 4.29)

Turn slightly to the right to do the circle up and to the rear to take the staff back. Turn slightly to the left to swing the staff down then forward with the lifting slice up. Keep the whole circle vertical.

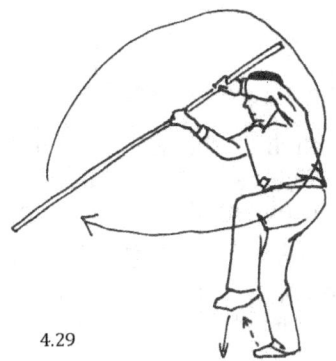

4.29

30. Left Side Lifting Slice Up   zuǒcè tíliāo gùn   左侧提撩棍

This is the same as move 28. (image 4.30)

4.30

31. Jumping Turn To Drop Stance Chop

tiàozhuàn pūbù pī gùn 跳转仆步劈棍

Push into the left foot to jump up, spinning around to the right. Lift the staff with the hands in front of the chest, staff tip pointing up. Look forward and down. (image 4.31a) Land on the right foot, then the left, bending the right knee and extending the left to take a left drop stance. Chop down with the staff, using both hands, hitting the ground with the fore-section. Look forward and down. (image 4.31b)

Turn quickly and land firmly. Chop strongly.

32. Bow Stance Snap

gōngbù bēng gùn 弓步崩棍

Push into the right leg to stand up. Bend the left knee forward and straighten the right knee to take a left bow stance. Snap the staff tip up forcefully with a raising, scooping, snap. The tip finishes slanting forward and upward. Look forward. (image 4.32)

Complete the snap as you complete the bow stance.

33. Jump To Bow Stance Cradle The Staff

tiào gōngbù bào gùn 跳弓步抱棍

Shift forward, stepping the right foot to the forward right. Bend the right leg and straighten the left. Hold the staff up, levelling it out somewhat. Look forward. (image 4.33a) Push into the left foot, then the right, to jump up. Land on the left foot, holding the right knee up. Circle the staff in both hands so that the tip goes up and to the left, to stop behind the left leg with the tip slanting down at the left side. Slide the left hand to the staff mid-section. Look to the rear left. (image 4.33b) Land the right foot to the forward right, bending the knee and straightening the left knee to take a right bow stance. Turn to the right. Circle the staff in both hands so that the tip goes down, then right and forward and up. The staff stops in front of the right side of the chest, with the tip slanting upwards. Look upwards, to the forward right. (image 4.33c)

Jump lightly and firmly into stance. Coordinate the completion of the cradling action with the taking of the stance.

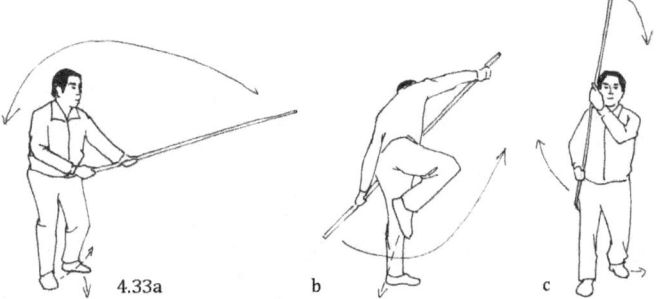

Section Five

34. Step Forward, Uppercut   shàngbù chāojǔ gùn   上步抄举棍

Shift forward and move the left foot to the forward left. Turn slightly leftward. Raise the staff up above the head, pointing forward. Look forward, to the left. (image 4.34a) Push into the right foot and shift leftward, pivoting both feet to the left. Circle the staff in both hands so that the shaft lowers, then goes left and to the front, raising above the head at the forward left. Look to the forward left. (image 4.34b)

When doing the uppercut, the tip lowers, then circles forward and up. Keep the circles soft, then finish with power.

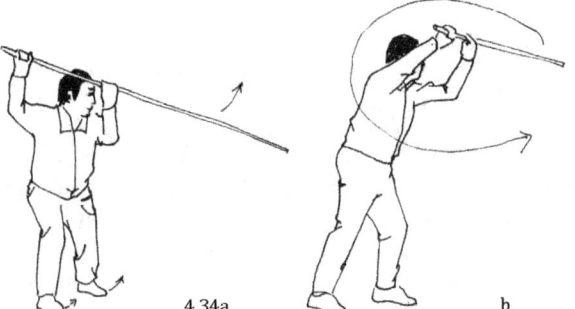

35. Left Jumping Turn With A Swing

zuǒ tiàozhuàn lūn gùn   左跳转抡棍

Without moving the feet, shift the weight back and forth between the right and left feet. Circle the staff in both hands, bring it from the forward left, more to the left, then over the head to the rear, then swing it up to the forward right. Look forward, to the right. (image 4.35a) Push into the right foot, then the left, jumping up and spinning around to the left. Land on the right foot and hold the left knee up. Continue to swing the staff in both hands around over the head to the left, making a full circle. Finish with the hands in front of the right side of the chest, elbows bent. Look forward. (image 4.35b)

Jump and spin lightly. Swing the staff with power.

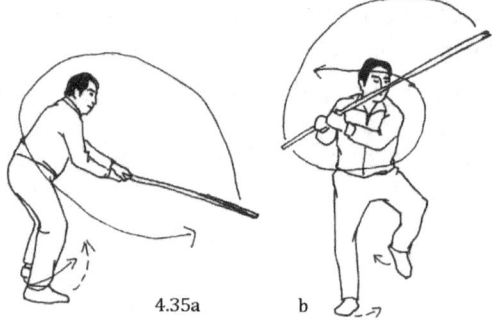

36. Bow Stance, Shoulder The Staff   gōngbù bēi gùn   弓步背棍

Land the left foot to the rear left, turning left. Bend the left knee and straighten the right to take a left bow stance. Circle the staff flat across to the left, holding it at the left shoulder. Look forward, to the right. (image 4.36)

Land the foot firmly, swing the staff with power.

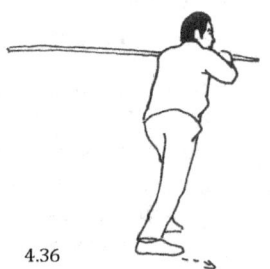

37. Right Jumping Turn With A Swing

yòu tiàozhuàn lūn gùn   右跳转抡棍

Push into the left foot and shift to the right, moving the right foot forward to the right and bending both legs. Turn slightly to the right. Lower the staff slightly, keeping it level. Look forward, to the right. (image 4.37a) Push into the left foot to shift to the right, and turn to the right. Circle the staff flat across to the left and forward to the forward right. Look to the forward right. (image 4.37b) Push into the left foot, then the right, to jump up and spin around to the right, spinning a full circle whilst airborne. Swing the staff with both hands so that it swings a full circle above the head, moving to the right. Look forward and down. (image 4.37c)

Jump and spin lightly. Swing the staff with power.

SHEPHERD'S STAFF

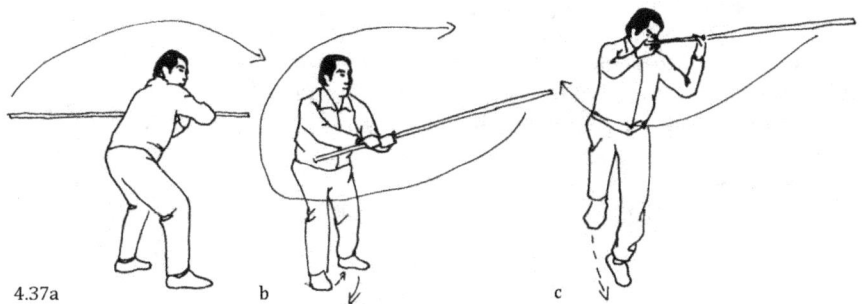

4.37a b c

38. Bow Stance, Shoulder The Staff   gōngbù bēi gùn   弓步背棍

Land the left foot, then the right, bending the right knee and straightening the left to take a right bow stance. Swing the staff in both hands flat across to the right, to stop at the right shoulder. Look forward, to the right. (image 4.38)

Land with good balance and swing the staff with power.

4.38

39. Left Rear Jumping Turn With A Swing
zuǒ hòu tiàozhuàn lūn gùn   左后跳转抡棍

Push into the right foot and pivot to the left on both feet, bending the knees and turning around to the left. Swing the staff with both hands, flat across to the left to in front of the body. Look forward, to the left. (image 4.39a) Push into the left foot, then the right, to jump up and spin around, turning around to the left. Land on the right foot, leaving the left leg up. Bend the arms, holding the staff up with the hands in front of the chest. Look forward. (image 4.39b)

Jump and spin lightly. Swing the staff with power.

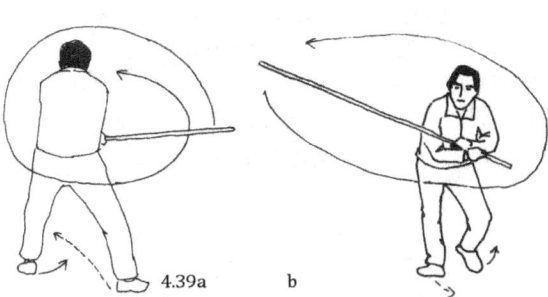

4.39a b

40. Bow Stance, Shoulder The Staff   gōngbù bēi gùn   弓步背棍

Land on the left foot, then the right, turning the right foot in. Bend the left knee forward and straighten the right, to take a left bow stance. Continue to turn the body around to the left, swinging the staff in both hands so that it circles flat across to the left to stop at the left shoulder. Look forward, to the right. (image 4.40)

Turn and set into stance with stability. Swing the staff with power.

4.40

41. Right Rear Jumping Turn With A Swing

yòu hòu tiàohuàn lūn gùn   右后跳换抡棍

Shift to the left and move the right foot back to the right, bending both knees slightly. Hold the staff out in front of the chest with the arms bent. Look forward, to the left. (image 4.41a) Push into the left foot, then the right, to jump up, spinning around to the right. Land the left foot, leaving the right knee up. Circle the staff in both hands flat around over the head, going to the right., finishing with the tip forward. Look forward. (image 4.41b)

Jump and spin lightly. Swing the staff with power.

4.41a   b

42. Bow Stance, Shoulder The Staff   gōngbù bēi gùn   弓步背棍

Land the right foot to the rear right, bending the knee and straightening the left knee to take a right bow stance. Continue to turn to the right. Swing the staff flat across to the right, using both hands, to lay it on the right shoulder. Look forward, to the left. (image 4.42)

Land with stability. Swing the staff with power.

4.42

SHEPHERD'S STAFF

43. Left Jumping Turn With A Swing

zuǒ tiàozhuàn lūn gùn   左跳转抡棍

Push into the left foot to shift right, then step the left foot to the forward left. Lean slightly forward and hold the staff in front of the body. Look forward. (image 4.43a) Push into the right foot, then the left, to jump up and spin around, turning left. Circle the staff to the left, swinging it a full circle above the head, using both hands.
Look forward, to the right.
(image 4.43b)

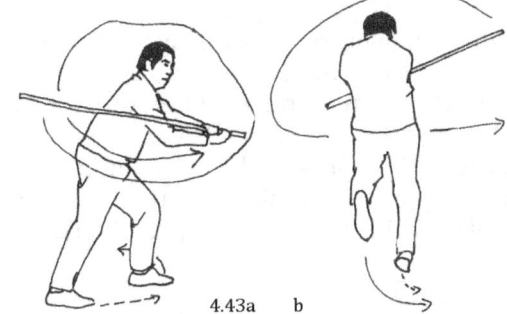

Jump and spin lightly. Swing the staff with power.

4.43a   b

44. Horse Stance Carry The Staff Level   mǎbù píngtuō gùn   马步平托棍

Continue to turn around to the left, landing on the right foot, then the left. Bend both legs to sit into a horse stance. Continue to swing the staff flat across to the left until it is at the left side of the body at waist height with the tip pointing left. Look forward, to the left. (image 4.44)

Turn and land with good balance. Swing the staff with power.

4.44

45. Turn Around, Thread The Staff Like A Shuttle

zhuànshēn chuānsuō gùn   转身穿梭棍

Without moving the feet, pull the staff to the right with the right hand, bringing it to chest height, and sliding the left hand along to the tip section. Look to the left. (image 4.45a) Still without moving the feet, turn right and thread the staff to the right side, sliding it through the hands until they are at to the tip section. Look to the right. (image 4.45b) Push into the right foot and shift to the left, turning around to the right. Step the right foot back to the right to stand up in an open stance. Switch the left hand to the staff midsection. Look to the left. (image 4.45c)

119

4.45a b c

Without moving the feet, thread the staff flat to the right, turning right. Slide the left hand to the grip section. Look to the right. (image 4.45d) Still in the open stance, turn right and thread the staff flat to the right, sliding it through the hands until they are at the grip section. Look to the right. (image 4.45e) Shift to the right and step the left foot to the right, turning right. Thread the staff flat to the left, sliding the staff through the hands until they are at the tip section. Look to the right. (image 4.45f)

4.45d e f

Push into the right foot and shift left, turning right. Step the right foot to the right and stand up in an open stance. Thread the staff flat to the right, sliding it through the hands until they are at the staff grip. Look forward. (image 4.45g)

Turn quickly. Step agilely. When turning and threading the staff, keep it level throughout, just under the jaw.

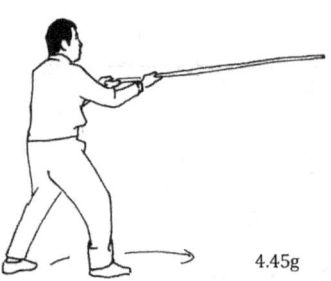

4.45g

46. Jump To Drop Stance Chop　　tiào pūbù pī gùn　　跳仆步劈棍

Push into the left foot and shift right, turning right, then step the left foot forward, bending the left knee and straightening the right. Thread the staff level to the right, switching the left hand to in front of the right. Look forward. (image 4.46a) Push into the right foot, then the left to jump up. Circle the staff with both hands so that it goes down, past the right leg, then out to the rear to finish lifted at the right, tip up. Look forward and up. (image 4.46b) Land on the right foot, then the left, squatting fully on the right leg and extending the left leg to take a left drop stance. Chop down in front using both hands, hitting the staff tip-section on the ground. Look forward. (image 4.46c)

Jump lightly and land into a solid stance. Chop with power.

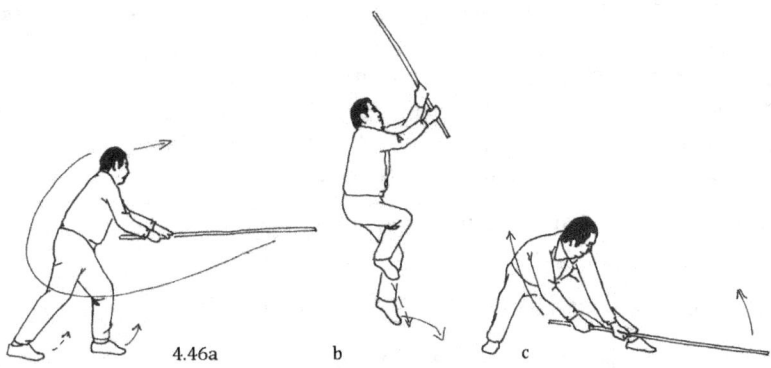

47. Turn Around To Bow Stance Chop

zhuànshēn gōngbù pī gùn   转身弓步劈棍

Push into both feet and stand up. Raise the staff in both hands above the head, sliding the left hand to the fore-section. Look forward, to the right. (image 4.47a) Without moving the feet, turn right, bending the right knee and straightening the left to take a right bow stance. Taking the staff in the right hand, swing it up and over to chop down at the right side, hitting the ground with the tip. Hold the left hand up over the head. Look forward, to the lower right. (image 4.47b)

Turn quickly, take a solid stance, and chop with power.

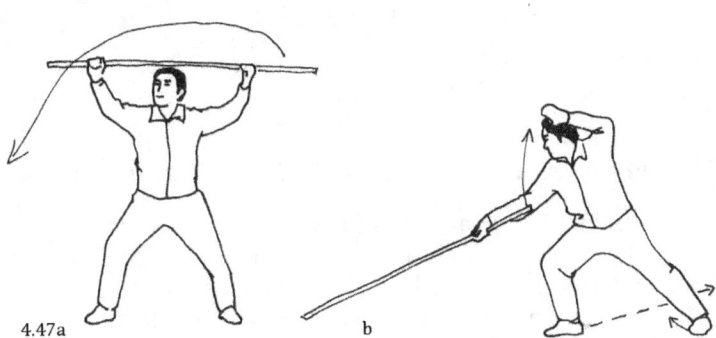

CHAQUAN, VOLUME III

Section Six

48. Raised Knee, Shoulder The Staff   tíxī bēi gùn   提膝背棍

Push into the right foot and shift back, then retreat the right foot behind and raise the left knee. Take the staff mid-section in the left hand and raise the staff in both hands back behind the head. The staff mid-section lies on the upper back, the butt pointing up. Look forward. (image 4.48) [tr. note: the image does not show the staff on the back, the image may be a transitional action.]

Stand firmly in the one-legged stance. Complete the placement of the staff with the raising of the knee.

4.48

49. Step Forward, Sweep   shàngbù sǎo gùn   上步扫棍

Land the left foot forward, bending the knee and almost straightening the right knee, leaning forward. Move the staff to outside the right shoulder, taking it in the right hand. Hold the left hand out to the left. Look forward and down. (image 4.49a) Push into the right foot and shift forward, turning left. Step the right foot forward keeping most weight on the left leg. Circle the staff across with a sweeping action to the right, forward, and down, tip striking the ground. Keep the left hand out to the side, at the back. Look forward and down. (image 4.49b)

Step forward quickly and sweep the staff with power.

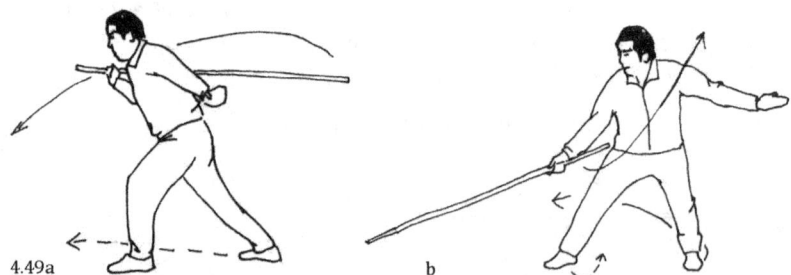

4.49a   b

50. Turn Around, Shoulder The Staff   zhuànshēn bēi gùn   转身背棍

Push into the left foot and shift forward. Pivot on the ball of the right foot and raise the left knee, turning the body around, turning left. Circle the staff in the right hand so that the shaft comes around to the left with the turn of the body. Catch the staff fore-section in the left hand and tuck the staff behind the upper back with both hands. Look forward and down. (image 4.50)

4.50

SHEPHERD'S STAFF

Spin around quickly, keeping steady on the right leg. Swing the staff with power, and tuck it firmly onto the back.

51. Step Forward, Sweep   shàngbù sǎo gùn   上步扫棍

Land the left foot forward, bending both knees. Hold the staff out to the rear right in the right hand. Hold the left hand out to the left side. Look forward. (image 4.51a) Push into the right foot and shift forward, turning left. Step the right foot forward, keeping the weight more on the left leg. Sweep the staff across on the right side to the lower front, hitting the tip on the ground. Hold the left hand out behind on the left side. Look forward and down. (image 4.51b)

Step quickly. Sweep the staff across with power.

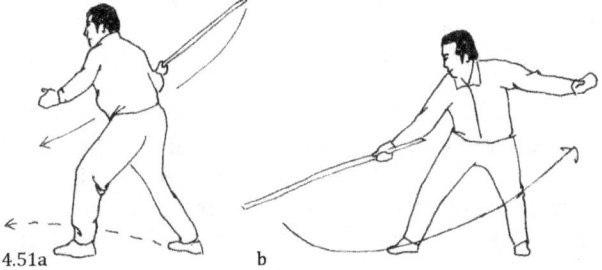

52. Turn Around, Shoulder The Staff   zhuànshēn bēi gùn   转身背棍

Push into the left foot and shift forward. Pivot on the right foot, raise the left knee, and turn around to the left. Swing the staff in the right hand around to the back with the turn. Catch the staff fore-section in the left hand and hold the staff on the upper back with both hands. Look forward and down. (image 4.52) [tr. note: in the image, the staff is not on the upper back, the image may be of a transitional action]

Spin around quickly, standing firmly on the right leg. Swing the staff with power and lay it on the upper back firmly.

53. Step Forward Sweep   shàngbù sǎo gùn   上步扫棍

Land the left foot forward and bend both knees. Hold the staff out behind on the right in the right hand. Hold the left hand out to the left side. Look forward. (image 4.53a) Push into the right foot and shift forward, turning left, then step the right foot forward, keeping the weight more on the left leg. Swing the staff around from the back to the lower front, sweeping it across with the tip hitting the ground. Hold the left hand out behind on the left side. Look forward and down. (image 4.53b)

Step quickly. Sweep the staff across with power.

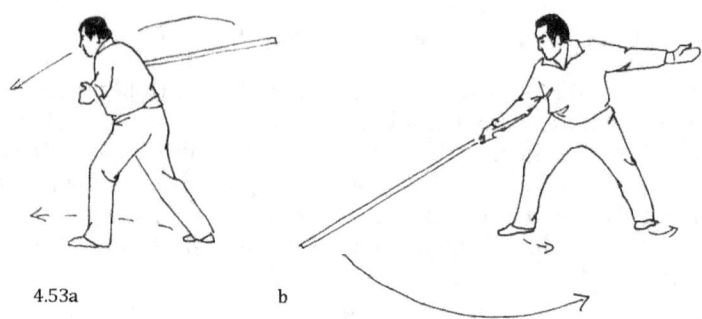

4.53a b

54. Bow Stance, Shoulder The Staff   gōngbù bēi gùn   弓步背棍

Push into the right foot and pivot around on the spot on both feet to turn around to the left. Swing the staff around in the right hand with the leftward turn of the body, holding it out in front. Catch the staff mid-section in the left hand, holding the tip up. Look forward. (image 4.54a) Push into the left foot to shift to the right, and raise the left knee. Circle the staff in both hands to bring the grip up behind to above the head, the shaft tight to the right flank. Look forward. (image 4.54b) Land the left foot to the left side, bending the knee and extending the right knee to take a left bow stance. Circle the staff in both hands to bring the grip to the left and down to tuck into the right upper back, the shaft tight to the back. The tip now slants up. Hold the left hand up to the left. Look forward, to the right. (image 4.54c)

Turn quickly. Take a firm bow stance. Tuck the staff onto the back with a smooth, gentle movement.

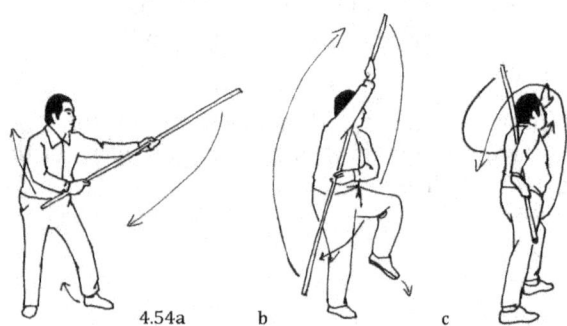

4.54a b c

55. Step Forward, Scoop   shàngbù tiǎo gùn   上步挑棍

Without moving the feet, lower the staff aft-section in the right hand to circle on the left side, then up, to hold it up at the right side. Grasp the fore-section in the left hand, and keep it in front of the chest. Look forward, to the right. (image 4.55a) Push into the right foot and shift to the left, then step the right foot forward to the left and stand up with the feet open. Circle the staff in both hands so that the grip drops down then circles up to the left

SHEPHERD'S STAFF

with a scooping action. The grip is up and the shaft slants along the left side of the chest. Look forward. (image 4.55b)

Step forward quickly. Circle the butt, then scoop up with the butt with power.

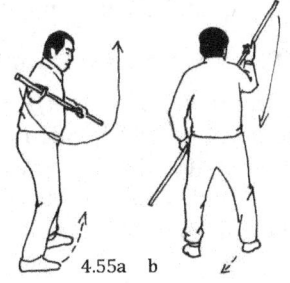

4.55a b

56. Bow Stance Press Down   gōngbù yā gùn   弓步压棍

Shift to the left and withdraw the right foot a half-step, touching down the foot and lifting the heel. Circle the staff in both hands, bring the grip forward then down to parry down outside the right leg, staff butt pointing down. Look down to the right. (image 4.56a) Retreat the right foot to the rear right, bend the left knee to the side, and straighten the right knee to take a left bow stance. Circle the staff in both hands so that the butt goes back then up, and then comes around and through to press down in front, butt hitting the ground. Look forward and down. (image 4.56b)

Retreat quickly and firmly. Circle and press down with the grip end of the staff with power.

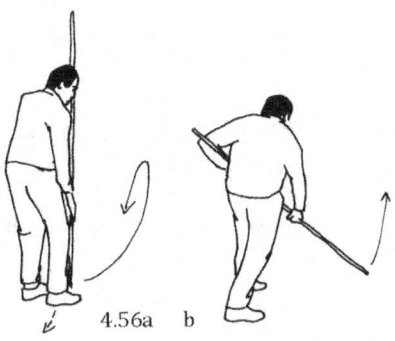

4.56a b

57. Turn Around, Stand The Staff   zhuànshēn lì gùn   转身立棍

Push into the left foot and shift right, turning right. Circle the staff in both hands to bring the grip end to the left, then scoop up above the head. The shaft is now vertical in front of the body. Look forward. (image 4.57a) Push into the left foot and shift to the right, turning right. Bring the left foot in to the right to take a closed stance. Circle the staff in both hands to bring the grip down on the right to stand the shaft at the right side. Look forward. (image 4.57b)

4.57a b

Turn quickly. Stand and place the staff upright firmly.

58. Withdraw Standing The Staff chèbù lì gùn 撤步立棍

Withdraw the left foot, touching down the foot with the heel lifted. With the staff in the right hand, hold it vertically at the right side. Lift the left hand to the left side. Look forward. (image 4.58a) Push into the right foot to shift back, and withdraw the right foot one step. Place the left hand on the foresection of the staff. Look forward. (image 4.58b) Bring the left foot in beside the right to take a closed stance. Stand to attention. Place the staff butt on the ground with the right hand. Hold the left arm down at the left side. Look left. (image 4.58c)

Step quickly and firmly. Coordinate the staff's actions with the body's actions.

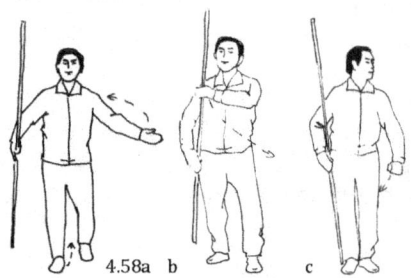

59. Closing Posture (Stand To Attention Holding The Staff)

shōu shì (lìzhèng chí gùn) 收势（立正持棍）

Look forward, standing to attention. (image 4.59)

CHA HOOKS

查钩

ABOUT THE CHA HOOKS

Each of a pair of hooks is made up of a complex blade and a grip near one end. The blade is made up of a spike, a crescent moon blade, a straight blade with two sharp edges, a hooking crown, and a hook tip. Silks, or flags, may be attached by the end of the grip.

The length of the hooks that an individual will use is determined by holding the hook by the grip, upright at the side with the arm straight, the flat of the blade tucked into the elbow crease. The crown should reach at least the top of the ear.

The blades are straight [until the hook at the end] and double-edged, and are usually made of metal. There is no weight restriction.

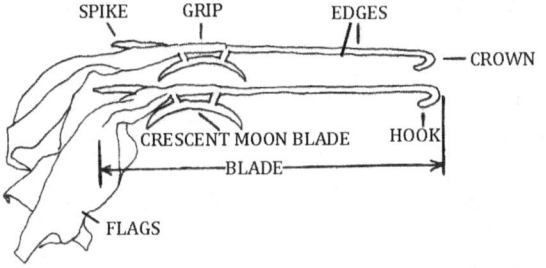

The usual manner of holding the hooks is to hold the grips, one in each hand. The hold on the grips can be relaxed or tight, according to needs of the techniques.

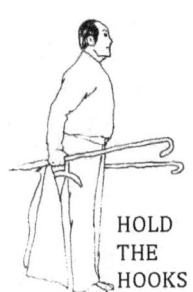

HOLD THE HOOKS

THE MAIN TECHNIQUES OF THE CHA HOOKS

Hook: A hook is a crossing hook, done with the blade flat, circling across in front to parry with the blade and hook to either side of the body.

Brush Aside: To circle forward and down from above, coming down and in to parry aside with the blade and hook.

Parry: To circle down and back from in front, to parry to the side, back and down.

Stab: To stab levelly forward with the spike, blade turned crescent moon side up.

Push: With the blade vertical, push forward with the crescent moon blade.

Slice up: Starting from behind, slice with the blade close to the side, moving down, then forward and up. May be done on either side.

Chop: To come down from above to cut with the edge of the blade.

Sweep: Cut across levelly, going from one side of the body, across the front, to the other side, power going to the blade edge.

NAMES OF THE MOVEMENTS OF THE CHA HOOKS FORM

Position Of Preparation
Section One
1. Step Forward Separate The Hooks
2. Straddle Step, Lash
3. Closed Stance Flash
4. Turn Around, Carry
5. Raised Knee Carry
6. Bow Stance Stab
7. Bow Stance Carry
8. Closed Stance Carry
9. Raised Knee Carry
10. Bow Stance Stab
11. Bow Stance Carry
12. Empty Stance Lash

Section Two
13. Bow Stance Stab
14. Raised Knee Lift
15. Right Side Slice Up
16. Left Side Slice Up
17. Right Side Slice Up
18. Turn Around To Drop Stance Chop
19. Bow Stance Framing Block And Stab
20. Bow Stance Push

Section Three
21. Step Forward, Right Push
22. Step Forward, Left Push
23. Double Drape To The Right
24. Double Drape To The Left
25. Double Drape To The Right
26. Turn Around, Bow Stance Lash

CHA HOOKS

27. Jumping Turn, Resting Stance Framing Block

Section Four

28. Single Drape To The Right
29. Single Drape To The Left
30. Single Drape To The Right
31. Step Forward, Slice Up
32. Raised Knee Carry
33. Bow Stance Carry
34. Walking Scoop
35. Jump, Parry And Chop
36. Empty Stance Push
37. Closed Stance Lash
38. Step Forward, Slice Up
39. Turn Around, Resting Stance Chop

Section Five

40. Retreat, Raised Knee Separate The Hooks
41. Empty Stance Cradle The Hooks
42. Framing Block, Jumping Kick
43. Turn Around, Sweep
44. Back-Cross Stance Double Lash
45. Roll Over, Chop
46. Closed Stance Lash
47. Turn Around, Scoop
48. Empty Stance Flash
49. Retreat, Press Down
50. Closing Posture (Stand To Attention Holding The Hooks)

0. **Position Of Preparation**   yù bèi shì   预备势

Stand to attention holding the hooks with the arms hanging down, one in each hand, level at either side of the body, the crescent blades and hook tips underneath. Look forward. (image 5.0a) Hold the hooks out to either side with the crowns pointing slightly inwards. Look to the left. (image 5.0b)

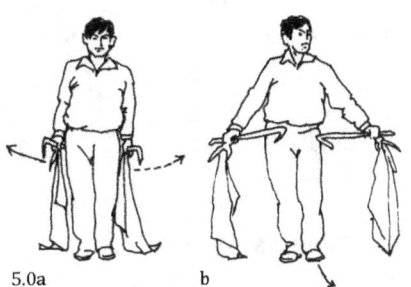

5.0a   b

Section One

1. **Step Forward Separate The Hooks**   shàngbù fēn gōu   上步分钩

Step the left foot forward and press into the knee. Look forward. (image 5.1a) Shift forward and step the right foot forward, pressing into the knee.

129

Cross the hooks at the fore-section, in front of the body. Look forward. (image 5.1b) Shift forward and bring the left foot up to the right to take a closed stance, standing up. Circle the hooks up and out to either side until the arms are level with the shoulders. The blades are vertical with the crowns up, the crescent blades out to the sides. Look to the right. (image 5.1c)

Coordinate the opening out of the hooks with the stepping and taking the stance.

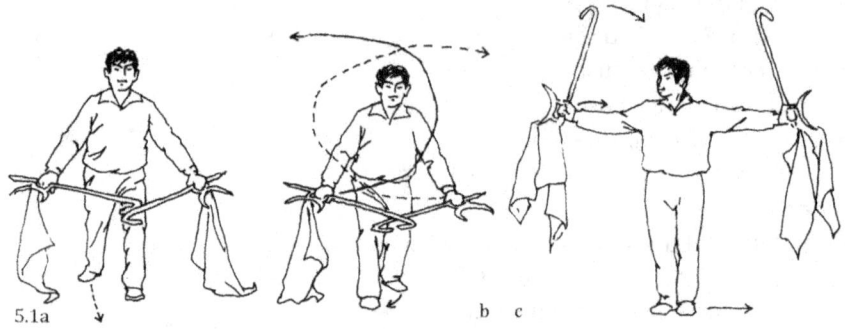

2. Straddle Step, Lash kuàbù bǎi gōu 跨步摆钩

Take a straddle step to the left with the left foot. Bend the right elbow to hold the hook up at the right side with the crown up and the crescent blade turned to the left. Look to the left. (image 5.2a) Push into the right foot and shift left, then bring the right foot up to meet the left in a closed stance. Stand up, turning left. Swing the right hook over to the left side. Both hooks are now at the left with the crowns up and the crescent blades on the left. Look to the left. (image 5.2b)

Step across and lash the hooks across in a coordinated action.

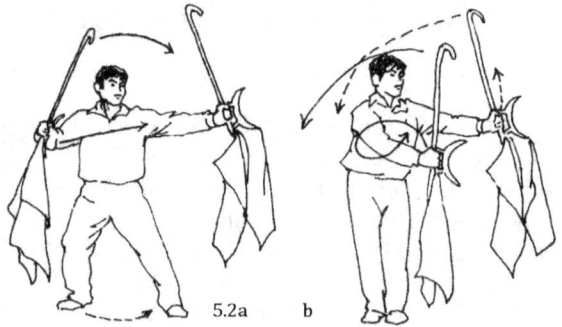

3. Closed Stance Flash bìngbù liàng gōu 并步亮钩

Keep standing up. Turn the left hook to lie flat at the left side with the flat of the blade tight to the left arm. Circle both hands up and to the right to cradle the hooks in front of the chest. Turn the hooks so that the crescent blades are up. The flat of the blade of the right hook is tight to the right arm. Look to the left. (image 5.3a) Still standing up, circle the right hook to lift it above the head at the right with the crescent blade up. Look to the left.

CHA HOOKS

(image 5.3b)

The circling and flashing actions are gentle. The final position should be expansive.

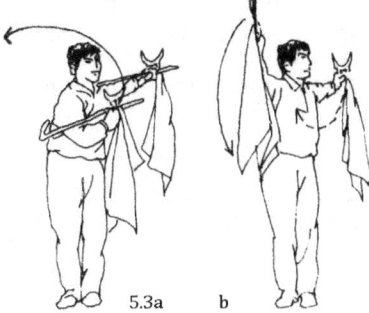

5.3a b

4. Turn Around, Carry zhuànshēn tuō gōu 转身托钩

Without moving the feet, turn right and lower the right hook down at the right side with the crown up and the crescent blade forward. Circle the left hook down and to the right to carry in front of the body. The left arm is straight at shoulder height, the crescent blade is up. Look forward, to the right. (image 5.4)

This position is open and expansive.

5.4

5. Raised Knee Carry tíxī tuō gōu 提膝托钩

Step the left foot forward and press into the knee. Bring the right hook forward to lift with the arm straight in front of the chest, crescent blade up. Bring the left hook down to stand upright at the left side, crown up, crescent blade forward. Look forward. (image 5.5a) Push into the right foot and shift forward, raising the right knee. Lower the right hook at the right side to stand with the crown up and the crescent blade forward. Lift the left hook up to carry in front with the arm straight, crescent blade up. Look forward. (image 5.5b)

Stand firmly on the left leg. Do the switch of left and right carrying of the hooks gently. Coordinate the carrying action of each hook with the stepping and lifting action of each leg.

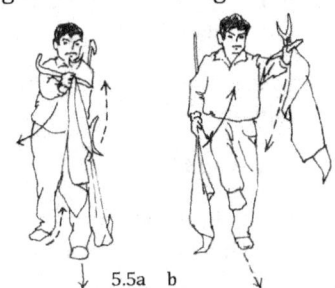

5.5a b

6. Bow Stance Stab gōngbù zhā gōu 弓步扎钩

Land the right foot forward, bending the knee and straightening the left to take right bow stance. Lift the right hook and stab the spike directly forward to shoulder height with the arm straight, crescent blade up. Bring

131

the left hook down to stand at the body, crown up, crescent blade forward. Look forward. (image 5.6)

Lift the spike first, then stab, so that the stab is directly forward.

5.6

| 7. | **Bow Stance Carry** | gōngbù tuō gōu | 弓步托钩 |

Push into the right foot and shift back. Pivot on both feet to turn around to the left, bending the left knee and straightening the right to take a left bow stance. Carry the left hook up to the left with the arm straight, slanting up from the shoulder, crescent blade up. Look forward, to the right. (image 5.7)

When pivoting on the feet, turn quickly and with good balance. Open out both arms.

5.7

| 8. | **Closed Stance Carry** | bìngbù tuō gōu | 并步托钩 |

Push into the right foot and shift left, turning left. Bring the right foot in to meet the left in a closed stance, and stand up. Lower the left hook to stand vertically at the left side, crown up, crescent blade forward. Carry the right hook up to the forward left with the arm straight at shoulder height, crescent blade up. Look forward, to the left. (image 5.8)

Complete the hook carry as the closed stance is completed.

5.8

| 9. | **Raised Knee Carry** | tíxī tuō gōu | 提膝托钩 |

Step the right foot forward to the left and bend the knee. Lower the right hook to the right side to stand vertically with the crown up and the crescent blade forward. Carry the left blade up in front with the arm straight at shoulder height, crescent blade up. Look forward, to the right. (image 5.9a) Push into the left foot and shift forward. Push off with the right foot to jump forward, landing with the left knee raised. Carry the right hook forward with the arm straight at shoulder height and the crescent blade up. Lower the left hook at the left side to stand vertically with the crown up and the crescent blade forward. Look forward, to the right. (image 5.9b)

CHA HOOKS

Step forward and jump with stability. Do continuous and smooth movements to complete first the left carry, then the right carry.

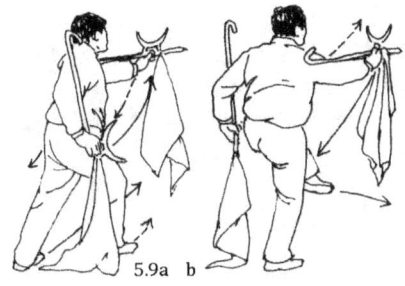

10. Bow Stance Stab   gōngbù zhā gōu   弓步扎钩

Land the left foot forward to the right, bending the left knee and straightening the right to take a left bow stance. Lower the right hook to stand at the right side, crown up and crescent blade forward. Stab the left hook spike forward to the right, arm straight at shoulder height, crescent blade up. Look forward, to the left. (image 5.10)

Put power into the spike when stabbing.

11. Bow Stance Carry   gōngbù tuō gōu   弓步托钩

Push into the left foot and shift back, pivoting on both feet around to the right. Bend the right knee and straighten the left to take a right bow stance. Carry the right hook up on the right with the arm straight, slanting up from the shoulder, crescent blade up. Look forward, to the left. (image 5.11)

Pivot quickly with good stability. Open out the arms in an expansive posture.

12. Empty Stance Lash   xūbù bǎi gōu   虚步摆钩

Without changing the bow stance, circle the right hook up and over to the left to in front of the left side of the chest, crown slanting up, crescent blade slanting down. Hold the left hook up on the left side with the blade upright, crown up, crescent blade to the left. Look behind, to the left. (image 5.12a) Push into the left foot and shift right. Step the left foot forward to the right, turning the foot out. Lower both hooks slightly. Look behind, to the left. (image 5.12b) Push into the right foot and shift forward. Step the right foot forward. Hold the hooks out to the left side, slanting downwards. Look behind, to the left. (image 5.12c)

133

CHAQUAN, VOLUME III

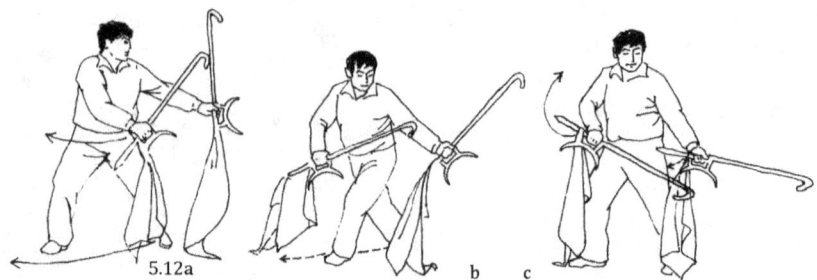

Without moving the feet, turn leftward. Circle the right hook down to the right then bring it up behind at the right, crescent blade slanting up. Look to the left. (image 5.12d) Push into the left foot and shift to the right, turning left. Bring the left foot in a half-step, lifting the heel with the ball of the foot touching down, bending both knees to take a left empty stance. Bring the right hook up over the head, circling to the left to stop in front of the body. Both hooks are standing upright with the crowns up and crescent blades forward. Look forward. (image 5.12e)

Coordinate the movements of the hooks with the stepping and sitting. Sit into a well-defined weighted / unweighted empty stance.

Section Two

13. Bow Stance Stab   gōngbù zhā gōu   弓步扎钩

Push into the left foot and raise the knee. Bring the hands up to place the hooks level in front of the chest with the flat of the blades lying along the arms, crescent blades up. Look forward. (image 5.13a) Land the left foot forward and bend the knee, straightening the right to take a left bow stance. Stab directly forward with the spikes of both hooks until the arms are straight at shoulder height. The crescent blades are up. Look forward. (image 5.13b)

Stab strongly into the spikes.

CHA HOOKS

14. Raised Knee Lift   tíxī jǔ gōu   提膝举钩

Push into the left foot and shift back, raising the left knee. Circle the hooks down and back, then lift and separate them, stopping the left in front of the chest and the right above the head. Both blades are level with the crescent blades up. Look forward, to the left. (image 5.14)

First circle the hook crowns from the rear, up and forward. Then circle them down and back, to parry and lift up. Do the one-legged stance with good balance.

5.14

15. Right Side Slice Up   yòucè liāo gōu   右侧撩钩

Land the left foot forward to the left and bend the knee. Circle the hooks to the right to parry downwards, crescent blades down. Look back, to the right. (image 5.15a) Push into the right foot and shift forward. Step the right foot forward, bending the knee. Do not change the position of the hooks relative to the body. Look back, to the right. (image 5.15b)

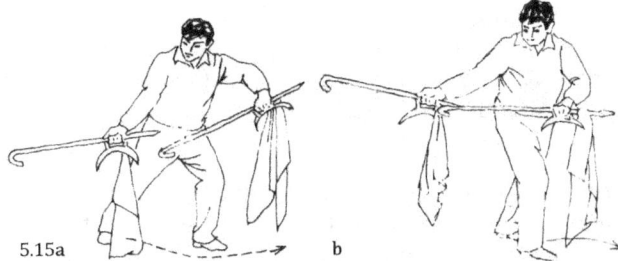

5.15a   b

Push into the left foot and shift forward, bending the knee. Start to lift the left hook up at the left side, holding it out at an angle. Look down. (image 5.15c) Push into the right foot and shift forward, turning left. Step the right foot forward. Circle both hooks forward and up towards the left to slice up. The left hook finishes above the head at the left. The right hook finishes up in front at the left. The blades are level, the crescent blades up. Look forward, to the right. (image 5.15d)

Keep the blades close to the body throughout the slicing action. Step forward and slice up in one smooth movement.

15c   d

16. Left Side Slice Up   zuǒcè liāo gōu   左侧撩钩

Push into the left foot and shift right, bending the right knee. Circle the hooks up, to the left, and down, holding them out at the left side, crescent blades down. Look back, to the left. (image 5.16a) Push into the left foot and shift right. Step the left foot forward with the foot turned out, bending the knee. Slice the right hook up to the front, crescent blade down. Look back, to the left. (image 5.16b) Push into the right foot and shift forward. Step the right foot forward, bending the knee. Continue to slice the right hook up to the front. Look back, to the left. (image 5.16c)

Push into the left foot and shift forward, turning right, and stepping the left foot forward. Circle the left hook down and to the right, to slice up in front at the right. Continue to slice up with the right hook until it is above the head. Both blades are level, crescent blades up. Look forward, to the left. (image 5.16d)

Keep the blades close to the body throughout the slicing actions. Coordinate the slicing with the stepping and turning.

17. Right Side Slice Up   yòucè liāo gōu   右侧撩钩

Push into the right foot and shift forward, moving the left foot forward, bending the left knee. Circle the hooks up and back on the right and down until they are in front of the body, crescent blades underneath. Look back, to the right. (image 5.17a) Push into the right foot and shift forward. Step the right foot forward with the foot turned out. Slice the left hook up at the left side. Look back, to the right. (image 5.17b) Push into the left foot and shift forward. Step the left foot forward, bending the knee. Continue to slice the left hook up in front at an angle. Look back and down, to the right. (image 5.17c)

CHA HOOKS

Push into the right foot and shift forward, turning left and stepping the right foot forward. Circle the right hook down to slice up in front along the left side. Continue to slice up with the left hook to over the head. Both blades are angled, the crowns slanting down. Look to the right. (image 5.17d)

5.17d

Keep the blades tight to the side of the body when slicing up. Step forward, turn, and slice in one coordinated whole.

18. Turn Around To Drop Stance Chop

zhuànshēn pūbù pī gōu 转身仆步劈钩

Push into the left foot and shift right, turning left and lifting the left foot up behind with the knee bent. Circle the hooks to bring them up and over to the left to in front of the body. The crowns are up with the crescent blades forward. Look forward. (image 5.18a) Land the left foot behind and squat fully, extending the right leg to take a right drop stance. Lean forward slightly. Continue to circle the hooks to bring them down with a chopping action. The blades are level with the hooks and crescent blades underneath. Look forward, to the right. (image 5.18b)

Turn quickly and drop into a stable stance. The chops are done with a circling action downwards.

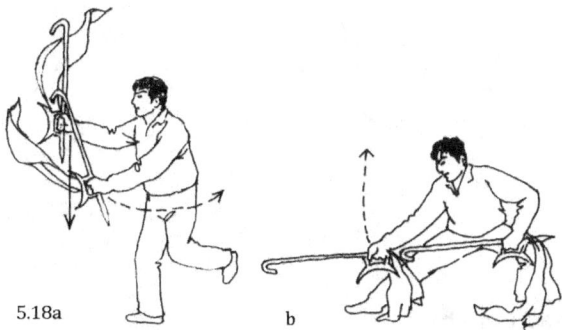

5.18a   b

19. Bow Stance Framing Block And Stab gōngbù jià zhā gōu 弓步架扎钩

Push into the left foot and stand up, bending the right knee. Bring the right hook up above the head, blade turned across the body. Hold the left hook out at the left side. Look forward. (image 5.19a) Push into the left foot and shift forward, bending the right knee and straightening the left to take a right bow stance. Do a framing block with the right hook above the head, crescent blade up. Stab forward with the left hook until the arm is straight at shoulder height. The crown is

5.19a   b

137

forward and the crescent blade underneath. Look forward. (image 5.19b)

This time the stab is done with the crown of the blade. Complete the stab with the completion of the bow stance.

20. Bow Stance Push gōngbù tuī gōu 弓步推钩

Push into the left foot and shift forward. Step the left foot forward. Circle the right hook out to the right side to stop outside the right hip, crescent blade down. Lift the left hook up in front at the left, crown up, crescent blade forward. Look forward. (image 5.20a) Push into the left foot to shift right, and step the left foot forward to the right, turned out. Push into the right heel, pressing the ball of the foot down. Hold the hooks out at their respective sides. Look forward and down. (image 5.20b) Push into the right foot and shift forward. Step the right foot forward to the right, bending the knee and straightening the left knee to take a right bow stance. Hold the right hook out by the right hip, blade level, crescent blade underneath. Push the left hook forward with the blade upright, the crown up, and the crescent blade forward. The left arm is straight, at shoulder height. Look forward. (image 5.20c)

Complete the push with the completion of the bow stance. Push with power.

Section Three

21. Step Forward, Right Push shàngbù yòu tuī gōu 上步右推钩

Push into the left foot and shift forward, turning left to face half-on. Place the left foot in front of the right and bend both knees. Press the left hook down with the blade tilted, crescent blade underneath. Look forward and down, to the left. (image 5.21a) Push into the right foot and step the left foot forward to the left. Bring the right foot up to meet the left, pressing down the ball of the foot with the heel lifted, both knees bent. Hold the left hook out to the left side, crescent blade down. Push the right hook forward to the left, crown slanting up and back, crescent blade forward. Look forward, to the left. (image 5.21b)

CHA HOOKS

Push into the crescent blade. As you push forward with the right blade, press the left blade down and back at the side to give power to the push.

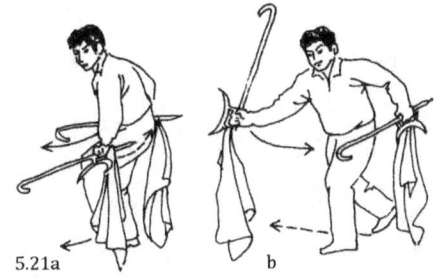

5.21a   b

22. Step Forward, Left Push shàngbù zuǒ tuī gōu 上步左推钩

Push into the right foot and shift forward, turning right. Step the right foot forward to the right. Hold the hands out at their respective sides with the crescent blades underneath. Look forward, to the right. (image 5.22a) Push into the left foot and shift to the right, turning right. Bring the left foot up behind the right foot, touching down the foot with the heel lifted, and bending both knees. Bring the right hook to the right hip, blade level, crescent blade down. Push forward with the left hook, blade vertical, crown up, crescent blade forward, and arm straight at shoulder height. Look forward, to the right. (image 5.22b)

Put power into the crescent blade for the push. As the left hook pushes, press the right down behind to assist with the power.

5.22a   b

23. Double Drape To The Right yòu shuāng dā gōu 右双搭钩

Push into the right foot and shift back, turning right. Retreat the right foot behind. Circle both hooks down, pulling them back to the right side, crowns slanting down to the right, crescent blades underneath. Look down to the right. (image 5.23a) Without moving the feet, turn slightly more to the right. Continue to circle the hooks rightward, continuing to above the head, turning the crescent blades to angle up. Look up. (image 5.23b) Push into the right foot and shift forward, turning left. Step the right foot forward and bend both knees to sit into a horse stance. Continue to circle the hooks forward with a double draping action, crowns angled to the upper front, crescent blades angled to the lower front. Look forward, to the right. (image 5.23c)

Step forward, turn the body, and drape with the hooks in one well coordinated movement.

CHAQUAN, VOLUME III

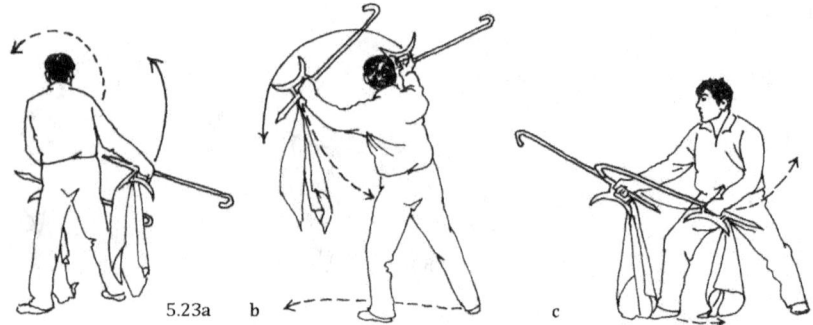

Note: The term 'double drape' is specific to the Chaquan system. Its meaning is to drape [tr. note: like draping clothes over a line] both weapons over an opponent's weapon, seizing the opportunity to attack.

24. Double Drape To The Left   zuǒ shuāng dā gōu   左双搭钩

Push into the right foot and shift to the left, turning left. Move the right foot towards the left foot and stand up. Circle the hooks down to the left side, crowns angled to the lower left and crescent blades underneath. Look to the left side. (image 5.24a) Push into the right foot and shift left, turning right and moving the right foot to the right. Continue to the circle the hooks to the left and up over the head. The crowns are angled to the upper rear, and the crescent blades are turned up. Look forward, to the right. (image 5.24b) Push into the left foot to shift right, and turn right. Step the left foot forward and bend both knees. Continue to circle the hooks to the left, over to the forward left. Finish with the crowns angled up in front and the crescent blades angled down. Look forward, to the left. (image 5.24c)

Step forward, turn, and drape the hooks in one smooth, well coordinated action.

25.   Double Drape To The Right   yòu shuāng dā gōu   右双搭钩

Push into the left foot to shift back, turn right, and move the left foot forward to the right. Circle the hooks down to in front of the belly, turning the crowns to face right, crescent blades underneath. Look back, to the right. (image 5.25a) Without moving the feet, shift left and turn left. Circle and lift the hooks to the right and up over the head, crowns angled back and crescent blades up. Look up and forward, to the left. (image 5.25b) Push into the right foot and shift forward, turning left, then step the right foot forward and bend both legs. Circle the hooks forward to hold them out in front on the right, crowns angled forward and up, crescent blades angled forward and down. Look to the lower front. (image 5.25c)

Step forward, turn, and drape the hooks all in one smooth movement.

26. Turn Around, Bow Stance Lash

zhuànshēn gōngbù bǎi gōu 转身弓步摆钩

Push into the left foot and shift right. Move the left foot towards the right foot and stand up. Look to the left. (image 5.26a) Move the left foot back to the left and turn left. Bend the left knee and straighten the right to take a left bow stance. Circle the hooks forward to bring them out in front at the left side of the body, crowns angled to the upper rear, crescent blades forward to the left. Look forward to the right. (image 5.26b)

Turn into the bow stance and lash the hooks all in one coordinated action.

27. Jumping Turn, Resting Stance Framing Block

tiàozhuàn xiēbù jià gōu 跳转歇步架钩

Push into the right foot to shift left, and turn right. Move the right foot towards the left foot. Hold the hooks out to the left side. Look forward, to the right. (image 5.27a) Step the right foot forward, shift forward, and raise the left knee, turning slightly rightward. Hold the hooks up in front of the chest, the crowns at the left and crescent blades forward. Look forward, to the right. (image 5.27b) Push into the right foot and jump up, spinning around to the right. Land on the left foot and raise the right knee. Carry the hooks around to the right, lifting them with the crowns pointing up to the right and the crescent blades up. Look up. (image 5.27c)

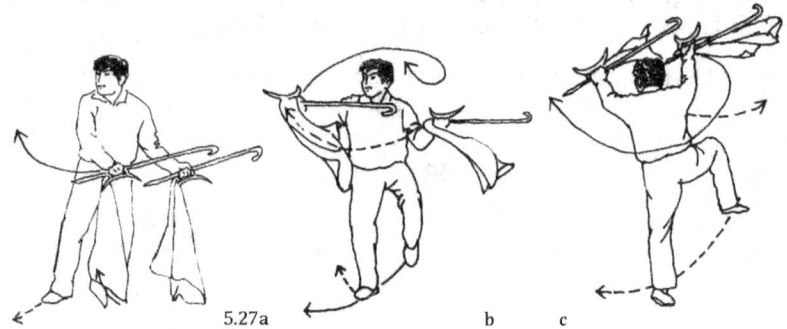

Spin around to the right, then land the right foot to the right side, standing up. Hold the hooks out to either side, crowns up, crescent blades out to their respective sides. Look to the left side. (image 5.27d) Push into the left foot to shift right, then step the left foot to the right side behind the right foot, with an insertion step, touching the ball of the foot down with the heel up. The legs are crossed and the knees bent, in a resting stance. Cross the hooks with framing blocks above the head. Look forward. (image 5.27e)

Be sure to keep control during the jumping spin. The hooks come around flat with the spin of the body, brandishing around over the head. Be sure to coordinate the whole move smoothly.

Section Four

28. **Single Drape To The Right**   yòu dān dā gōu   右单搭钩

Push into both feet to stand up. Step the left foot forward and bend the knee. Do a framing block up in front with the left hook with the blade level and crown pointing right, crescent blade up. Hold the right hook out behind. Look forward. (images 5.28a, 28b) Push into the right foot and shift forward. Step the right foot forward, bending the knee and straightening the left to take a right bow stance. Turn left. Do a framing block with the left hook over the head, crescent blade up. Lower the right hook and circle it forward to drape, turning it left, crescent blade to the left. Look forward. (image 5.28c)

Step forward, block with the left hook, and drape with the right hook in a well coordinated movement.

Note: The term 'single drape' is specific to the Chaquan system. Its meaning is to drape the weapon over an opponent's weapon, like draping clothes over a line, thus creating an opportunity to attack.

29. Single Drape To The Left   zuǒ dān dā gōu   左单搭钩

Push into the right foot and shift back. Move the right foot towards the left foot and bend both knees. Circle the hooks up and to the left, to hold them out at the left side, blades vertical, crowns up, crescent blades to the rear left. Look forward, to the right. (image 5.29a) Push into the right foot and shift left, then step the right foot forward to the right, bending the knee. Turn slightly to the right. Circle the right hook down and to the right, to do a framing block across above and forward, crown to the left, crescent blade up. Hold the left hook back on the left, slanting down. Look forward, to the right. (image 5.29b) Push into the left foot and shift forward. Step the left foot forward and bend the knee, straightening the right knee to take a left bow stance. Continue the right framing block to over the head, crescent blade up. Circle the left hook from the rear to the left, then to the right with a level drape, the crescent blade to the right. Turn right. Look forward. (image 5.29c)

Step forward, block up, and drape in one coordinated action.

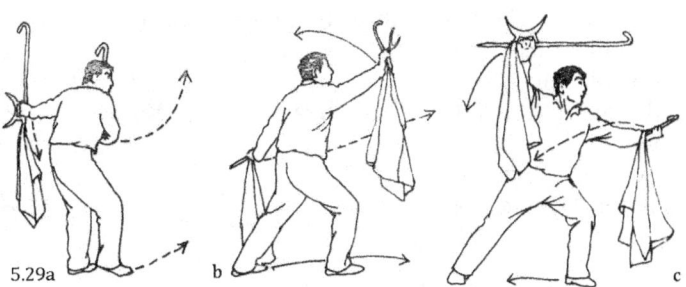

30. Single Drape To The Right   yòu dān dā gōu   右单搭钩

Push into the left foot and shift back, moving the left foot towards the right foot and bending both legs. Circle the hooks up and over to the right side of the body, crowns angled up and crescent blades to the rear. Look forward, to the left. (image 5.30a) Push into the left foot and shift to the right. Step the left foot forward and pushing into the knee. Circle the left hook down and to the left, then forward and up to do a framing block across, crown to the right, crescent blade up. Look forward, to the left. (image 5.30b) Push into the right foot and shift forward, turning left. Step the right foot forward and bend the knee, straightening the left knee. Lift the left hook to do a framing block above the head, crescent blade up. Circle the right hook down and to the left with a draping action, crescent blade left. Look forward, to the right. (image 5.30c)

Step forward, block up with the left, and drape with the right, all as one coordinated action.

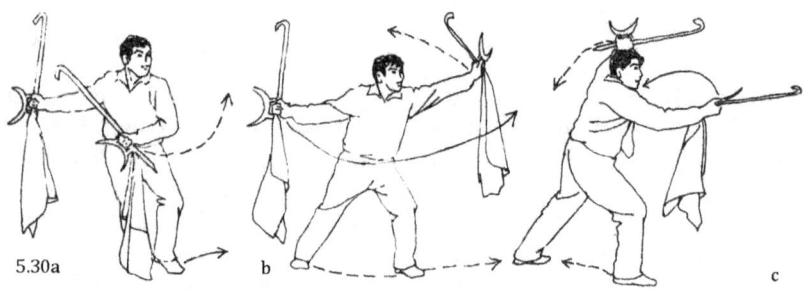

31. Step Forward, Slice Up   shàngbù liāo gōu   上步撩钩

Push into the right foot and shift back, moving the right foot towards the left foot. Circle the hooks up and over to the rear, holding them out at the left side, crowns up, crescent blades back. Look forward, to the right. (image 5.31a) Push into the left foot to shift forward, and step the left foot forward. Do not change the position of the hooks relative to the body. Look to the left side. (image 5.31b) Push into the right foot to shift forward, and step the right foot forward. Circle both hooks to the left and down, then slice up to the front. The right hook slices up in front to vertical, crown down, crescent blade forward. The left hook slices out to the rear at the left, crown back, crescent blade down. Look forward, to the right. (image 5.31c)

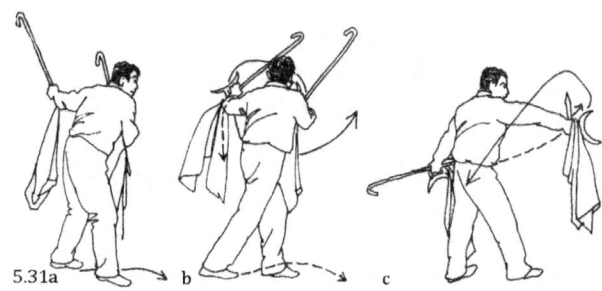

CHA HOOKS

When slicing forward, lead with the crescent blade and the cutting edge of the long blade on that side. Step forward and slice in one smooth action.

32. Raised Knee Carry   tíxī tuō gōu   提膝托钩

Push into the left foot to shift right, lift the left heel with the ball of the foot touching down, and turn right. Circle the right hook forward, up, and over to the rear, stopping at the right side with the blade vertical, flat of the blade on the right arm. The crown is up and the crescent blade forward. Circle the left hook down and forward, stopping with a carry in front, with the blade level, flat of the blade along the left arm. The crescent blade is up. Look forward. (image 5.32a) Push into the left foot to shift forward, and raise the left knee. Carry the right hook level in front, arm straight, crescent blade up. Lower the left hook to stand at the left side, crown up, crescent blade forward. Look forward, to the right. (image 5.32b)

Stay stable when stepping into the one-legged stance. When doing a carry with the hooks, the crescent blade edge is always up.

33. Bow Stance Carry   gōngbù tuō gōu   弓步托钩

Land the left foot behind to the left, bending the knee and straightening the right knee. Lift the left hook out to the left side, higher than the shoulder. Look forward, to the right. (image 5.33)

The carrying posture should be open and expansive.

34. Walking Scoop   xíngbù tiǎo gōu   行步挑钩

Push into the right foot to shift left, and step the right foot in front of the left, turning to the left. Circle the right hook down, to the left, then carry up at the left, arm straight, crescent blade angled up. Hold the left hook vertical at the left side of the body, crown up, crescent blade forward. Look forward and up. (image 5.34a) Push into the left foot and shift forward, then step the left foot in an arcing step to the forward right. Hold the position of the hooks relative to the body. Look forward. (image 5.34b) Push into the right foot and shift forward, then step the right foot in an arcing step to the forward right. Land with the foot turned out, and turn the body to the right. Do not change the position of the hooks relative to the body. Look forward, to the right. (image 5.34c) Push into the left foot and shift forward, turning right. Step the left foot in an arcing step to the forward right, then bend the knee. Still do not change the position of the hooks relative to the body. Look to the upper right. (image 5.34d)

Step with a continuous, smooth, walk, following a curving line.

35. Jump, Parry And Chop   tiào guàpī gōu   跳挂劈钩

Push into the right foot to shift to the left, and raise the right knee. Hook and parry the right hook down and to the right to the outside of the right leg, crescent blade underneath. Hold the left hook up above the head, crown up, crescent blade forward. Look down to the right. (image 5.35a) Push into the left foot to jump up, then land on the right foot and stand with the left knee raised. Lash the right hook out and up to the right. Press the left hook forward and down across, to outside the left knee, crown to the left, crescent blade forward and down. Look down in front. (image 5.35b) Land the left foot forward, bending the knee and straightening the right knee to take a left bow stance. Hook and parry the left hook out to the left side, blade level, crown forward, crescent blade underneath. Bring the right hook over to chop forward and down, crown angled to the upper front, crescent blade angled to the lower front. Look forward. (image 5.35c)

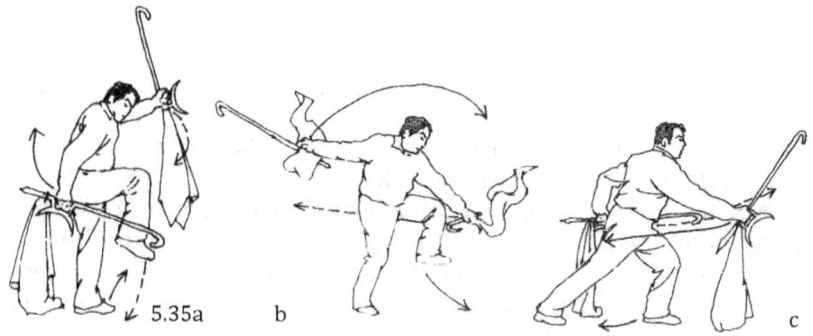

Jump into the bow stance with good balance. Put power to the crescent blade side of the long blade for both parrying and chopping. When doing the parry and chop, complete the parry first, then chop.

36. Empty Stance Push   xūbù tuī gōu   虚步推钩

Push into the left foot to shift back, shift the left foot towards the right foot, lifting the heel and sitting into a left empty stance. Bring the right hook in and back, to hold it out at the right side, crown pointing forward, crescent blade underneath. Push the left hook forward into the crescent blade edge, crown pointing up. Look forward. (image 5.36)

Sit into a well-defined empty stance. Push the left hook with power.

37. Closed Stance Lash   bìngbù bǎi gōu   并步摆钩

Push into the left foot and stand up, turning right. Bring the left foot in beside the right foot to take a closed stance. Push the right hook forward, then immediately circle both hooks up and over to the rear, so that they stand vertically at the right side. The crowns are up and the crescent blades face right. Look forward, to the right. (image 5.37)

The closed stance, turn, and double lash are all done as one coordinated action.

38. Step Forward, Slice Up   shàngbù liāo gōu   上步撩钩

Push into the right foot and step the left foot across to the left side, bending the knee. Circle the hooks down to the right, holding them out at the right side of the body, blades level, crowns pointing right, crescent blades underneath. Look down to the right. (image 5.38a) Push into the right foot to shift left, turn left, and step the right foot forward. Circle the hooks down and to the left, then slice up in front, the crowns pointing right, the crescent blades up. Look to the upper right. (image 5.38b)

Step forward, turn, and slice up as one coordinated action.

CHAQUAN, VOLUME III

39. Turn Around, Resting Stance Chop

zhuànshēn xiēbù pī gōu　　　　　　　　　　转身歇步劈钩

Push into the left foot, shift right, turn left, and raise the left knee. Bring the hooks up and over to the left to chop down in front [tr. note: front means facing in the new direction]. The left hook is level at the left side of the body, crown forward, crescent blade underneath. The right hook is in front with the crown angled up and the crescent blade angled down. Look to the lower front. (image 5.39a) Land the left foot forward, turned out, crossing the legs and sitting into both legs in a resting stance. Lift the left hook further out to the rear left, crown pointing forward and down, crescent blade underneath. Keep the right hook where it is. Look to the lower front. (image 5.39b)

Turn around and settle into the resting stance with good control. The stance is expansive. Chop forward and down with the crescent blade side of the long blade.

5.39a　　　　　　　　　　b

Section Five

40. Retreat, Raised Knee Separate The Hooks

tuìbù tíxī fēn gōu　　　　　　　　　　退步提膝分钩

Push into both feet to stand up, retreating the left foot, then the right. Hold the hooks in front of the belly, crescent blades out to either side, tips crossing in front of the body. Look forward and down. (image 5.40a) Push into the left foot to shift back, and raise the left knee. Raise the hooks, crossed, up in front of and above the head. Look forward. (image 5.40b) Keeping the left knee raised, separate the hooks out to either side to shoulder height with the arms straight. The blades are vertical, the crowns up, and the crescent blades are out to either side. Look

5.40a　　b　　　　c

CHA HOOKS

forward. (image 5.40c)

Stay stable when retreating to the one-legged stance. Complete the upper framing block with the hooks before separating them out to their respective sides. These actions are gentle and smooth.

41. Empty Stance Cradle The Hooks   xūbù bào gōu   虚步抱钩

Land the left foot forward and shift towards to the left leg. Circle the hooks around to go up and forward with the crescent blades angled forward and up and the crowns angled back and up. Look forward. (image 5.41a) Push into the right foot to shift forward, and step the right foot forward, bending into the knee. Circle the hooks down to separate out to their respective sides, crescent blades underneath, crowns angled forward and up. Look forward. (image 5.41b) Push into the left foot and shift forward, then step the left foot forward. Touch down the ball of the left foot with the heel up, and bend both knees to sit into a left empty stance. Circle the hooks forward from the sides, to hold them vertically in front of the body, crescent blades facing each other. Look forward. (image 5.41c)

Be sure to have clear-cut weighting in the empty stance. Circle the hooks when lifting them to cradle [tr. note: this is not a push].

5.41a   b   c

42. Framing Block, Jumping Kick   jià gōu tiàotī   架钩跳踢

Push into the right foot to shift forward, and step the right foot forward. Lower the hooks to cross the blades in front. Look forward. (image 5.42a) Push into the left foot and shift forward, bending the right knee. With the hooks holding each other, lift the blades above the head in front, crescent blades up. Look forward and up. (image 5.42b) Push into the left foot to shift forward, and raise the left knee. Uncross the hooks and hold the blades out in front. Look forward. (image 5.42c) Push into the right foot to jump up. Land on the left foot and do a snap kick forward with the right leg. Hook the blades again and do framing blocks above the head. Look forward. (image 5.42d)

When doing the framing blocks, the blades hook together, then lift. Jump lightly. Kick with power.

5.42a b c d

43. Turn Around, Sweep zhuànshēn sǎo gōu 转身扫钩

Land the right foot forward and bend both knees Do not change the position of the hooks relative to the body. Look forward. (image 5.43a)

With the left blade hooked in the right blade, sweep the two together in the right hand, around to the rear. Hold the left hand out to the side. Look forward, to the right. (image 5.43b) Push into the left foot to shift to the right, turn left, and raise the left knee. Continue to sweep the hooks in the right hand to the left side in a flat sweeping circle. Look forward, to the left. (image 5.43c)

5.43a

5.43b c

Pivot on the right foot around to the rear left, turning the body around leftward, to land the left foot to the rear left. Bend both knees. Continue to sweep the two hooks in the right hand flat around to the left. Reach the left hand out to the front on the left side [tr. note: preparing for the catch]. Look forward and down, to the left. (image 5.43d)

Turn and move the feet quickly and with good stability. Sweep the blades in the right hand in one line, turning flat.

5.43d

CHA HOOKS

44. Back-Cross Stance Double Lash chābù shuāng bǎi gōu 叉步双摆钩

Without moving the feet, continue to sweep the hooks flat around to the left with the right hand. Catch the grip of the far hook with the left hand. Look forward, to the right. (image 5.44a) Lash the hooks, now separated, to the lower left, turning left. The crowns are angled down and the crescent blades down. Look down to the left. (image 5.44b) Push into the left foot to shift right, and step the left foot behind the right leg to the right side with an insertion step, touching down the foot with the heel lifted. The legs are crossed and bent. Turn right. Lash the hooks to the left, up, and over, circling to the right side, finishing with the crowns up and crescent blades to the right. Look to the right side. (image 5.44c)

Time the lash of the hooks with the completion of the back-cross stance.

45. Roll Over, Chop fānshēn pī gōu 翻身劈钩

Swivel on both feet on the spot to turn and roll over to the left, keeping the legs fairly straight. Circle the hooks around with the turn, down, left, and up and over, the crowns to the right and crescent blades up. Look up to the right. (image 5.45a) Continue to swivel the feet on the spot around to the left, turning left. Circle the hooks over to chop down to the left, crowns angled forward and up, crescent blades angled forward and down. Look forward, to the right. (image 5.45b)

Roll over quickly. Swivel with good balance. Chop forward with the crescent blade sides of the whole blades.

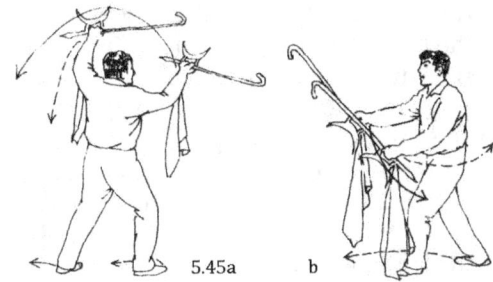

46. Closed Stance Lash bìngbù bǎi gōu 并步摆钩

Push into the right foot to shift forward, and step the right foot forward, turning left. Circle the hooks to lash down and out to the left side of the body. The crowns point left and the crescent blades are underneath. Look

151

down to the right. (image 5.46a) Push into the left foot to shift right, and bring the left foot up to meet the right foot in a closed stance. Circle the hooks to the left, up and over to lash out to the right. The blades are vertical, the crowns up, and the crescent blades on the right. Look to the right side. (image 5.46b)

Complete the double lash as you complete the closed stance.

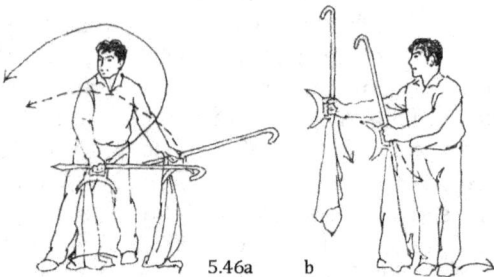

47. Turn Around, Scoop   zhuànshēn tiǎo gōu   转身挑钩

Stride the left foot across to the left side, taking an open stance. Circle the hooks down and out in front of the legs. Look to the left side. (image 5.47a) Push into the right foot to shift to the left, and bring the right foot in beside the left foot in a closed stance, standing up. Take the hooks over to the left with a circling scoop up, turning the body slightly to the left. The blades are vertical, the crowns up, and the crescent blades to the left. Look to the left side. (image 5.47b)

Coordinate the stepping with the action of the hooks.

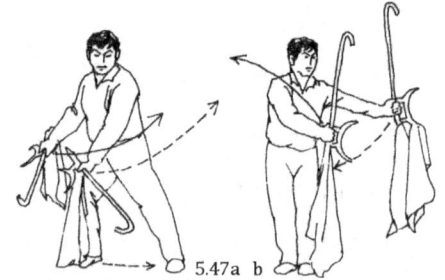

48. Empty Stance Flash   xūbù liàng gōu   虚步亮钩

Withdraw the right foot to the rear right. Lift the right hook up, lying the flat of the blade on the right arm, crescent blade up. Place the left hook upright at the left side of the body, crown up, crescent blade forward. Look forward, to the left. (image 5.48a) Push into the left foot to shift right, and move the left foot over to the right, touching the ball of the foot down and lifting the heel. Sit to take a left empty stance. Hold the right hook up to the right above the head. Hold the left hook out to the left side, slanting downwards. Look forward, to the left. (image 5.48b)

Do a well-defined empty stance.

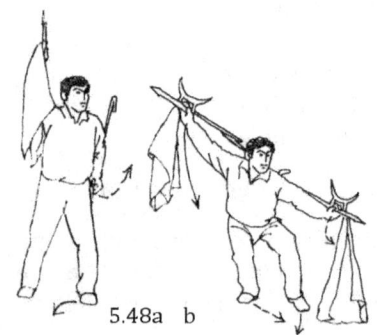

CHA HOOKS

49. Retreat, Press Down tuìbù yā gōu 退步压钩

Push into the left foot to shift right, and retreat the left foot behind, keeping both legs bent. Press the hooks down in front with the fore-section of the blades crossed. Look forward and down. (image 5.49a) Push into the right foot to shift back, and retreat the right foot behind, standing up a bit. Lift the hooks slightly. Look forward. (image 5.49b) Push into the left foot to shift back, bring the left foot towards the right foot to take a closed stance, and stand up. Lower the hooks in front, holding the blades flat and tilted down. Look to the left. (image 5.49c)

Coordinate the press down with the retreating step.

50. Closing Posture (Stand To Attention Holding The Hooks)

shōu shì (lìzhèng wò gōu) 收势（立正握钩）

Lower the hooks to either side, the arms hanging down and the blades level. Look forward. (image 5.50)

153

HORSE CONTROLLING BATONS

拦马橛

ABOUT THE HORSE CONTROLLING BATONS

The batons are wooden sticks with a base end, or butt, a hole for the tassel, a grip area, and a tip. The whole baton is differentiated into the fore-section – the third nearest the tip, the mid-section, and the aft-section – the third nearest the grip. The base end is thicker than the tip. The grip is near the base end, but forward of the hole.

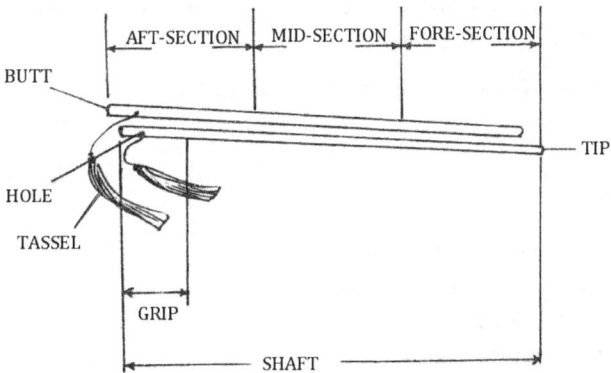

The length of the baton is when it is standing on the ground, it just reaches chest height. The baton is usually made of a waxwood tree, but may be of other wood. There is no weight restriction.

Tassels are usually attached, using the hole near the butt. The hole is the size of a horse's nostril.

The batons are held at the grip, ahead of the hole.

HOLD THE BATONS

THE MAIN TECHNIQUES OF THE HORSE CONTROLLING BATONS

Chop: A double chop is with both batons, while a single chop is with one. Similar to the Cha sabre and sword, a chop circles down from above to chop down, power going to the fore-section.

Stab: To stab quickly directly forward into the tip, the baton level.

Slice up: Similar to slicing with the sabre and sword, a slice moves forward and up, passing along close to the side, with the power going to the fore-section.

Intercept: A double intercept is with both batons; a single intercept is with one. For a single intercept, one hand circles down from above to strike. A double intercept, both hands cross the batons, and strike down from above, or up from below.

Sweep: This is a low technique, with one baton, the hand holding it below the knee with the baton level. The baton circles by the side to the front, to sweep across to the other side. The power goes to the fore-section.

Brandish: With one or two batons, circle the baton over the head in a full, level, circle.

Strike: This is similar to a chop, but the power is shorter. The strike is to the tip.

Flowers: With both batons, circle them in vertical or horizontal circles, alternating the left and right, continuously.

NAMES OF THE MOVEMENTS OF THE HORSE CONTROLLING BATONS FORM

Position Of Preparation
Section One
1. Step Forward, Separate The Batons
2. Step Astride, Stand The Batons
3. Step Forward, Chop
4. Back-Cross Step, Chop
5. Roll Over, Chop
6. Turn Around, Left And Right Chop
7. Back-Cross Step, Chop
8. Roll Over, Chop
9. Step Forward, Push

Section Two
10. Right Dodge, Left And Right Chops
11. Left Dodge, Right And Left Chops
12. Right Dodge, Left And Right Chops
13. Turn Around, Bow Stance Lash
14. Jumping Turn, Brandish And Lash

Section Three
15. Empty Stance Slice Up And Snap
16. Right Bow Stance Framing Block And Pierce
17. Left Bow Stance Framing Block And Pierce
18. Right Bow Stance Framing Block And Pierce
19. Withdraw, Double Lash
20. Jumping Turn To Drop Stance Chop
21. Bow Stance Framing Block And Pierce

22. Bow Stance Push

Section Four

23. Left Dodge, Left And Right Chops
24. Turn Around, Present The Batons
25. Raised Knee Low Intercept
26. Jumping Step, Chop
27. Bow Stance Low Intercept
28. Horse Stance, Plant Down, High Framing Blocks
29. Plant The Batons, Side Kick
30. Plant The Batons, Turn Around, Side Kick
31. Left And Right Flowers, Chop
32. Back-Cross Step, Chop
33. Turn Around, Raised Knee Present The Batons

Section Five

34. Empty Stance Press Down
35. Step Forward, Framing Block And Sweep
36. Turn Around, Framing Block And Sweep
37. Turn Around, Framing Block And Sweep
38. Left And Right Flowers, Chops
39. Back-Cross Step, Chops
40. Roll Over, Chop
41. Left And Right Flowers, Chops
42. Back-Cross Step, Chop
43. Roll Over, Chop
44. Step Forward, Double Lash
45. Step Astride, Scoop Up
46. Empty Stance Present The Batons
47. Closing Posture (Stand To Attention Holding The Batons)

0. Position Of Preparation   yùbèi shì   预备势

Stand to attention, holding the batons, one in each hand, at the side of the body with the arms hanging down. The batons are level with the tips pointing forward. Look forward. (image 6.0a) Without moving the feet or the body, lift the batons out to the sides, the arms slanting down and baton tips slanting in and down. Look to the left. (image 6.0b)

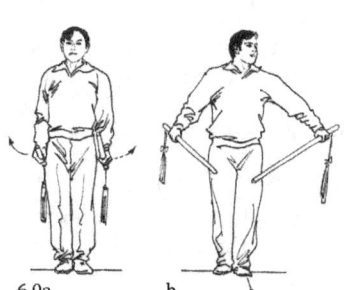

6.0a   b

CHAQUAN, VOLUME III

Section One

1.   Step Forward, Separate The Batons   shàngbù fēn jué   上步分概

Step the left foot forward and shift forward. Look forward. (image 6.1a) Push into the right foot to shift forward, then step the right foot forward. Circle the batons forward and up above the head, tips slanting up. Look forward. (image 6.1b) Push into the left foot to shift forward, and step the left foot up to meet the right foot in a closed stance. Stand up straight. Separate the batons out to their respective sides, holding the arms straight at shoulder height. The batons are vertical with the tips up. Look to the right. (image 6.1c)

Coordinate the stepping with the separation of the batons.

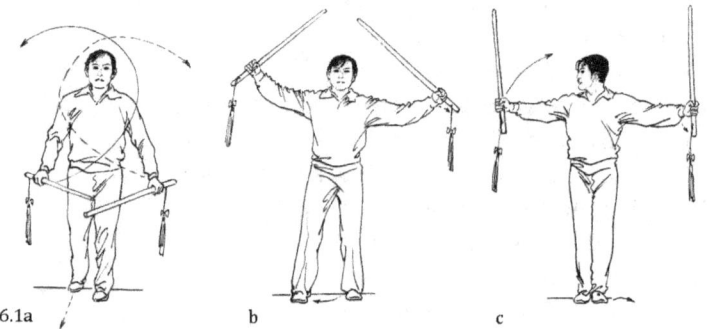

6.1a   b   c

2.   Step Astride, Stand The Batons   kuàbù lì jué   跨步立概

Stride the left foot out to the left, keeping both legs straight. Turn the left baton over to point down. Hold the right baton up over the head. Turn slightly to the left. Look to the left. (image 6.2a) Push into the right foot and shift left, then bring the right foot up beside the left foot in a closed stance. Turn the torso to the left. Place the tip of the left baton on the ground. Place the butt of the right baton on top of the butt of the left baton at the left side. Look to the left. (image 6.2b)

Step to the side and place the batons standing in one smooth action.

6.2a b

3.   Step Forward, Chop   shàngbù pī jué   上步劈概

Step the right foot in front, to the right, and turn left. Hold the batons out on the left side. Hold the left baton outside the left hip with the tip pointing forward. Hold the right baton at the left shoulder with the tip slanting down to the rear. Look forward, to the right. (image 6.3a) Push into the left foot and shift right, bending the right knee. Circle the right baton up and over to chop down in front at the right, tip slanting up. Look forward, to the right. (image 6.3b) Without moving the feet, place the right baton outside the right hip. Circle the left baton around on the left and up, coming over to the front to chop at the right, the baton slanting up. Turn right. Look forward. (image 6.3c)

Step forward and chop, each action coordinated smoothly. Put power into the chops.

6.3a　　b　　c

4. **Back-Cross Step, Chop**　　chābù pī jué　　叉步劈橛

Push into the left leg, shift forward, turn right, and step the left foot forward to the right. Stand up in an open stance. Hold the left baton out at the left side. Bring the right baton over to the rear right. Look forward, to the left (image 6.4a) Push into the left foot to shift left, and step the right foot behind the left leg to the forward left in a back-cross step. Turn right, press the left ball of the foot into the ground and lift the heel, and bend both legs in the crossed stance. Circle the left baton so that the tip turns to press down in front of the body, tip to the right. Circle the right baton up and over to chop down at the left in front of the body, tip pointing left. The right baton is above the left. Look to the left. (image 6.4b)

Step into the back-cross stance with good balance. Press the left baton down while chopping with the right baton. Do a strong chop.

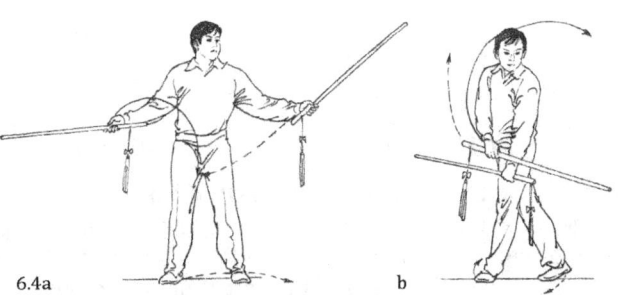

6.4a　　b

5. **Roll Over, Chop**　　fānshēn pī jué　　翻身劈橛

Pivot to the right on the spot, rolling the body into the back, over to the right, standing up with the body leaning back, the chest up. Bring the batons around to the right and up to cross above the head. Look up. (image 6.5a) Push into the right foot to shift left, turn right, and move the right foot to the right. Bend into the right knee and straighten the left to take a right bow stance. Circle the batons to the right, holding them out to the right side. The left baton stands outside the right arm, tip up. Look forward, to the right.

CHAQUAN, VOLUME III

(image 6.5b)

Keep good balance whilst pivoting around on both feet. Roll over quickly. Complete the body roll at the same time as you stand the batons to the side.

6.5a   b

6. Turn Around, Left And Right Chop

zhuànshēn zuǒyòu pī jué   转身左右劈橛

Push into the right foot to shift left, and turn the torso left, bending the left knee and pushing into it. Lash the right baton out to the rear right. Look forward, to the left. (image 6.6a) Push into the right foot to shift forward, turn the torso left, and step the right foot forward. Lower the left baton in front of the body. Circle the right baton over to chop out to the front, tip slanting up. Look forward, to the right. (image 6.6b)

Turn around and step quickly. Chop both left and right strongly.

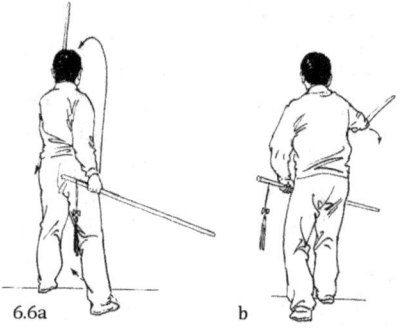

6.6a   b

7. Back-Cross Step, Chop   chābù pī jué   叉步劈橛

Hold out the batons at their respective sides, moving the left baton behind. (image 6.7a) Push into the left foot, turn right, then step the left foot behind the right leg to the right, turning left. The legs are crossed and bent, the left heel lifted with the ball of the foot touching down. Circle the right baton down and around on the left to behind the left arm, tip up. Circle the left baton up then over to chop outside the right leg, tip slanting down. Look down to the right. (image 6.7b)

Step firmly, chop strongly.

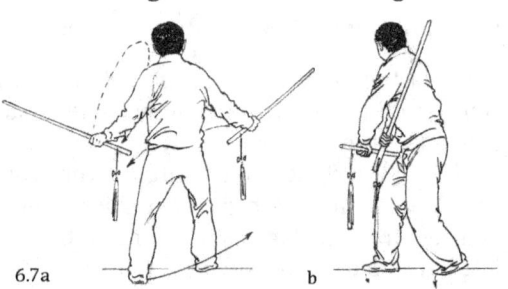

6.7a   b

160

HORSE CONTROLLING BATONS

8. Roll Over, Chop   fānshēn pī jué   翻身劈橛

Pivot to the left on both feet on the spot and roll over into the back to the left, standing up and leaning back. Circle the batons up on the left, crossing them over the head. Look up. (image 6.8a) Push into the left foot to shift right, and turn the torso left. Move the left foot to the rear left, bending the knee and straightening the right knee to take a left bow stance. Circle the batons to the left to hold them out to the left side. The right baton is outside the left arm, tip up. Look forward, to the right. (image 6.8b)

Pivot with stability. Roll over quickly. Complete the roll and the placement of the batons at the same time.

9. Step Forward, Push   shàngbù tuī jué   上步推橛

Push into the left foot to shift right, and turn right. Bring the left foot in a half-step and bend both legs. Circle the batons down and out to the rear, lifting them out at each side with the tips slanting forward and down. Look forward, to the left. (image 6.9a) Push into the left foot to shift right, then step the left foot forward to the right with the foot turned out. Cross the legs in a relatively open stance. Lean forward slightly. Keep the batons opened out to the sides. Look forward, to the left. (image 6.9b) Push into the right foot to shift forward, then step the right foot forward to the right. Bend the right knee and straighten the left to set into a right bow stance. Push the left baton forward to the right, tip slanting up. Look forward, to the left. (image 6.9c)

Turn, step, and push as one smooth action.

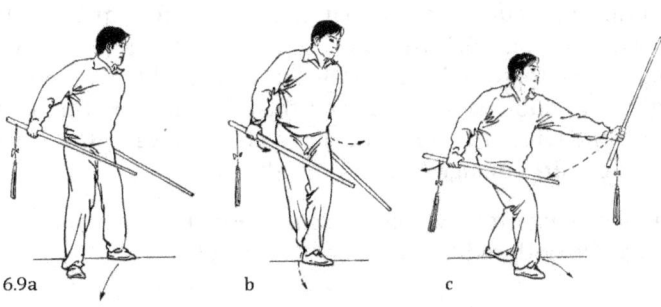

Section Two

10. Right Dodge, Left And Right Chops

yòushǎn zuǒyòu pī jué　　　　　　　　　右闪左右劈概

Push into the left foot to shift forward, and step the left foot forward to the right, standing up. Circle the batons down and back on the right, tips slanting down to the rear right. Look forward, to the left. (image 6.10a) Push into the left foot to shift back, and then move the right foot forward, bending the left knee. Circle the left baton up and over to chop down in front, tip forward, slanting up. Look forward. (image 6.10b) Push into the right foot to shift forward, and step the right foot forward, turning left. Lower the left baton to the rear left. Circle the right baton up and over to chop forward, tip forward and up. Look forward. (image 6.10c)

Take arcing steps with the left foot, then the right, when stepping forward, and dodge the body to the right. Do both left and right chops with power.

11. Left Dodge, Right And Left Chops

zuǒshǎn yòuzuǒ pī jué　　　　　　　　　左闪右左劈概

Push into the right foot to shift back, then move the right foot towards the left foot and stand up. Circle the batons down and over to the rear left, tips slanting down and back to the left. Look forward, to the right. (image 6.11a) Push into the right foot to shift left, then step the right foot in a curving step to the forward left, bending the knee and turning the torso to the right. Circle the right baton up and over to chop in front at the right, tip forward, slanting up. Turn the left baton to point forward, slanting down. Look forward. (image 6.11b) Take a curving step forward with the left foot, turning the torso right. Bend the left knee and straighten the right. Lash the right baton down to the rear on the right, tip pointing forward and down. Circle the left baton up and over to chop forward, tip forward, slanting up. Look forward. (image 6.11c)

Take curving steps when stepping forward. Turn the body to the left to dodge. Do both right and left chops strongly.

HORSE CONTROLLING BATONS

12. Right Dodge, Left And Right Chops

yòushǎn zuǒyòu pī jué   右闪左右劈橛

Push into the left foot to shift back, then move the left foot towards the right foot and stand up. Circle the batons down, holding them out to the rear right, tips pointing to the lower rear right. Look forward, to the left. (image 6.12a) Push into the left foot to shift right, and step the left foot forward, bending the knee. Circle the left baton up and over to chop out to the left, tip forward, slanting upwards. Look forward. (image 6.12b) Step the right foot forward with an arcing step, turning left. Bend the right knee and straighten the left. Place the left baton outside the left hip, tip forward and down. Circle the right baton up and over to chop in front, tip forward, slanting up. Look forward. (image 6.12c)

Both the left and right steps arc as they go forward, drawing a curved line. Dodge the body to the right. Do both left and right chops with power.

13. Turn Around, Bow Stance Lash

zhuànshēn gōngbù bǎi jué   转身弓步摆橛

Push into the right foot to shift back, and pivot on the spot on both feet around to the left, turning left and bending both knees. Swing the right baton flat over to the front, above the head. Look forward, to the left. (image 6.13a) Push into the left foot to shift right, turn left, then move the left foot to the rear left, bending the knee to the side. Lash the right baton across flat to the left to stop in front, tip slanting up. Circle the left baton out to the rear left and up, tip pointing to the rear left, slanting upwards. Look forward, to the right. (image 6.13b) Push into the right foot to shift left, and bend the left knee, straightening the right. Circle the right baton to the left, holding it out at the left under the left arm, baton level, tip pointing back. Look forward. (image 6.13c)

Turn quickly. Stay steady when moving the feet. Lash the batons strongly.

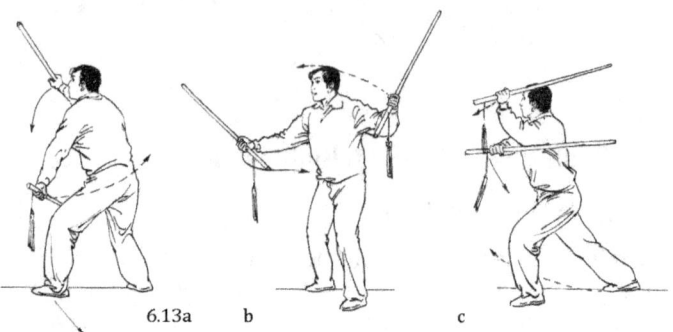

14. Jumping Turn, Brandish And Lash

tiàozhuàn yúnbǎi jué   跳转云摆概

Push into the right foot to shift left, then step the right foot forward to the right, bending into the knee. Lift the left baton at the forward left, above head height. Look forward, to the right. (image 6.14a) Without moving the feet, circle the left baton with a brandishing action to the right to in front of the head, tip pointing right. Look forward to the right. (image 6.14b) Push into the left foot and jump up, spinning around to the right whilst airborne. As the body turns, swing both batons flat around to the right, brandishing in front of the head. Look forward. (image 6.14c) Continue to spin to the right, then land on the left foot, keeping the right knee raised. Look forward. (image 6.14d)

Pivot the left foot on the spot to continue to turn to the right. Land the right foot to the rear right, bending into the knee and straightening the left leg to take a right bow stance. Brandish both batons around to the rear right. Stop

HORSE CONTROLLING BATONS

the right baton above the head, pointing left. Stop the left baton under the right armpit, tip pointing to the rear right. Look forward, to the left. (image 6.14e)

Jump and spin quickly. Land firmly. Brandish the batons with power.

6.14e

Section Three

15. Empty Stance Slice Up And Snap xūbù liāobēng jué 虚步撩崩橛

Push into the left foot to shift right, and step the left foot forward, bending into the knee. Circle the left baton down to come through to slice up forward, tip forward. Look forward. (image 6.15a) Push into the left foot to shift back, and move the left foot towards the right foot, touching down the foot with the heel lifted. Sit into a left empty stance. Lower the right baton by the right hip, tip forward. Snap the left baton upwards at the front. The tip is now slanting up. Look forward. (image 6.15b)

Sit into a distinctly weighted / unweighted empty stance. Set the left wrist down to snap the baton upwards.

16. Right Bow Stance Framing Block And Pierce

yòu gōngbù jiàcì jué 右弓步架刺橛

Step the left foot forward, both knees bent. Press the left baton down until the tip slants down in front. Look forward. (image 6.16a) Push into the left foot to shift back, then move the left foot forward. Block the left baton up in front the head with a framing block above head height, the tip slanting to the upper right. Look forward. (image 6.16b) Push into the right foot to shift forward, turn left, and step the right foot forward, bending into the knee and straightening the left knee to take a right bow stance. Pierce directly forwards with the right baton. Do a framing block above the head with the left baton, holding the baton flat with the tip pointing forward. Look forward. (image 6.16c)

The first action – the press down and high framing block – is a defensive move. Then do another framing block and a fierce pierce forward.

6.16a   b   c

17. Left Bow Stance Framing Block And Pierce

zuǒ gōngbù jiàcì jué   左弓步架刺橛

Push into the right foot to shift back, then move the right foot towards the left foot. Bring the left baton down and hold it out at the left side, tip slanting to the lower front. Press down with the right baton in front, the tip also slanting to the lower front. Look to the lower front. (image 6.17a) Push into the right foot to shift back, then move the right foot forward. Lift the right baton, holding it across in front, up above the head. Look forward. (image 6.17b) Push into the left foot to shift forward, turn right, and step the left foot forward. Bend the left knee, straighten the right, and set into a left bow stance. Pierce directly forward with the left baton and hold the right baton up above the head with a framing block, baton level with the tip forward. Look forward. (image 6.17c)

The first press down and block up is a defensive move. The following framing block is simultaneous with a fierce forward pierce.

6.17a   b   c

18. Right Bow Stance Framing Block And Pierce

yòu gōngbù jiàcì jué   右弓步架刺橛

Push into the left foot to shift back, then move the left foot towards the right foot. Lower the right baton to outside the right hip, tip forward and down. Press the left baton down in front at the left side of the body, with the tip held forward and down. Look to the lower front. (image 6.18a) Push into the left foot to shift to the right, then step the left foot forward. Lift the left baton with a framing block in front of and above the head, tip slanting to the upper right. Look forward. (image 6.18b) Push into the right foot to shift forward, turn the torso left, then step the right foot forward. Bend the right knee and straighten the left to take a right bow stance. Pierce directly forward with the right baton. Continue the framing block up above the head with the left baton, keeping it level with the tip pointing forward. Look forward. (image 6.18c)

The press down and upper framing block done with the left baton are defensive moves. As the framing block continues up, the right baton pierces forward forcefully.

19. Withdraw, Double Lash　　　chèbù shuāng bǎi jué　　撤步双摆橛

Push into the right foot to shift back, turn right, then step the right foot behind. Pull the left baton back, circling it downwards to hold it high in front. Lift the right baton up in front, above head height. Both batons point forward. Look forward. (image 6.19a) Push into the left foot to shift right, and turn right. Bring the left foot back to meet the right foot in a closed stance, standing up. Circle both batons together from the upper front, up, and across to the right side, tips up. Look to the right side. (image 6.19b)

Retreat, turn, and lash the batons as one coordinated movement.

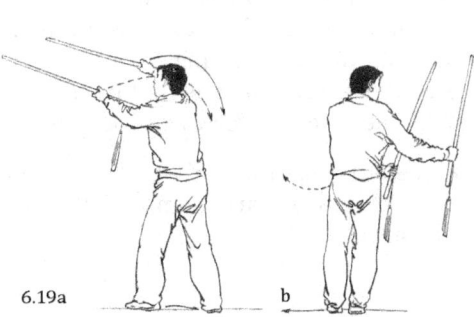

20. Jumping Turn To Drop Stance Chop

tiàozhuàn pūbù pī jué   跳转仆步劈橛

Stride the left foot across to the left, bending the knee out to the side. Circle the batons down to hold them out at the right, tips slanting down. Look to the lower right. (image 6.20a) Push into the right foot to shift forward, and pivot on the ball of the left foot to turn to the left, raising the right knee. Circle the batons to the left, holding them level up above the head with the tips pointing to the right. Look to the lower right. (image 6.20b) Push into the left foot and jump up, spinning around to the left. Land on the right foot, then the left, squatting fully on the left leg and extending the right leg along the ground, in a right drop stance. Swing both batons down at the left and over to chop down in front of the legs, tips slanting to the lower right. Look to the lower right. (image 6.20c)

Jump and spin quickly. Land into a firm stance. Chop down strongly with both batons. Coordinate all the actions well together – the jump, the spin, the drop stance, and the chops.

21. Bow Stance Framing Block And Pierce

gōngbù jiàcì jué   弓步架刺橛

Push into the left foot and stand up, turning slightly rightward. Turn in the left foot and bend the right knee. Do a framing block across above the head to the front, tip pointing upward to the left. Look forward. (image 6.21a) Push into the left foot to shift right, bend the right knee forward and straighten the left, turning the body rightward to take a right bow stance. Pierce the left baton directly forward until the arm is straight at shoulder height, the baton tip forward. Look forward. (image 6.21b)

Complete the right baton's full framing block upwards before doing the left baton's pierce forward. Complete the pierce simultaneous with the set into bow stance.

HORSE CONTROLLING BATONS

6.21a   b

22. Bow Stance Push   gōngbù tuī jué   弓步推橛

Push into the right foot to shift back, turn the torso right, and move the right foot to the right. Lower the batons and hold them out to either side, tips forward, slanting down. Look forward, to the left. (image 6.22a) Push into the right foot to shift right, then step the left foot forward to the right, bending the knee. Lower the right baton to outside the right hip, tip forward, slanting down. Hold the left baton in front of the body, tip forward, slanting up. Look forward, to the left. (image 6.22b) Push into the right foot to shift forward, and step the right foot forward to the right, bending the knee and straightening the left to take a right bow stance. Push the left baton forward, holding it vertical, tip up. Look forward, to the left. (image 6.22c)

Complete the set into bow stance and the final push together.

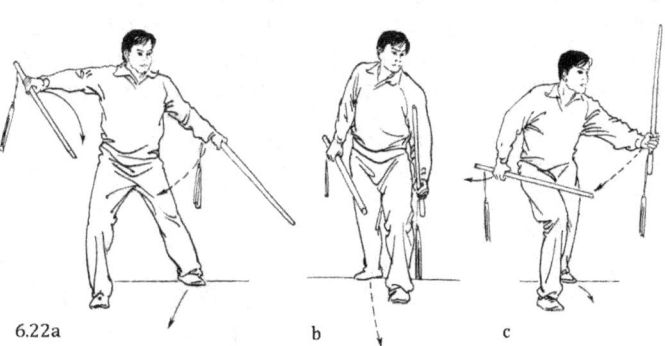

6.22a   b   c

Section Four

23. Left Dodge, Left And Right Chops

zuǒshǎn zuǒyòu pī jué   左闪左右劈橛

Push into the left foot to shift forward, and step the left foot forward to the left, standing up. Circle the batons down and over to the right side with the tips slanting to the lower right. Look to the left side. (image 6.23a) Push into the left foot to shift to the right, and move the left foot forward, to the left, bending the knee. Circle the left baton to the right and up to chop down at the left, tip forward, slanting to the upper left. Look forward, to the left. (image 6.23b) Push into the right foot to shift forward, turn left, and step

169

the right foot forward. Bend the right knee and straighten the left, to take a right bow stance. Circle the right baton from the rear, up and over to chop down in front, tip forward, slanting up. Hold the left baton outside the left hip. Look forward. (image 6.23c)

The right step arcs as it goes forward, and the body dodges to the left. Step and dodge quickly. Be sure to chop strongly for both the left and right chops. Coordinate the whole move as one – the step, the dodge, and the chops.

24. Turn Around, Present The Batons   zhuànshēn jǔ jué   转身举橛

Push into the right foot to shift to the left, and pivot around on both feet to the left on the spot. Circle the batons down to hold them in front of the body, tips slanting to the lower right. Look forward, to the right. (image 6.24a) Push into the right foot to shift left, and bend the left knee to the left side, straightening the right. Hold the left baton up over the head at the left, tip slanting up to the right. Hold the right baton in front of the right side of the chest, tip forward to the right. Look forward, to the right. (image 6.24b)

Pivot on both feet with good stability, turning quickly. Fully coordinate the pivot, the turn, and presentation of the batons.

25. Raised Knee Low Intercept   tíxī xiàjié   提膝下截

Push into the right foot to shift left, turn right, and raise the right knee. Circle the right baton down to intercept outside the right leg, tip slanting down. Hold the left baton up over the head. Look forward, to the right. (image 6.25)

HORSE CONTROLLING BATONS

Turn quickly and stand firmly. Intercept with power. Complete the turn, knee raise, and intercept as one action.

26. Jumping Step, Chop   tiàobù pī jué   跳步劈橛

Push into the left foot and jump up, spinning to the right. Land on the right foot, holding the left knee raised. Hold the right baton out to the rear right, tip pointing up to the rear right. Circle the left baton forward, turning it across to press down in front of the left knee, tip to the left. Look forward and down. (image 6.26a) Land the left foot forward, bending the knee forward and straightening the right knee. Circle the right baton up and over to chop down in the front, the tip forward and up. Look forward. (image 6.26b)

Jump and turn quickly. Land firmly. Chop forward with the right baton after the left baton has completed the crossing press down. Chop strongly.

27. Bow Stance Low Intercept   gōngbù xiàjié   弓步下截

Push into the left foot to shift back, turn right, and pivot to the right on both feet, on the spot. Bend the right knee to the side and straighten the left, taking a right bow stance. Hold the right hand up over the head at the right, the baton vertical with the tip up. Hold the left baton out in front, intercepting down to the left, tip pointing down. Look forward. (image 6.27)

Turn quickly. Intercept with power. Complete the interception with the completion of the turn into bow stance.

28. Horse Stance, Plant Down, High Framing Blocks
mǎbù xiàzāi shàngjià jué   马步下栽上架橛

Push into the left foot to shift right, turn left, and move the left foot to the left. Bend both knees to sit into a horse stance. Cross the batons in front of the body to plant them down, tips on the ground. Look forward and down. (image 6.28a) Keeping the knees bent to stay in the horse stance, raise the torso slightly. Keeping the batons crossed, lift them up above the head in front. Look forward and up. (image 6.28b)

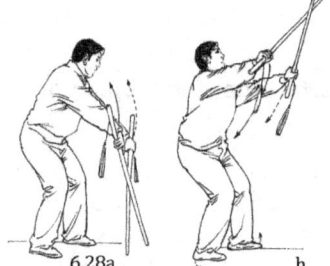

Turn and lower the batons smoothly. Keep the batons crossed throughout when moving from the low plant down to the high framing blocks.

6.28a   b

29. Plant The Batons, Side Kick   zāi jué chuāituǐ   栽橛踹腿

Push into the right foot and pivot on both feet on the spot, to the left. Turn to the left. The legs are now crossed and bent. Circle the batons to the left and down to plant down with the tips on the ground. Look to the right. (image 6.29a) Push into the right foot to shift left, raise the right knee, then do a sidekick out to the right side. Lean the torso slightly to the left and kick the leg out at waist height. Keep the baton tips on the ground. Look to the right. (image 6.29b)

Turn quickly. Plant the batons firmly. Kick into the heel with power.

6.29a   b

30. Plant The Batons, Turn Around, Side Kick

zāi jué zhuànshēn chuāituǐ   栽橛转身踹腿

Land the right foot and bend both knees to squat, keeping both batons on the ground. Look to the right. (image 6.30a) Push into the right foot to shift left, move the right foot towards the left foot, and turn left. Raise the left knee, then do a left sidekick to waist height to the left. Look to the left. (image 6.30b)

Turn quickly. So the sidekick with power, with the focus into the heel.

HORSE CONTROLLING BATONS

31. Left And Right Flowers, Chop zuǒyòu wǔhuā pī jué 左右舞花劈橛

Land the left foot and stand up. Hold the batons out to the rear right, tips slanting down to the rear right. Look to the left. (image 6.31a) Push into the left foot to shift right, and move the left foot to the left. Circle the left baton to the right and up, coming over to chop forward at the left, tip forward and slanting up. Look forward, to the left. (image 6.31b) Push into the right foot to shift forward, and turn to the left, pivoting around on the spot with both feet. Circle the right baton up, forward, and to the left to chop down with a full swinging chop in front. The arm is at shoulder height. The baton tip is forward. Lower the left baton slightly. Look forward, to the right. (image 6.31c)

Push into the right foot to shift to the left, and step the right foot to the right. Lower the left baton and circle it to the rear left, to hold it out at the upper left. Circle the right baton down, then out to the left side, tip pointing left. Look forward, to the right. (image 6.31d) Push into the left foot to shift right, and pivot on both feet around the right, crossing the legs. Lift the left heel, pressing the ball of the foot into the ground. Circle the left baton to the left and up, to come forward to chop to the lower right. The tip slants down at the rear right. Turn the torso to the right and lean forward slightly. Look to the left. (image 6.31e) Push into the left foot to shift forward, and step the left foot forward, bending the knee. Circle the left baton to the right and up, to come over to chop to the left, tip in front and slanting up. Circle the right baton down then back behind on the right. Look forward. (image 6.31f)

CHAQUAN, VOLUME III

6.31d e f

This is a stepping-left-and-right flowers. The batons keep moving until the chop is completed. The wrists are relaxed to do the flowers. Do the flowers with vertical circles close to each side of the body. The turn of the body while stepping and circling the batons keeps it all coordinated.

32. Back-Cross Step, Chop   chābù pī jué   叉步劈橛

Push into the right foot to shift forward, and pivot on the spot on the toes to the right, turning to the right. Step the right foot to the left behind the left foot with the heel lifted and ball of the foot touching down. This is a back-cross step, with the legs bent and crossed. Lower the left baton in a circle, to take it out to the right side. Bring the right baton from the right, up, and forward to chop on the left side, tip slanting down. Look down to the left. (image 6.32)

Turn, step, and chop as one coordinated action.

6.32

33. Turn Around, Raised Knee Present The Batons

zhuànshēn tíxī jǔ jué   转身提膝举橛

Push into both legs to stand up, then pivot on the spot to the right, turning around to the right. Circle the batons to the right with the turn, lifting them up at the right, tips forward and tilted up. Look forward and up. (image 6.33a) Push into the left foot to shift right, and raise the left knee. Hold the batons up over the head in front, tips forward. Look forward. (image 6.33b)

Turn, raise the knee, and present the batons in one well coordinated action. Stay steady when raising the knee.

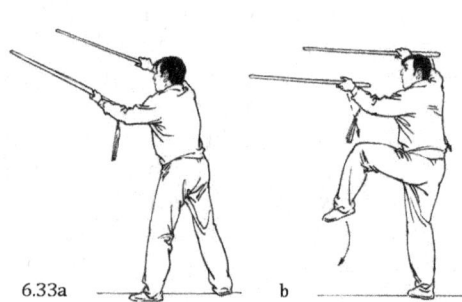

6.33a   b

174

HORSE CONTROLLING BATONS

Section Five

34. Empty Stance Press Down   xūbù yā jué   虚步压橛

Land the left foot, touching down the ball with the heel lifted. Bend both legs to take a left empty stance. Lower both batons to press down level at waist height, tips forward. Look forward. (image 6.34)

Sit into a distinctly weighted/unweighted empty stance. Press down with both batons at the same time that you take the stance.

6.34

35. Step Forward, Framing Block And Sweep

shàngbù jià sǎo jué   上步架扫橛

Step the left foot forward, bending into the knee. Do a framing block with the right baton in front of the head, baton crossing above, tip to the left. Hold the left baton in front of the belly, tip to the right. Look forward. (image 6.35a) Without moving the feet, circle the right baton back and hold it out at the right, tip tilted up. Continue into a framing block with the left baton, crossing upwards to the forward left. Look forward. (image 6.35b) Push into the right foot to shift forward, and pivot around on both feet on the spot to turn left. Bend the torso forward while turning left. Circle the right baton from the upper right, down, and left, to sweep out to the forward right, tip forward and down. Look to the lower front, to the right. (image 6.35c)

Step and turn quickly. Sweep the right baton across in front after the left baton has completed the upwards framing block. Sweep with power.

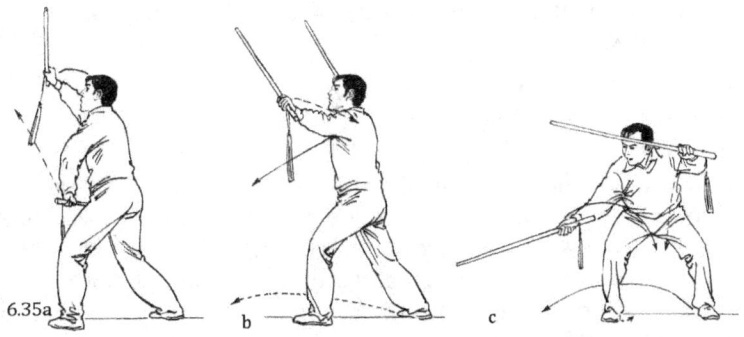
6.35a   b   c

36. Turn Around, Framing Block And Sweep

zhuànshēn jià sǎo jué　　　　　　　　　　　转身架扫橛

Turn in the right foot. Push into the left foot to shift to the right, turning left. The legs are now crossed in an insertion stance, the left behind the right with the heel lifted. Both legs are crossed and bent. Cross the batons and place them in front of the right knee. Look to the lower front. (image 6.36a) Pivot around on the spot to turn left, turning the body around to the left and standing up. Keep the batons crossed and hold them out in front of the belly. Look forward. (image 6.36b) Turn the left foot out and turn left. Do a framing block up with the right baton in front of and above the head. Look forward.
(image 6.36c)

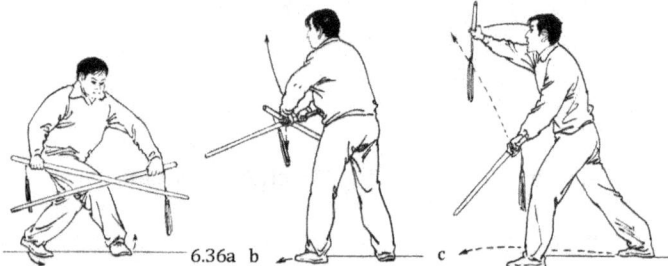

Push into the right foot to shift forward, and turn slightly to the left. Step the right foot forward. Circle the right baton back to hold it out to the upper right. Lift the left baton up in front of and above the head. Look forward. (image 6.36d) Turn the right foot in and bend both knees to sit down. Circle the right baton up to the right, then down across to the left with a sweep. The tip points forward and down. Look to the lower right front. (image 6.36e)

Step and turn quickly. Wait to do the right sweep across in front until you have completed the upper framing block with the left baton. Sweep the baton across with power.

37. Turn Around, Framing Block And Sweep

zhuànshēn jiàsǎo jué　　　　　　　　　　　转身架扫橛

Pivot around to the left on the spot of both feet, turning left. Circle the batons down and to the left, holding them down in front of the body. Look forward, to the left. (image 6.37a) Pivot both feet further to the left on the spot, turning the body further to the left and crossing the legs. Lift the right heel and press the ball of the foot into the ground. Hold the batons out to their respective sides, tips pointing forward and down. Look to the left.

(image 6.37b) Pivot further to the left on the left foot, staying on the spot, and turn the body further to the left. Circle the right foot around to step forward, bending both legs. Bring the left baton across, holding it across in front of the right leg, tip to the right. Circle the right baton to the left then do a crossing framing block up in front, above the head, tip to the left. Look forward. (image 6.37c) Push into the left foot, lifting the heel and pressing the ball of the foot into the ground, to shift forward. Circle the right baton behind to hold it out at the right side. Do a crossing framing block with the left baton in front, above the head, tip to the right. Look forward. (image 6.37d)

6.37a   b   c   d

Pivot to the left on the spot with both feet to turn the body to the left, leaning forward slightly. Bend the legs to a half-squat. Circle the right baton from the upper right to the lower left, to sweep across in front to the left, tip pointing forward and down. Look forward, to the lower right. (image 6.37e)

6.37e

Turn and step quickly. Complete the framing block before doing the sweep across. Sweep the baton with power.

38. Left And Right Flowers, Chops

zuǒyòu wǔhuā pī jué 　　　　　　　　　　左右舞花劈橛

Push into the right foot to shift left, and turn to the right, standing up. Step the right foot back. Circle the right baton down and to the rear, holding it out at the rear right, tip pointing to the rear right. Hold the left baton in front with the tip pointing forward and tilted up. Look forward, to the left. (image 6.38a) Pivot both feet to the left on the spot, turning the body left to cross the legs, lifting the right heel with the ball of the foot touching down. Circle the right baton up and over to the front, tip slanting down. Look forward and down. (image 6.38b) Push into the right foot to shift forward, turn left, and step the right foot forward. Circle the right baton down in front, to the left, then up and over to chop down in front at the right, tip forward. Circle the left baton down and out to the rear left. Look forward, to the right. (image 6.38c)

Push into the left foot to shift right, turn right, and step the left foot forward. Circle the left baton over from the back to the forward right to chop forward, tip slanting down. Tuck the right baton into the left armpit. Look forward. (image 6.38d) Push into the right foot to shift forward, turn right, and step the right foot behind the left leg to the left side, in a back-cross step. The right heel is lifted, the ball of the foot touching down, and the legs are crossed. Circle the left baton down, to the right, then up to do a swinging chop to the front, tip pointing forward, to the left. Circle the right baton down, to the right, and out to the right side. Look forward, to the left. (image 6.38e)

Both batons do swinging chops. Keep the batons close to the body to do the vertical flowers at the left side and the right side. Relax the grip of the hands and relax the wrists to do the flowers.

39. Back-Cross Step, Chops   chābù pī jué   叉步劈橛

Squat a bit into the back-cross stance. Circle the left baton down, then over to the right to in front of the left leg, pointing down. Circle the right baton up and over to the left to chop down to the left, tip slanting down. Look to the lower left. (image 6.39)

Chop the right baton down strongly.

HORSE CONTROLLING BATONS

40. Roll Over, Chop   fānshēn pī jué   翻身劈橛

Pivot both feet on the spot to the right to turn around to the right, rolling over. Hold the batons up in front over the head. Look up, to the right. (image 6.40a) Circle the right baton up and over to the right to chop down in front, at the right, tip forward and tilted up. Hold the left baton out at the left side, tip tilted up. Look forward, to the right. (image 6.40b)

Pivot quickly and with good balance, to roll over quickly. Chop the right baton down strongly.

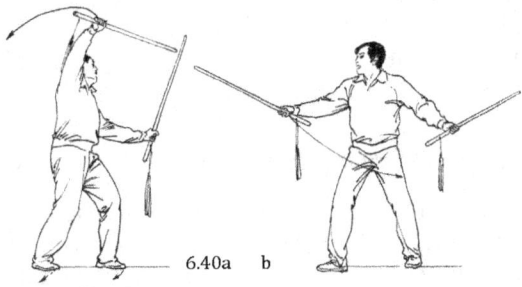

6.40a b

41. Left And Right Flowers, Chops

zuǒyòu wǔhuā pī jué   左右舞花劈橛

Without moving the feet, circle the right baton down and to the left at the left side of the body, tip tilted down to the left. Hold the left baton out, tilted down. Look forward, to the right. (image 6.41a) Still without moving the feet, circle the right baton to the left, up and over to chop at the right, the tip forward and right. Hold the left baton out behind at the left. Look forward, to the right. (image 6.41b) Push into the left foot to shift forward, turn right, and step the left foot forward. Circle the left baton up from behind, then over to the front, down, then back to the right, and then forward, in a swinging chop. The tip is forward, tilted up. Circle the right baton down and out to the rear at the right side. Look forward. (image 6.41c)

6.41a   b   c

Push into the right foot to shift forward, turn left, and step the right foot forward. Hold the left baton out down in front, in front of the belly, tip forward. Circle the right baton up and over to the front, then down, to the left and over again to chop down in front, tip up. Look forward. (image 6.41d) Without moving the feet, circle the left baton down, along the left to

179

Both batons do swinging chops, left and right. The flowers are vertical circles close to the body at either side. When doing the flowers, the hands grip loosely and the wrists are relaxed.

6.41d e

42. Back-Cross Step, Chop   chābù pījué   叉步劈橛

Push into the left foot to shift right, and step the left foot behind the right foot towards the right with a back-cross step. The legs are crossed, the left heel lifted with the ball of the foot touching down. Circle the right baton down and over to the left to tuck into the left armpit, tip up. Bring the left baton up and over to chop down at the right, tip slanting down. Look to the lower right. (image 6.42)

Step and sit into stance as the left baton chops down, in one coordinated action. Chop strongly.

6.42

43. Roll Over, Chop   fānshēn pī jué   翻身劈橛

Pivot both feet on the spot to the left, turning left, leaning back to roll over. Hold the batons out and up with the roll. Look forward and up. (image 6.43a) Continue to pivot both feet around to the left, turning left. Bend the left knee and straighten the right. Circle the left baton up and over to the left and down to the left side, tip forward and down. Circle the right baton up and over to the left to chop forward, tip forward and up. Look forward. (image 6.43b)

Turn quickly, pivoting with good balance. Chop the right baton strongly.

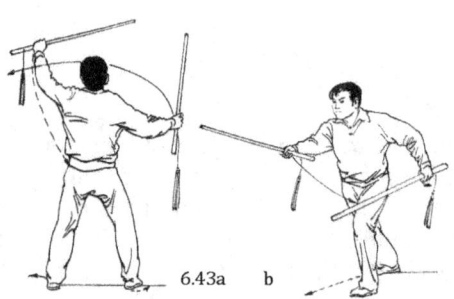

6.43a b

HORSE CONTROLLING BATONS

44. Step Forward, Double Lash   shàngbù shuāngbǎi jué   上步双摆橛

Push into the right foot to shift forward, turn left, and step the right foot forward. Circle the batons down and over to the lower left, tips slanting down. Look down to the right. (image 6.44a) Push into the left foot to shift right, turn right, and bring the left foot up to the right foot into a closed stance. Circle the batons to the left, up, and over to lash to the right, batons vertical with the tips up. Look to the right side. (image 6.44b)

Keep the wrists relaxed to do the lashing actions. Complete the closed stance as the batons arrive at the right side.

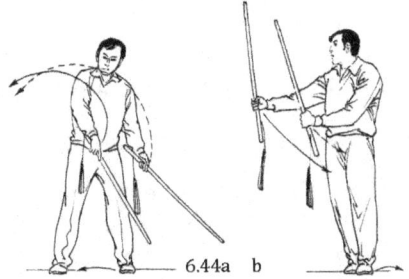

45. Step Astride, Scoop Up   kuàbù tiǎo jué   跨步挑橛

Stride the left foot across to the left. Circle the batons to the right and down to the lower left, slanting down towards the left. Look to the left side. (image 6.45a) Push into the right foot to shift left, and bring the right foot to the left foot into a closed stance, turning the body leftward. Circle the batons to the left, then scoop up on the left side, batons vertical with the tips up. Look to the left side. (image 6.45b)

Turn and step into the closed stance quickly. Relax the wrists to bring the batons down. Tighten up the grasp to scoop up to the left side.

46. Empty Stance Present The Batons   xūbù jǔ jué   虚步举橛

Retreat the right foot behind and turn right. Hold the right baton standing at the right side, tip up. Lift the grip of the left baton to present it in front of the body, level, and along the left arm, tip back. Look forward. (image 6.62a) Push into the left foot to shift back, and lift the left heel, pressing the ball of foot into the ground. Bend both knees to take a left empty stance. Hold the right baton up at the right side, grip up, tip down. Place the left baton vertically at the left side, tip up. Look to the left side. (image 6.46b)

Sit into a well-defined empty stance. Keep the batons snug to their respective arms.

47. Closing Posture (Stand To Attention Holding The Batons)

shōu shì (lìzhèng wò jué)　　　　　　　收势（立正握概）

Retreat the left foot behind, placing the ball of the foot on the ground with the heel lifted. Cross the batons in front of the body. Look forward. (image 6.47a) Push into the right foot to shift back, and bring the right foot back to the left foot to take a closed stance. Stand up. Place the batons at either side of the body, holding them level with the tips forward. Look forward. (image 6.47b)

Place the batons at their respective sides as the stepping is completed.

TWO-HANDED CUTTER

双手带

About the Two-Handed Cutter

The cutter, or cutter body, is made up of a hilt or handle, a guard, and a head, or curved blade. The blade is about a third of the total length, and its parts are the spine, the cutting edge, and the tip. The end of the hilt is called the base, on which is usually a metal loop. [tr. note: in English, the cutter is often called a horse cutter]

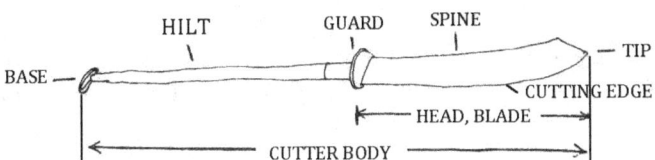

The length of the cutter that an individual will use is determined by standing with the cutter's base on the ground by the side. The tip should reach at least the top of the head.

The curved blade is made of metal, with a single cutting edge. The hilt is wooden, and there is no weight restriction. It may have metal rings on the loop at the base, but not always.

A smooth grasp is when both thumb webs smoothly face the blade. For various techniques, the grasp may change according to need. Sometimes a one-handed grasp is used, sometimes a two-handed grasp, and sometimes the hands may slide along the hilt.

HOLD

When a hand is not holding the cutter it generally holds the shape of a tight palm. The palm is held with the thumb bent and tucked in (though it may be held open). The fingers are held together, straight, and pulled back.

HAND

The Main Techniques of the Two-Handed Cutter

Chop: With both hands on the hilt, come forward and down from above with the power going to the cutting edge. It can also come down at an angle, chopping from above at one side to below at the other side.

Slice up: With both hands on the hilt, circle down and forward, to slice up from behind with the cutting edge turned up, power going to the cutting edge.

Hack: With both hands on the hilt, with the cutter body level at the chest, cut across in front, from one side to the other, with a flat cut. This is a short, strong, action – power going to the cutting edge.

Smear: The action is similar to a cut, but the power is softer. The cutter is level at chest height, or may have the blade slanting downward. From one side to the other side, in front, the blade cuts across level with a smearing action that arcs slightly back. This is done softly, with the power to the cutting edge.

Parry: With both hands on the hilt, circle the blade spine down to the side from the front towards the rear to parry or hook. Power goes to the blade spine, using the non-sharp side to catch or deflect.

Sweep: With both hands on the hilt, the cutter is level, and turns with the leftward or rightward turn of the body, sliding the right hand along to meet the left hand, so that the blade edge sweeps flat across in front from one side to the other. Power goes to the blade edge.

Brandish: With both hands on the hilt, with the cutter in front of and higher than the head, circle it left to right, keeping it level.

Flowers: With both hands on the hilt, draw vertical circles alternating at both sides of the body, or draw level circles above the head.

NAMES OF THE MOVEMENTS OF THE TWO-HANDED CUTTER FORM

Position Of Preparation (Stand To Attention Holding The Cutter)
Section One
1. Step Forward, Lash The Hand
2. Stomp And Present The Cutter
3. Snap Kick
4. Bow Stance, Shoulder The Cutter
5. Right Side Slice Up
6. Left Side Slice Up
7. Jump To Bow Stance Hack
8. Turn Around, Smear

Section Two
9. Empty Stance Slice Up
10. Raised Knee, Present The Cutter
11. Walking Smear
12. Turn Around, Raised Knee, Present The Cutter

Section Three

13. Left Parry And Chop
14. Jumping Turn To Chop
15. Jumping Turn To Chop
16. Stomp And Hack
17. Turn Around, Bow Stance, Shoulder The Cutter

Section Four

18. Left Jumping Brandishing Turn And Hack
19. Right Jumping Brandishing Turn And Hack
20. Left Side Parry
21. Right Side Parry
22. Resting Stance Chop
23. Roll Over And Chop
24. Reverse Bow Stance Framing Block
25. Turn Around, Bow Stance, Present The Cutter

Section Five

26. Step Forward, Press Down With The Hilt
27. Back-Cross Stance, Stir With The Hilt
28. Step Forward, Flat Hack
29. Turn Around, Flat Hack
30. Step Forward, Smear To The Left
31. Step Forward Push And Hack
32. Turn Around, Bow Stance Lift
33. Closed Stance, Present The Cutter

Section Six

34. Step Forward, Jumping Turn To Chop
35. Retreat, Brandish And Smear
36. Turn Around, Brandish And Smear
37. Turn Around, Brandish And Smear
38. Turn Around, Bow Stance Chop
39. Turn Around, Parry
40. Turn Around, Bow Stance Stab
41. Stomp, Bow Stance Hack
42. Retreat To Closed Stance Present The Cutter
43. Step Forward, Raised Knee Slice Up
44. Horse Stance, Present The Cutter
45. Horse Stance, Stand The Cutter
46. Raised Knee Half-Squat Carry
47. Bow Stance Carry The Cutter And Push The Hand
48. Toss The Cutter
49. Bow Stance Lift The Cutter And Push The Hand

50. Closed Stance, Present The Cutter
51. Retreat, Stand The Cutter
52. Closing Posture (Stand To Attention Holding The Cutter)

0.   Position Of Preparation (Stand To Attention Holding The Cutter)

yùbèi shì (lìzhèng chí dài)   预备势（立正持带）

Stand to attention, holding the cutter with the right hand in the middle, standing it at the right side of the body. The cutting edge faces forward, the tip points upward, the base is on the ground. Look forward. (image 7.0a). Without moving the feet, lift the cutter slightly in the right hand, keeping it vertical at the right side. Open the left hand out slightly to the left. Look left. (image 7.0b)

Coordinate the actions as one – stand straight, lift the cutter, and open out the left hand.

Section One

1.   Step Forward, Lash The Hand   shàngbù bǎizhǎng   上步摆掌

Push into the right foot to shift forward, and step the left foot forward, lifting the right heel, keeping the ball of the foot on the ground. Lift the cutter in the right hand. Lift the left hand further out to the left side. Look to the left. (image 7.1a) Push into the right foot to shift forward, and step the right foot forward. Lift the left hand further up at the left side. Keep looking to the left. (image 7.1b) Push into the left foot to shift forward, and step the left foot up to meet the right, taking a closed stance. Circle the left hand forward and across to grasp the cutter hilt under the right hand. Look to the left. (image 7.1c)

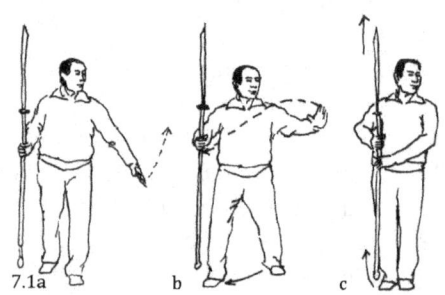

Coordinate the stepping with the action of the left hand.

2.   Stomp And Present The Cutter   zhēnjiǎo jǔ dài   震脚举带

Push into the right foot to shift left, and raise the right knee. Lift the cutter slightly in both hands. Look to the left. (image 7.2a) Land the right foot with a stomp, immediately and quickly lifting the left foot to stand on the right leg. Lift the cutter upwards with the edge to the left and tip up. Look to the left. (image 7.2b)

Stomp with power. Stand firmly on in the one-legged stance.

TWO-HANDED CUTTER

3. Snap Kick   tántuǐ   弹腿

Still standing firmly on the right leg, do a snap kick with the left leg, extending it straight out to the left to chest height, putting power into the shin and instep. Look to the left. (image 7.3)

Stand with good balance. Kick with power.

4. Bow Stance, Shoulder The Cutter   gōngbù bēi dài   弓步背带

Land the left foot forward, bending the knee and straightening the right knee. Chop forward to level, using both hands. Look forward. (image 7.4a) Push into the right foot to shift forward, and step the right foot forward, turning the foot out and bending both legs. Circle the cutter in both hands, down and back to hold it out at the right behind the body, edge down. Look behind to the right. (image 7.4b) Push into the left foot to shift forward, and step the left foot forward, bending the left knee and straightening the right to take a left bow stance. Circle the cutter in both hands, up and over to cut forward and down, holding it out behind at the right side. The hilt is now lying on the right upper back and side, tip slanting down. Place the left hand up in front, fingers up. Look forward. (image 7.4c)

Step forward lightly, take a stable bow stance. Circle the cutter smoothly onto the back with a vertical circle at the right side.

CHAQUAN, VOLUME III

5. Right Side Slice Up yòucè liāo dài 右侧撩带

Push into the right foot to shift forward, and move the right foot forward slightly. Bring the right hand forward to circle the cutter up in front, tip slanting up, edge slanting down. Bring the left hand to take the cutter hilt near the base end, tucking it into the right ribs. Look forward. (image 7.5a) Push into the right foot to shift forward and step the right foot forward, lifting the left heel with the ball of the foot touching down. Circle the cutter in both hands up and over to the rear to hold it at the right side to the rear, edge down. Turn the torso slightly to the right. Look back, to the right. (image 7.5b) Without moving the feet, turn left. Circle the cutter in both hands down and forward to slice it up in front of the body, blade edge up, tip slanting upward. Look forward and up. (image 7.5c)

The cutting edge of the blade must lead when doing a slice up. Step forward and turn the body to bring the cutter close to the body in a well coordinated action.

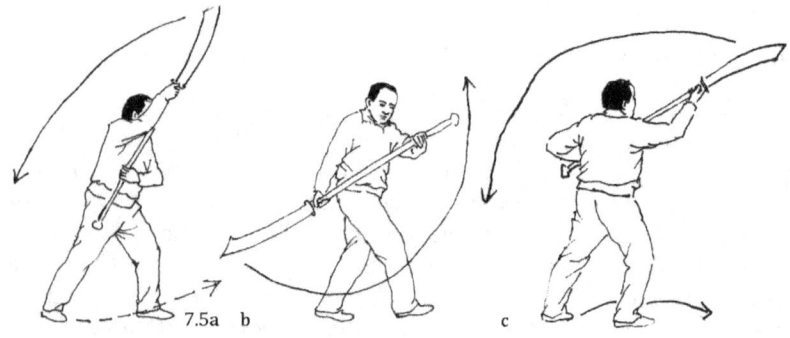

6. Left Side Slice Up zuǒcè liāo dài 左侧撩带

Push into the left foot to shift to the right, and step the left foot forward. Turn to the left, bending and twisting the torso. Circle the cutter with both hands up and over to the rear to hold it out behind at the left side, tip slanting down. The arms are crossed in front of the belly. Look to the lower left. (image 7.6a) Push into the right foot to shift forward, and raise the

TWO-HANDED CUTTER

right knee. Standing on the left leg, lift the heel, pushing into the ground with the ball of the foot. Turn the torso to the right. Circle the cutter with both hands down and across to the front to come through slicing up to above the head. The tip finishes up with the cutting edge to the rear. Look to the lower front. (image 7.6b)

Throughout the slice on the left side, the cutting edge must lead, going forward and up. Coordinate the knee raise with the final slice up.

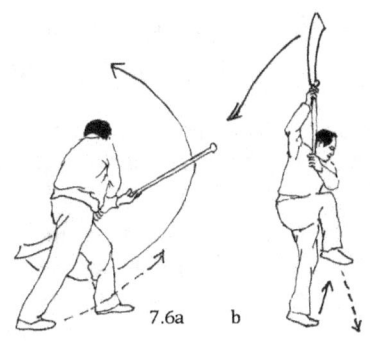

7.6a b

7. **Jump To Bow Stance Hack**   tiào gōngbù zhǎn dài   跳弓步斩带

Push into the left foot to jump up, landing on the right foot and stopping with the left knee raised. Hold the cutter up to the rear right in both hands, cutting edge slanting up. Look to the lower front. (image 7.7a) Land the left foot forward to the left and bend the knee forward, straightening the right leg to take a left bow stance. Cut across in front to the left with a level hack, edge to the left, tip forward. Look forward, to the left. (image 7.7b)

Jump lightly. Coordinate the hack with the completion of the bow stance. Hack strongly, cutting into the blade edge.

7.7a b

8. **Turn Around, Smear**   zhuànshēn mǒ dài   转身抹带

Push into the left foot to shift back, and pivot on the spot on both feet, turning around to the right. Bend the right knee and straighten the left, to take a right bow stance. Medially rotate the right forearm and take the cutter in both hands from the forward left around to the right, behind the body. This is a level, smearing, action, finishing front of the body at the right, as it turns. with the edge to the right and tip to the forward right. The left hand tucks the hilt into the left ribs. Look forward, to the right. (image 7.8)

Turn quickly. Take a solid bow stance. Keep the turn and the smear soft.

7.8

CHAQUAN, VOLUME III

Section Two

9. Empty Stance Slice Up   xūbù liāo dài   虚步撩带

Push into the right foot to shift back, and move the right foot across to the left. Bend both legs, putting the weight more on the left leg, in a right empty stance. Circle the cutter in both hands down and across to the left, then slice up along the inside of the right leg, edge out, tip down. Look to the lower front. (image 7.9)

Take a distinct empty stance with evident weighted and unweighted legs. Circle the cutter across, then slice up forward with the cutting edge forward.

7.9

10. Raised Knee, Present The Cutter   tíxī jǔ dài   提膝举带

Push into the right foot to shift back, and raise the right knee. Lift the cutter up to present it inside the right knee. Look down to the right front. (image 7.10)

Stand firmly in the one-legged stance.

7.10

11. Walking Smear   xíngbù mǒ dài   行步抹带

Land the right foot to the forward right, bending both legs slightly and turning the torso slightly to the right. Medially rotate the right forearm and circle the cutter down, to the right, to smear across over in front towards the right side, tip slanting down, cutting edge to the right. Bend the left arm to hold the cutter in front of the chest. Look down to the right front. (image 7.11a) Push into the left foot to shift forward, turn the right foot out, and take a curving step to the forward right with the left foot. Keep both legs bent. Smear with the cutter in both hands across to the right, staying slanted. Look forward, to the right. (image 7.11b) Push into the right foot to shift forward, and step the left foot forward. Smear the cutter further to the right in both hands, still slanting. Look forward, to the lower right. (image 7.11c)

TWO-HANDED CUTTER

7.11a b   c

Push into the left foot to shift forward, turn the right foot out, and step the left foot to the forward right. Turn around to the right. Circle the cutter in both hands to smear around to the right, keeping it slanted at the right side of the body. Look down to the right side. (image 7.11d)

7.11d

Take continuous, connected steps to walk around. Smear with the blade angled downwards, drawing a circle in front of the body. Walk and turn to enable the slanting smear to come around with the body.

12. Turn Around, Raised Knee, Present The Cutter

zhuànshēn tíxī jǔ dài   转身提膝举带

Push into the right foot shift to the left, turn the left foot in, then pivot on the ball of the left foot to turn around the right. Turn the torso around to the right and raise the right knee. Smear with both hands around to the right, cutter tip slanting down, edge going to the rear in the direction of travel. Bring the left hand to hold the cutter in front of the left side of the chest. Look down to the rear right. (image 7.12a) Land the right foot to the rear right and raise the left knee. Lift the cutter in both hands to present it above the head, hilt vertical in front of the body, tip up, edge forward. Look forward, to the left. (image 7.12b)

Keep the cutting edge leading whilst turning and smearing. Raise the knee and present the cutter in one coordinated action.

7.12a   b

Section Three

13. Left Parry And Chop zuǒ guàpī dài 左挂劈带

Land the left foot forward to the left, turning out the foot and bending both legs. Circle the cutter in both hands down in front to parry to the left at the left side of the body, tip down, blade spine in. Tuck the hilt with the left hand under the right upper arm. Turn the torso to the left and lean forward slightly. Look down to the left. (image 7.13a) Push into the right foot to shift forward, and step the right foot forward. Circle the cutter in both hands down at the left, then back and up above the head. The cutter is now vertical at the right side of the body. Look forward, to the right. (image 7.13b) Bend both legs and sit. Bring the cutter in both hands down to chop level in front at waist height, cutting edge down. Look forward, to the right. (image 7.13c)

The parry uses the blade spine, circling it back with a turning, hooking action. Turn the blade to chop down with the cutting edge forward. Follow an arcing line to do the parry. Chop with power.

14. Jumping Turn To Chop tiàozhuàn pī dài 跳转劈带

Push into the left foot to shift right, and raise the left knee. Circle the cutter down in both hands, and to the left, to hold it out at the left side. Lean forward to the right. Look down, to the right. (image 7.14a) Push into the right foot to jump up, spinning around to turn around to the left whilst airborne. Hold the cutter in both hands to circle it up and over above the head with the body turn. Look up. (image 7.14b) Continue to spin around to the left, landing on the left foot, then the right, and sitting into a horse stance. Bring the cutter over, using both hands to chop down to the left at waist height, cutting edge down, tip to the right. Look to the right side. (image 7.14c)

Stay well balanced during the spin, jump and landing. Chop strongly.

TWO-HANDED CUTTER

7.14a   b   c

15. Jumping Turn To Chop   tiàozhuàn pī dài   跳转劈带

Push into the left foot to shift to the right, and raise the left knee. Turn around to the left with a roll over. Circle the cutter in both hands down, left, then up to hold it out at the right side. Look to the right. (image 7.15a) Push into the right foot to jump up, spinning around to the left whilst airborne. Hold the cutter in both hands over the head. Look to the lower front. (image 7.15b) Continue to turn to the left and land on the left foot, then the right. Bend both legs to sit into a horse stance. Bring the cutter in both hands to chop down at waist height in front, cutting edge down, tip to the right. Look to the right. (image 7.15c)

Jump, spin, and land with good stability. Chop strongly.

7.15a   b   c

16. Stomp And Hack   zhènbù zhǎn dài   震步斩带

Push into the right foot to shift back and raise the right knee. Lift the cutter in both hands, pulling it back towards the head. This is a parry with the blade spine, the tip pointing up and the cutting edge slanting down. Look forward. (image 7.16a) Push into the left foot to jump, landing with a stomp on the right foot and lifting the left knee. Pull the hands in to the chest, to further parry inwards. Look forward. (image 7.16b) Land the left foot forward and bend the knee, straightening the right to take a left bow stance. Hack the cutter to the forward left with both hands, tip forward, cutting edge angled down. Look forward. (image 7.16c)

CHAQUAN, VOLUME III

Settle down the weight when you stomp. Hack strongly.

17. Turn Around, Bow Stance, Shoulder The Cutter

zhuànshēn gōngbù bēi dài 转身弓步背带

Push into the left foot to shift back, then pivot on both feet on the spot, turning around to the right. Circle the cutter in both hands to the right, lifting it up over the head to lie level, with the cutting edge up and tip pointing right. Look forward and up. (image 7.17a) Push into the right foot to shift back, and step the right foot behind to the right. Then step the left foot across in front of the right foot towards the right, landing with the foot turned out. Lift the right heel, pushing the ball of the foot into the ground, and turn the body right. Circle the cutter with both hands circling and holding it level above the head, then lift the tip at the upper left with the cutting edge forward. Look forward. (image 7.17b) Step the right foot to the forward right and shift forward, lifting the left heel and pressing the ball of the foot into the ground. Circle the cutter in both hands so that it goes forward and down to tuck behind the right arm. The hilt is tucked along the right upper back, and the tip is slanting down. Hold the left hand, elbow bent, in front of the chest. Look forward. (image 7.17c) Withdraw the left foot a half-step, bend the right knee and straighten the left, to take a right bow stance. Push the left hand forward. Look forward. (image 7.17d)

Keep the movement soft to do the turn, brandish, and placement of the cutter along the back. Coordinate the placement of the cutter with the turning action.

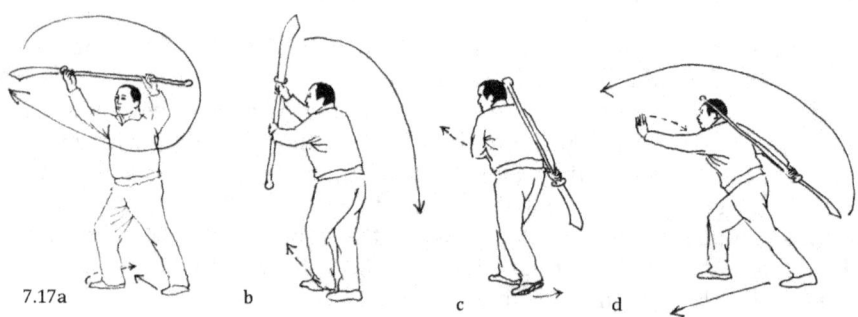

TWO-HANDED CUTTER

Section Four

18. Left Jumping Brandishing Turn And Hack

zuǒ tiào yún zhuàn zhǎn dài   左跳云转斩带

Push into the left foot to shift forward, and step the left foot forward, to the left. Circle the cutter in the right hand over and up to hold it at the right in front of the body, tip forward, edge to the right. Bring the left hand to grasp the hilt. Look forward, to the left. (image 7.18a) Push into the right foot to shift forward, then push into the left foot to jump up and spin around, turning left. Brandish the cutter to the left and back over the head in both hands, edge up, tip to the right. Look up. (image 7.18b) Land, still spinning to the left, and stand on the right leg, keeping the left knee raised. Hold the cutter in both hands over the head at the right. Look forward, to the left. (image 7.18c) Continue to turn to the left and land the left foot to the forward left. Bend the left knee and straighten the right, to take a left bow stance. Hack with the cutter in both hands to the forward left, hilt angled down from the blade, tip forward, cutting edge angled down. Look forward. (image 7.18d)

Jump and spin lightly. Land into a firm bow stance. Hack strongly.

19. Right Jumping Brandishing Turn And Hack

yòu tiào yún zhuàn zhǎn dài   右跳云转斩带

Push into the right foot to shift forward, and step the right foot forward, to the right. Circle the cutter with both hands from the forward left to up over the head at the right. Look forward, to the left. (image 7.19a) Push into the left foot to shift to the right, then raise the left knee. Turn the torso to the right. Circle the cutter in both hands flat above the head to the right, in front of the head. Look forward, to the right. (image 7.19b) Push into the right foot and jump up, spinning around to the right. Land on the left foot and settle into the ball of the foot. Circle the cutter with both hands flat to the rear left, holding it in front of the head. Look forward, to the right. (image 7.19c) Spin to the right and land the right foot, bending the knee and straightening the left knee to take a right bow stance. Circle the cutter in both hands across to the rear right to hack at an angle, tip forward, cutting edge to the lower front right. Tuck the cutter hilt with the left hand under the right armpit. Look forward. (image 7.19d)

Jump and spin lightly. Land into a solid bow stance. Hack strongly.

20. Left Side Parry   zuǒcè guà dài   左侧挂带

Push into the right foot to shift back, and retreat the right foot in a half-step, turning the left foot out. Circle the cutter with both hands to parry down and to the rear, to hold it out at the left, slanting with the blade down. The arms are crossed in front of the belly. Look to the lower front. (image 7.20a) Push into the right foot to shift left, and raise the right knee. Circle the cutter with both hands to the left and up, to continue to parry over the head, tip up, edge to the left. Look up. (image 7.20b)

When doing a parry, the blade must hook with the spine along an arcing line. The one-legged stance should be well balanced.

21. Right Side Parry   yòucè guà dài   右侧挂带

Land the right foot to the right with the foot pointing forward. Circle the cutter with both hands to bring it around to the right and down, to parry out at the right in front, blade spine down, and edge up. Look forward, to the right. (image 7.21a) Push into the left foot to shift right, turn right, and step the left foot forward into an open stance. Circle the cutter with both hands to bring it down and to the rear right with a parrying action, carrying on to above the head at the right. Look forward, to the left. (image 7.21b)

The parry must use the blade

TWO-HANDED CUTTER

spine, hooking in an arcing line. Coordinate the parry with the step and turn.

22. Resting Stance Chop   xiēbù pī dài   歇步劈带

Push into the right foot to shift left, and step the right foot behind the left foot towards the left, touching down the foot with the heel lifted. The legs are crossed and bent in a back-cross step. Circle the cutter with both hands to the left to chop down at the left side, cutting edge down, tip to the left. The arms are crossed in front of the belly. Look down to the left. (image 7.22)

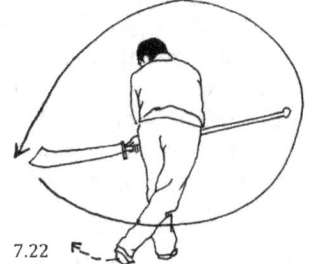

7.22

In the resting stance, the right knee is tucked into the depression behind the left knee. Complete the chop strongly.

23. Roll Over And Chop   fānshēn pī dài   翻身劈带

Push into both feet to pivot around to the right, rolling over into the back and turning around to the right, then move the right foot forward, bending both legs. Circle the cutter with both hands down, right, and up, to end up chopping flat at the right. The cutting edge is down, the tip forward. Slide the hands along the hilt, separating the right up to the guard and the left to near the base. Look forward, to the right. (image 7.23)

7.23

Roll over quickly. Chop strongly.

24. Reverse Bow Stance Framing Block

àogōngbù jià dài   拗弓步架带

Push into the right foot, then the left, to jump up. Land with the right foot stomping, and the left knee raised. Cradle the cutter in both hands in front of the chest, the tip forward and cutting edge up. Look forward. (image 7.24a) Land the left foot forward with the foot turned out, and lift the right heel slightly. Turn the torso to the left. Do a framing block with the cutter above and to the left of the head. Look back to the left. (image 7.24b)

Stomp strongly. Step forward, turn the body, and block up in one coordinated action.

7.24a   b

197

25. Turn Around, Bow Stance, Present The Cutter

zhuànshēn gōngbù jǔ dài　　转身弓步举带

Push into the right foot to shift forward, and turn the left foot in. Spin around to the right and raise the right knee. Hold the cutter in both hands in front of the body, tip up. Look forward. (image 7.25a) Continue to spin around to the right, then land the right foot behind on the right, bending the knee and straightening the left knee to take a right bow stance. Circle the cutter across to the rear right with the spin, focussing on the hilt, to finish presented on the right side of the body, tip up. Look forward, to the left. (image 7.25b)

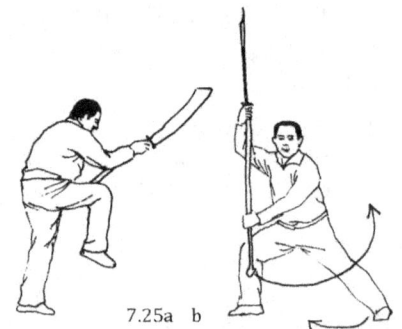

7.25a b

Turn and take the bow stance with good balance. As the body turns, the cutter comes around vertically to the right, circling until it is presented at the right side.

Section Five

26. Step Forward, Press Down With The Hilt   shàngbù yābà　上步压把

Push into the left foot to shift to the right, and move the left foot up towards the right foot. Bend both knees slightly. Bring the cutter with both hands so that the base end moves across to the left, up, then forward to press down. The hilt is level at belly height. Look to the left. (image 7.26)

7.26

Press down with the base as the left foot comes in.

27. Back-Cross Stance, Stir With The Hilt   chābù jiǎobà　叉步绞把

Push into the right foot to shift left, then step the right foot behind the left with an insertion step, touching down the foot with the heel lifted. The legs are crossed and bent. Using the base end of the cutter, circle it in both hands to with a stirring action at the left side of the body, down and to the left. Look to the left side. (image 7.27a) Step the left foot across to the left into an open stance with the knees bent. Circle the base end of the cutter to the left and up to stir at belly height. Look to the left. (image 7.27b)

Do the back-cross step quickly. Stir softly but with power.

TWO-HANDED CUTTER

28. Step Forward, Flat Hack shàngbù píngzhǎn 上步平斩

Push into the right foot to shift left, turn the torso leftward, and step the right foot forward. Circle the cutter with both hands to the right from the rear, to hack level in front, cutting towards the left. Slide the right hand to the middle of the hilt. The blade tip is forward with the cutting edge to the left. Look forward, to the right. (image 7.28)

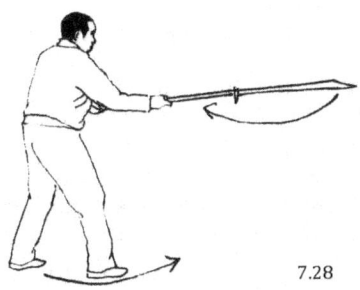

Turn and step quickly. Start the hack softly, and finish with strength.

29. Turn Around, Flat Hack zhuànshēn píngzhǎn 转身平斩

Push into the left foot to shift right, and step the left foot behind the right foot, moving to the right with an insertion step, touching down the foot with the heel lifted. Turn the torso slightly to the left. Pull the cutter in with both hands, moving it to the left and turning it over. Look back to the left. (image 7.29a) Pivot on the spot on both feet, turning around to the left. Circle the cutter with both hands to bring it flat across to the left, turning it over, placing it at the belly. Look forward, to the left. (image 7.29b) Push into the right foot to shift left, then step the right foot forward. Turn to the left and circle the cutter flat across in both hands to the front, hacking to the left. Slide the right hand to the middle of the hilt. The blade tip points forward, the cutting edge to the left. Look forward, to the right. (image 7.29c)

Turn quickly. Start the hack softly and complete it strongly.

30. Step Forward, Smear To The Left   shàngbù zuǒmǒ   上步左抹

Push into the left foot to shift right, and step the left foot forward. Bend the left knee and straighten the right. Circle the cutter in both hands to smear at an angle to the left. The cutting edge faces left, the tip forward. Look forward, to the right. (image 7.30)

Draw the blade back at an angle to smear with the cutting edge. The power is gentle but powerful.

31. Step Forward Push And Hack   shàngbù tuīzhǎn   上步推斩

Push into the right foot to shift forward, and step the right foot forward, bending both legs slightly. Circle the cutter in both hands to bring it to the left, then press it down in front at the right. The hilt is at the belly, tip forward, blade flat with the cutting edge left. Look forward, to the right. (image 7.31a) Push into the left foot to shift right, and bring the left foot up to meet the right foot in a closed stance. Push the cutter forward with both hands to do a flat hack at chest height. Straighten the right arm and bend the left in front of the chest. Look forward, to the right. (image 7.31b)

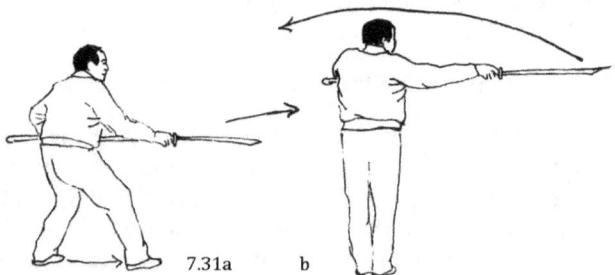

Step quickly. Push into the hack with power.

32. Turn Around, Bow Stance Lift

zhuànshēn gōngbù tí dài   转身弓步提带

Without moving the feet, turn the torso to the left. Circle the cutter up and over from the right to the left with both hands, placing it at an angle with the tip up and the cutting edge forward and

down. The arms are crossed in front of the chest. Look forward, to the left. (image 7.32a) Step the left foot across to the left side and bend the knee. Straighten the right leg to take a left bow stance. Circle the cutter forward, down, and back with both hands, placing it outside the right hip, edge down, tip forward. Push the left hand forward, to the left. Look forward, to the left. (image 7.32b)

Turn and step into the bow stance as the cutter circles, so that the placement is simultaneous with the stance.

33. Closed Stance, Present The Cutter   bìngbù jǔ dài   并步举带

Without changing the bow stance, push the cutter forward with the right hand, tip slanting forward and up, edge down. Bring the left hand in to grasp near the base. Look forward, to the left. (image 7.33a) Push into the left foot to shift back, turn the torso right, and step the left foot in beside the right foot in a closed stance. Present the cutter in both hands at the right side, tip up, edge forward, to the left. Look to the left. (image 7.33b)

Section Six

34. Step Forward, Jumping Turn To Chop

shàngbù tiàozhuàn pī dài   上步跳转劈带

Step the left foot to the left, bending the knee and straightening the right knee. Circle the cutter in both hands to the right and down, to hold it out slanting down, edge down and tip pointing to the lower right. Turn the torso slightly to the right. Look back, to the right. (image 7.34a) Push into the right foot to shift left, turn the torso left, and raise the right knee.

Circle the cutter with both hands from the back, down, and up on the left, to slice up and hold it up in front, at the left. Look forward and down. (image 7.34b) Push into the left foot to jump up and spin around to the left. Circle the cutter in both hands up and over above the body, edge angled forward and down. Look forward and down. (image 7.34c)

Land on the right foot, then the left, bending both knees to sit into a horse stance. Circle the cutter with both hands down, left, then up to chop level at the right side. The hilt is tucked into the belly, cutting edge down, tip to the right. Look forward, to the right. (image 7.34d)

7.34d

Jump and spin lightly. Land stably. Chop with power.

35. Retreat, Brandish And Smear   tuìbù yúnmǒ dài   退步云抹带

Push into the right foot to shift left, turn the torso right, and retreat the right foot to the rear. Circle the cutter with both hands from the front towards the right, and up to hold it above the head, slanting with the tip up and the edge forward. The arms are crossed in front of the body. Look forward. (image 7.35a) Lean forward, turning right and bending both legs. Circle the cutter with both hands, going left and forward to in front of the body, down to the left. Look forward, to the lower left. (image 7.35b)

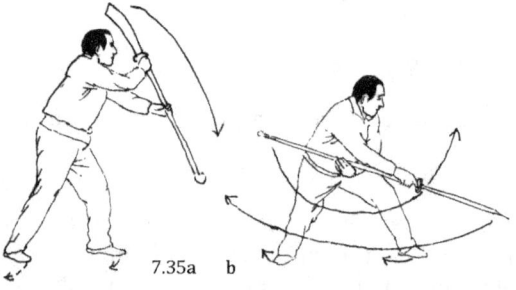

7.35a   b

The cutting edge must lead when doing a smear. Retreat and smear at the same time.

36. Turn Around, Brandish And Smear

zhuànshēn yúnmǒ dài   转身云抹带

Push into the left foot to shift right, and pivot around to the right on both feet on the spot. Stand up, and bring the cutter in both hands to bring the base in front of the body to the left side. Then smear down to the rear right at an angle. Look forward, to the lower right. (image 7.36a) Push into the left foot to shift right, and take a curving step to the right with the left foot, turning right. Circle the cutter in both hands from the rear right, upwards, to brandish above the head, hilt flat, tip to the right, edge up. Look forward and up. (image 7.36b) Push into the right foot to shift left, turn around to

TWO-HANDED CUTTER

the right, and move the right foot back, standing up in a parallel open stance. Circle the cutter with both hands to the rear right, still above the head. Look to the left side. (image 7.36c)

7.36a   b   c

Sit down, bending both legs, and lean forward slightly. Circle the cutter in both hands to the left and down to smear at an angle at the side of the body, cutting edge to the left, tip forward. The arms are crossed in front of the body. Look to the lower front. (image 7.36d)

Turn and brandish quickly and softly. Smear with the cutting edge leading. Coordinate the cutter techniques with the steps and the turn.

7.36d

37. Turn Around, Brandish And Smear

zhuànshēn yúnmǒ dài   转身云抹带

Push into the left foot to shift right, and pivot to the right on the spot on both feet, turning right. Circle the cutter in both hands to bring the base across in front of the body to the left side. Then do an angled smearing action to the rear right. Look forward [tr. note: towards the cutter, called the rear previously], to the lower right. (image 7.37a) Push into the left foot to shift right, step the left foot to the right side, and turn around to the right. Circle the cutter with both hands up to brandish above the head, with the hilt level and tip to the right, edge up. Look forward and up. (image 7.37b) Push into the left foot to shift right, and pivot on both feet on the spot to the right, bending the knees and sitting mostly to the right leg. Turn the torso to the right. Circle the cutter with both hands to brandish flat to the right, crossing over the head in front. Look forward and up. (image 7.37c)

CHAQUAN, VOLUME III

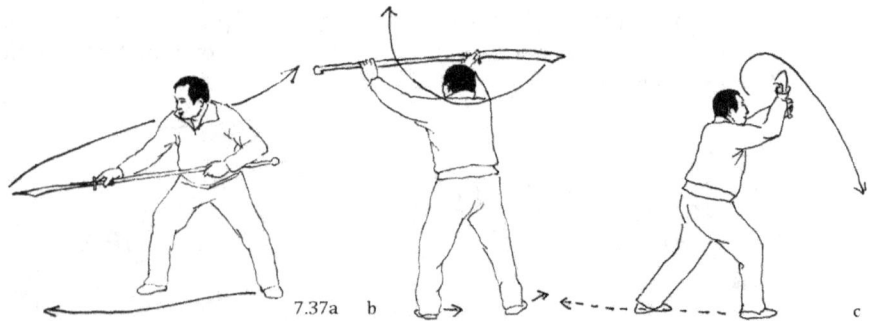

7.37a b c

Push into the right foot to shift left, and step the right foot behind. Bend both legs and lean forward. Circle the cutter with both hands to the right, back, and to the left, to brandish and smear to the front and down. The cutting edge faces left, and the tip points forward and down to the left. The arms are crossed in front of the body. Look forward and down. (image 7.37d)

7.37d

Turn and brandish the cutter quickly and softly. The cutting edge must lead in the smear. Coordinate the stepping and bodywork with the techniques of the cutter.

38. Turn Around, Bow Stance Chop

zhuànshēn gōngbù zhā dài   转身弓步扎带

Push into the left foot to shift right, and pivot to the right on both feet on the spot. Bend into the right knee and straighten the left, to take a right bow stance. Circle the cutter with both hands to go up and over to the rear, to chop down at an angle. The cutting edge is down, the tip forward. Look forward. (image 7.38)

Turn quickly. Take a firm bow stance. Chop strongly.

7.38

39. Turn Around, Parry   zhuànshēn guà dài   转身挂带

Push into the right foot to shift back, and pivot on the left foot around to the left, turning the body around the left. Then immediately push into the left foot to shift right, and raise the left knee. Bring the cutter in both hands up and across to the left, holding it out at the upper left, edge up, tip to the left. Tuck the hilt with the left hand onto the right flank. Look forward, to the left. (image 7.39a) Land the left foot forward, turned out, and press into the ball of the right foot, lifting the heel. Circle the cutter with both hands down and to the left side to parry outside the left leg. The cutting edge is down, the tip points back. Lean forward to the left. Look back, to the left. (image 7.39b) Push into the left foot to shift forward, and step the right foot forward. Circle the cutter in both hands to the left, back, and up and over to push it up in front of the body at the right, cutting edge angled up. Look forward, to the right. (image 7.39c)

The blade spine must lead to do the parry throughout the circle. Turn and step well coordinated with the parrying technique.

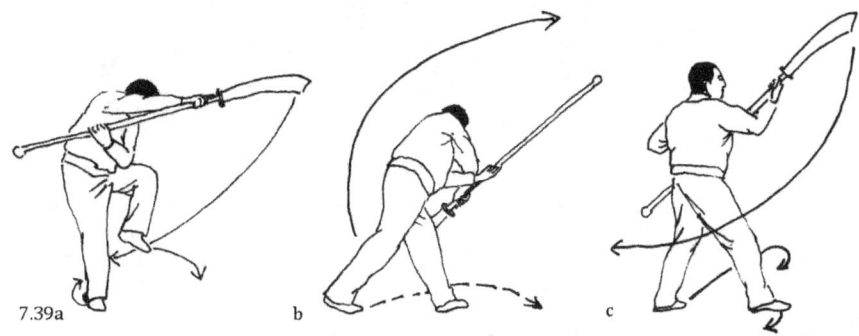

40. Turn Around, Bow Stance Stab

zhuànshēn gōngbù zhā dài   转身弓步扎带

Push into the left foot to shift right, and pivot on the right foot to the right, raising the left knee and turning the body around to the right. Circle the cutter down in front, and back to the lower right, edge down, tip slanting down. Look down to the right. (image 7.40a) Turn the body further to the right and land the left foot forward, bending the knee. Straighten the right leg to take a left bow stance. Stab the cutter with both hands directly forward, edge up, tip forward. Look forward. (image 7.40b)

Turn quickly and take a firm stance. Stab strongly.

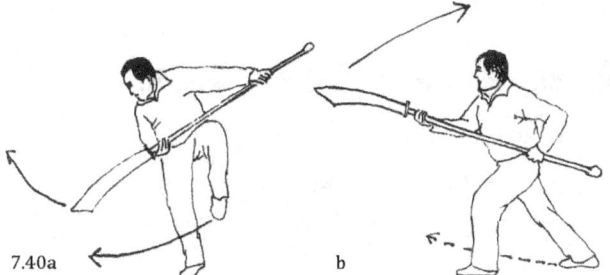

41. Stomp, Bow Stance Hack   zhèn gōngbù zhǎn dài   震弓步斩带

Push into the right foot to shift forward, and raise the right knee. Present the cutter with both hands in front of the chest, tip up, edge forward. Look forward. (image 7.41a) Push into the left foot to jump up. Look forward. (image 7.41b) Land firmly on the right foot and step the left foot forward, bending the left knee and straightening the right, to take a left bow stance. Hack forward to the left, edge slanting down, tip forward. Look forward. (image 7.41c)

Land the right foot with an audible thump. Take a solid bow stance. Hack strongly.

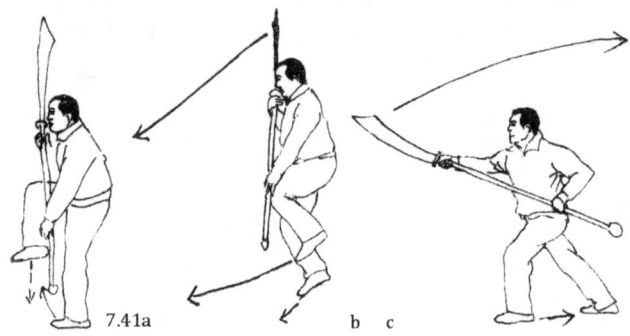

42. Retreat To Closed Stance Present The Cutter

tuì bìngbù jǔ dài

退并步举带

Push into the left foot to shift back, then bring the left foot to the right foot in a closed stance. Turn the torso to the right. Hold the cutter in both hands up at the right side, edge to the right, tip up. Look to the left side. (image 7.42)

Coordinate the stepping with the cutter technique, completing all as one action.

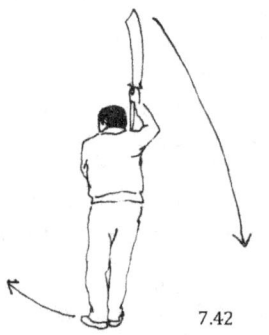

43. Step Forward, Raised Knee Slice Up

shàngbù tíxī liāo dài

上步提膝撩带

Step the left foot to the left, bending the knee and straightening the right leg. Circle the cutter with both hands back, then down along to outside the right leg, edge down, tip slanting to the rear. Look to the left side. (image 7.43a) Push into the right foot to shift forward, then raise the right knee. Turn the torso to the left. Circle

TWO-HANDED CUTTER

the cutter up to the forward left to slice up in front, edge up, tip forward. Look forward, to the right. (image 7.43b)

Step forward and raise the knee with good balance. When slicing, the edge must lead. The action is soft.

44. Horse Stance, Present The Cutter   mǎbù jǔ dài   马步举带

Pivot on the spot on the left foot to the left, then step the right foot forward. Turn to the left, then sit into a horse stance. Present the cutter in front of the body in both hands, tip up, edge to the left, hilt vertical. Bring the hands together on the hilt. Look to the left. (image 7.44)

Coordinate the turn, sit, and presentation of the cutter as one move.

45. Horse Stance, Stand The Cutter   mǎbù lì dài   马步立带

Without changing the stance, place the cutter base on the ground. Slide the hands to the guard and middle of the hilt. The cutting edge is on the left, the tip up. Look to the left. (image 7.45)

The cutter is standing vertically on the ground.

46. Raised Knee Half-Squat Carry   tíxī bàndūn tuō dài   提膝半蹲托带

Push into the right foot to shift left, then raise the right knee. Keep the left leg bent. Circle the cutter with both hands back to the right and down, to present it at the right side of the body. Tuck the hilt into the crook of the right arm, following the line of the forearm. The cutting edge is up and the tip points to the left. Look to the left. (image 7.46)

Keep the bent one-legged stance well balanced.

47. Bow Stance Carry The Cutter And Push The Hand

gōngbù tí dài tuīzhǎng   弓步提带推掌

Step the right foot to the right, bending the knee and straightening the left knee to take a right bow stance. Keep carrying the cutter in the crook of the right arm, lying it on the forearm. Push the left hand directly out to the left side. Look to the left. (image 7.47)

Complete the bow stance simultaneous with the push.

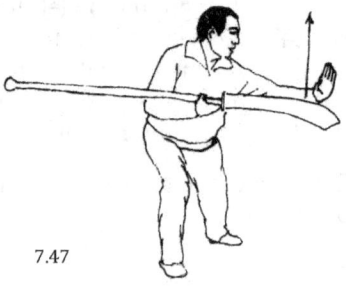

48. Toss The Cutter   pāo dài   抛带

Push into the right foot to shift back, then move the right foot back. Toss the cutter up with the right hand. Look at the cutter. (image 7.48a) Catch the cutter in the right hand. Look at the cutter. (image 7.48b)

Use the right forearm as well as the hand to toss the cutter up with good power. Wait to catch the cutter until it has come down to meet the hand.

49. Bow Stance Lift The Cutter And Push The Hand

gōngbù tí dài tuīzhǎng   弓步提带推掌

After catching the cutter in the right hand, place it at the right hip, cutting edge down, tip forward, to the left. Raise the left knee. Bring the left hand to the belly. Look forward, to the left. (image 7.49a) Step the left foot forward, bending the knee and straightening the right knee to take a left bow stance. Push the left hand out to the left. Look forward, to the left. (image 7.49b)

Complete the step with the push.

TWO-HANDED CUTTER

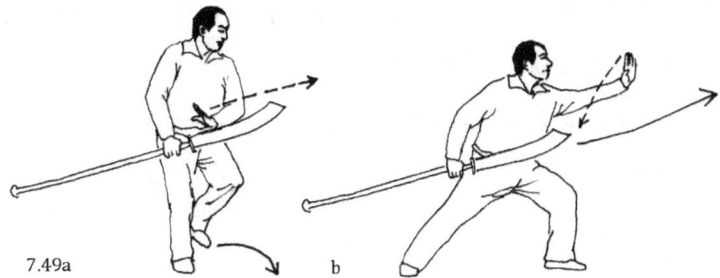

7.49a   b

50. Closed Stance, Present The Cutter   bìngbù jǔ dài   并步举带

Without changing the stance, push the cutter to the left with the right hand, edge down, tip to the left. Bring the left hand to the lower end of the hilt. Look forward, to the left. (image 7.50a) Push into the left foot to shift back, turn right, and bring the left foot in beside the right foot to a closed stance. Stand to attention. Bring the cutter in both hands to present it on the right side. Look to the left. (image 7.50b)

7.50a   b

51. Retreat, Stand The Cutter   tuìbù lì dài   退步立带

Retreat the left foot to the rear. Take the cutter to the right side with both hands, then lower the left hand. Look to the left. (image 7.51a) Bring the right foot in to meet the left in a closed stance. Stand to attention. Place the cutter base on the ground. Let the left arm hang in a relaxed manner. Look left. (image 7.51b)

Step and lower the cutter lightly and softly.

7.51 b

52. Closing Posture (Stand To Attention Holding The Cutter)

shōu shì (lìzhèng chídài)　　　　　　收势（立正持带）

Look forward. (image 7.52)

CRESCENT MOON BLADE

偃月刀

ABOUT THE CRESCENT MOON BLADE

The crescent moon blade is made up of a hilt or handle, a guard, and a head, or blade. The blade is quite wide, and its parts are the cutting edge, the spine, a hook on the spine, and the curving tip. There is usually a tassel attached to the hook on the spine.

The length of the crescent moon blade is determined by standing it by the side and reaching an arm straight up. The tip should reach at least the top of the fingers. The curved blade is single-edged, and made of metal. The hilt is usually wooden, and there is usually a metal base, shaped as a spike. There is no weight restriction.

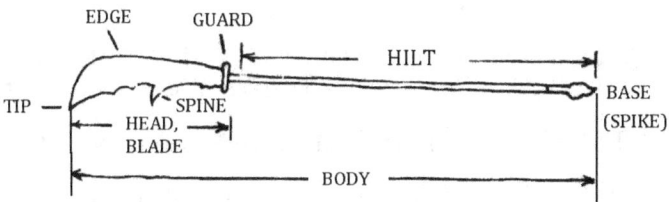

A smooth grasp is when both thumbs smoothly face the blade. For various techniques, the grasp may change, according to need. Sometimes a one-handed grasp is used, sometimes a two-handed grasp, and sometimes the hands may slide along the hilt.

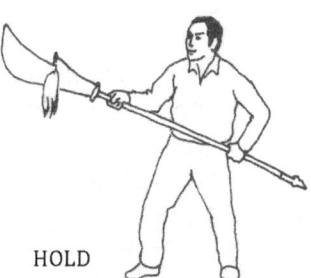

HOLD

THE MAIN TECHNIQUES OF THE CRESCENT MOON BLADE

Chop: With both hands on the hilt, come forward and down from above with the power going to the cutting edge of the blade. It can also come down at an angle, chopping from above at one side to below at the other side.

Hack: With both hands on the hilt, with the cutter body level at the chest, cut across in front, from one side to the other, with a flat cut. This is a short, strong, action, with power going to the cutting edge.

Slice up: With both hands on the hilt, circle from behind to go down and forward, to slice up with the cutting edge turned up, power going to the cutting edge.

Parry: With both hands on the hilt, circle the blade spine down to the side from the front towards the rear to parry or hook. Power goes to the blade spine.

Smear: With both hands on the hilt, with the blade body level at the chest, cut across in front, from one side to the other, with a flat cut or a slanting cut downwards. The blade cuts across level with a smearing action that circles slightly inwards. This is done softly, with the power to the cutting edge.

Sweep: With both hands on the hilt, hold the hilt level, turn the body leftward or rightward, and sweep the blade edge flat across in front from one side to the other. The right hand slides along to meet the left hand near the base. Power goes to the blade edge.

Brandish: With both hands on the hilt, with the hilt above the head, circle it left to right, keeping it level.

Flowers: With both hands on the hilt, draw vertical circles alternating at both sides of the body, or draw continuous level circles above the head.

NAMES OF THE MOVEMENTS OF THE CRESCENT MOON BLADE FORM

Position Of Preparation (Stand To Attention Holding the Blade)
Section One
1. Step Forward Holding The Blade
2. Bow Stance Carry
3. Retreat And Brandish
4. Bow Stance Shoulder The Blade
5. Step Forward, Left And Right Slices Up
6. Jump To Bow Stance Hack
7. Turn Around, Smear
8. Raised Knee Slice Up And Present The Blade
9. Walking Turn Around With A Smear
10. Raised Knee Present The Blade

Section Two
11. Horse Stance Parry And Chop
12. Roll Over To Bow Stance Chop
13. Turn Around, Sideways Bow Stance, Present The Blade
14. Jump To Bow Stance Chop
15. Left And Right Smears
16. Empty Stance Covering Chop
17. Roll Over To Bow Stance Stab
18. Retreat, Slice Up And Chop

19. Roll Over, Jump To Bow Stance Chop

Section Three

20. Empty Stance Cradle The Blade
21. Jump To Bow Stance Stab
22. Left And Right Smears
23. Empty Stance Cover And Chop
24. Turn Around And Chop
25. Walk To Bow Stance Shoulder The Blade
26. Jump To Bow Stance Hack
27. Turn Around, Smear
28. Step Forward, Raised Knee Push
29. Turn Around, Step Forward, Slice Up And Present The Blade (Haul Up A Banner)

Section Four

30. Left Parry And Chop
31. Roll Over And Chop
32. Empty Stance Cradle The Blade
33. Jump To Bow Stance Stab
34. Bow Stance, Left And Right Smear
35. Empty Stance, Cover And Chop
36. Turn Around And Chop
37. Turn Around, Step Forward, Smear
38. Empty Stance, Hide The Blade
39. Step Forward, Deflect With The Hilt
40. Turn Around To Bow Stance Hack

Section Five

41. Turn Around, Smear
42. Step Forward, Raised Knee Push
43. Turn Around, Slice Up
44. Jump To Bow Stance Hack
45. Closed Stance Push
46. Turn Around, Slice Up
47. Raised Knee Push

Section Six

48. Turn Around, Parry
49. Turn Around, Slice Up And Stab
50. Jump To Bow Stance Hack
51. Turn Around, Smear
52. Jump To Bow Stance Hack
53. Turn Around, Smear
54. Empty Stance Cradle The Blade

55. Withdraw, Stand The Blade
56. Closing Posture (Stand To Attention Holding The Blade)

0. Position Of Preparation (Stand To Attention Holding the Blade)
yùbèi shì (lìzhèng chí dāo)　　　　预备势（立正持刀）

Stand to attention holding the hilt in the right hand. It is standing upright at the right side with the base on the ground. Look straight ahead. (image 8.0a) Open the left arm out slightly, turning the fingers inwards, palm down. Look to the left. (image 8.0b)

Stand straight up, open the left hand, and turn the head to look to the side as one well coordinated action.

Section One

1. Step Forward Holding The Blade　　shàngbù chí dāo　　上步持刀

Step the left foot forward and shift forward, lifting the right heel, touching down the ball of the foot. Lift the blade with the right hand. Hold the left hand out to the left side, slanting down from the shoulder. Look to the left. (image 8.1a) Push into the right foot to shift forward, lifting the left heel with the ball of the foot touching down. Lift the left hand to level. Look forward, to the left. (image 8.1b) Bring the left foot up to meet the right foot in a closed stance and stand straight. Place the base of the blade on the ground. Bring the left hand in to beside the right hand, which is holding the hilt. Look to the left side. (image 8.1c)

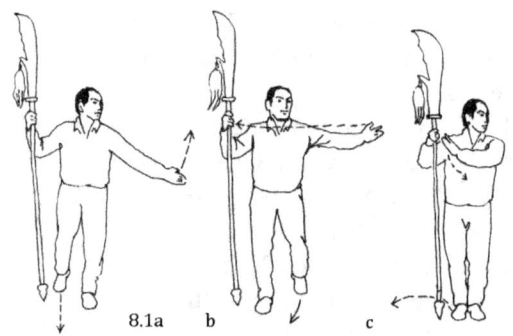

Coordinate the stepping with the swing of the left arm.

2. Bow Stance Carry　　gōngbù tuō dāo　　弓步托刀

Push into the right foot to shift to the left, lifting the right leg slightly, out to the right side. Place the left hand in front of the chest. Look to the left. (image 8.2a) Kick the base of the hilt with the right foot towards the left side, suspending the right leg in the air. Place the left hand on the lower section of the hilt. Look to the lower left. (image 8.2b) Step the right foot to the left, then step the left foot past it to the left. Bend the left knee forward and straighten the right, to take a left bow stance. Circle the blade with both hands so that the blade goes back from above, down, then slices up forward

CRESCENT MOON BLADE

to be carried in front. The hilt is level with the shoulders, the cutting edge up, the tip forward. Look forward. (image 8.2c)

Do not kick the hilt too hard. Complete the bow stance as the carrying action is completed.

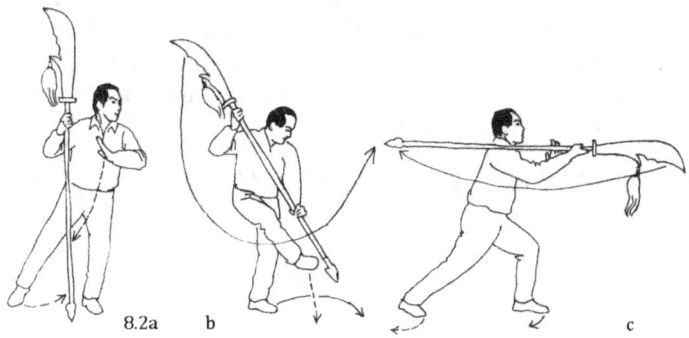

8.2a b c

3. Retreat And Brandish   tuìbù yún dāo   退步云刀

Push into the left foot to shift back, and pivot on both feet on the spot to the right, turning right. Circle the blade with both hands to the right and back, to brandish it over the head with the hilt level, the tip to the right, and the edge up. Open the hands to hold the hilt loosely. Look forward. (image 8.3a) Push into the left foot to shift right, then step the left foot in front of the right shin, towards the right, with the foot turned out. Lift the right heel, keeping the ball of the foot on the ground. The legs are crossed and bent. Circle the blade in both hands back from the right, towards the left, to continue to brandish downwards to the left, turning in front of the belly. the edge is down, the tip to the left. Look down to the right. (image 8.3b)

Keep the hilt level during the brandishing turn. Complete the brandish with the retreating step.

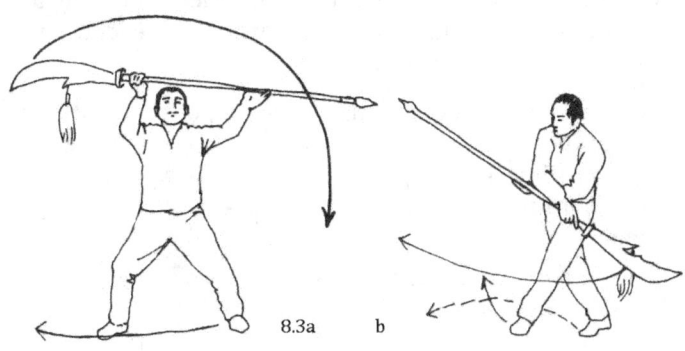

8.3a b

CHAQUAN, VOLUME III

4. Bow Stance Shoulder The Blade   gōngbù bēi dāo   弓步背刀

Push into the right foot to shift to the right, and step the right foot to the right, raising the left knee. Circle the blade with both hands down and across to the right, to slice up at the right side. Place the left hand in front of the right side of the chest. Look to the lower right. (image 8.4a) Step the left foot to the left side, bending the left knee and straightening the right, to take a left bow stance. Bring the hilt up to lie across the upper back, slanted down, lying along behind the right arm. Hold the left hand up to the left. Look down to the right. (image 8.4b)

Complete the placement of the blade with the setting into stance.

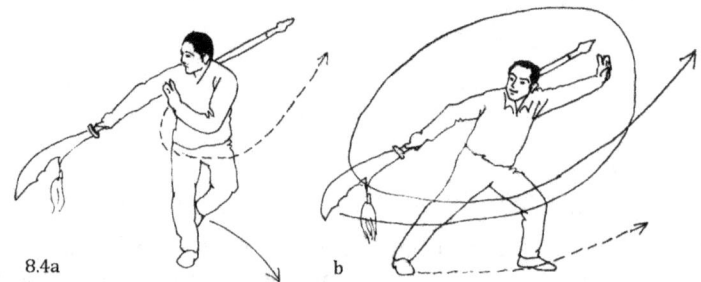

5. Step Forward, Left And Right Slices Up

    shàngbù zuǒyòu liāo dāo   上步左右撩刀

Push into the right foot to shift forward, and step the right foot forward, turning to the left. Circle the blade with the hilt in the right hand down from behind, to move forward, then up and over, to come through again from behind, to slice forward and up to the forward left. The cutting edge is up. Take the lower part of the hilt in the left hand. Look forward, to the right. (image 8.5a) Push into the left foot to shift right, turning right, and step the left foot forward. Circle the hilt in both hands to take the blade up and over to the rear, then down and past the left side of the body to slice out in front. Tuck the left hand into the right armpit. The cutting edge is up. Look forward and down. (image 8.5b)

Be sure to lead with the cutting edge on both the left and right slices. Step forward, turn, and slice, each time in a well coordinated manner.

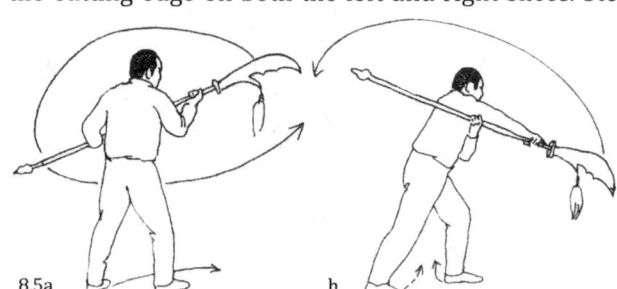

CRESCENT MOON BLADE

6. **Jump To Bow Stance Hack**   tiào gōngbù zhǎn dāo   跳弓步斩刀

Push into the right foot to shift forward, bending into the knee and lifting the left heel with the ball of the foot touching down. Circle the hilt with both hands up and over to the rear, to hold the blade up behind on the right. Look forward and down. (image 8.6a) Push into the left foot and jump up. Continue to circle the hilt with both hands further back and down, to come to lie at an angle at the right side. Look forward and down. (image 8.6b) Land on the right foot, then the left, bending into the left knee and straightening the right, to take a left bow stance. Do a level hack, using both hands, across in front to the left, the cutting edge slanting to the left, the tip forward. Look forward, to the left. (image 8.6c)

Stay stable whilst jumping and setting to stance. Hack strongly.

8.6a   b   c

7. **Turn Around, Smear**   zhuànshēn mǒ dāo   转身抹刀

Push into the left foot to shift back, then pivot on the spot around to the right on both feet. Bend the right knee and straighten the left to take a right bow stance. Draw a flat circle with the blade around to the right and rear, smearing over to the rear right with the edge to the right. Look forward, to the right. (image 8.7)

Turn quickly and take a firm stance. When smearing, the cutting edge must lead. The movement is soft.

8.7

8. **Raised Knee Slice Up And Present The Blade**

   tíxī liāo jǔ dāo   转身撩举刀

Push into the right foot to shift back, then move the foot towards the left foot, touching down the foot with the heel up. Bend both knees to sit into a right empty stance. Circle the hilt in both hands to bring the blade down and over to the left to slice up on in front of the right leg. The cutting edge is forward and the tip down. Look to the lower front. (image 8.8a) Raise the right knee. Lift the blade slightly in both hands. Look forward. (image 8.8b)

Keep good balance. Slice up and present softly.

9. Walking Turn Around With A Smear

xíngbù zhuànshēn mǒ dāo   行步转身抹刀

Land the right foot forward and shift towards the right leg. Push the blade forward with both hands. Look forward. (image 8.9a) Push into the left foot to shift forward, then take an arcing step with the left foot in front of the right, turning the torso slightly to the right. Look forward to the lower right. (image 8.9b) Push into the right foot to shift forward. Take an arcing step with the right foot to the forward right, turning the foot out. Do not change the relative position of the hands and blade. Turn the torso rightward. Look forward, to the right. (image 8.9c) Push into the left foot to shift forward, then step the left foot forward. Look to the lower right. (image 8.9d) Push into the right foot to shift forward. Pivot on the ball of the left foot to turn the body around to the right, sliding the right foot to the rear right to an open stance. Keep both knees bent. Circle the blade to the right and around to the rear to smear with the blade to the rear of the body, tip angled down, edge to the right. Look forward, to the right. (image 8.9e)

Keep the blade outwards when smearing. Circle and turn to smear, using the stepping to turn the body and smear with the blade in a coordinated manner.

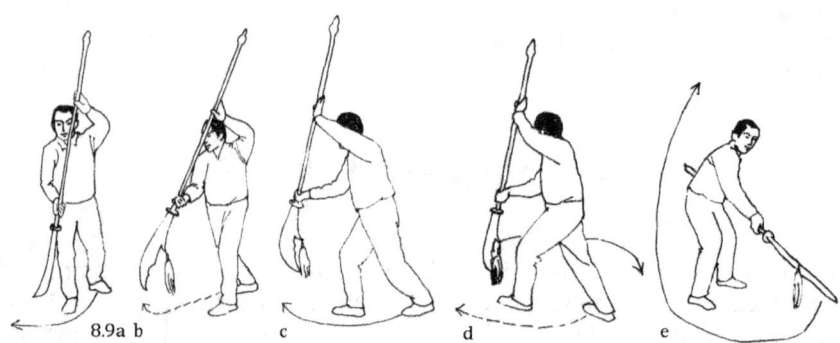

CRESCENT MOON BLADE

10. Raised Knee Present The Blade　　tíxī jǔ dāo　　提膝举刀

Push into the left foot to shift to the right, then raise the left knee. Circle the blade across to the right, then back, and finally lift it up at the right. Hold the hilt vertically with the tip up and the cutting edge to the left. Look forward, to the left. (image 8.10)

Stand with good balance when raising the knee. Coordinate the timing of the knee raise with the final lift of the blade.

8.10

Section Two

11. Horse Stance Parry And Chop　　mǎbù guàpī dāo　　马步挂劈刀

Land the left foot forward with the foot turned out, lifting the right heel with the ball of the foot on the ground. Turn to the left and shift forward. Circle the blade forward and down to parry it outside the left leg, tip down. Look down to the left. (image 8.11a) Step the right foot to the right side and bend both knees to take a horse stance. Circle the blade to the left, then up and over to chop level in front. The hilt is at waist height, the cutting edge down, and the tip to the right. Look to the right side. (image 8.11b)

The cutting edge must lead throughout the parry and chop. Complete the horse stance with the chop. Chop down into the cutting edge strongly.

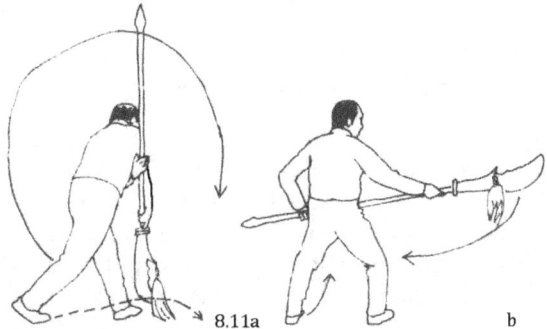
8.11a　　b

12. Roll Over To Bow Stance Chop

　　fānshēn gōngbù pī dāo　　翻身弓步劈刀

Push into the left foot to shift to the right, then raise the left knee out to the side. Circle the blade down, over to the left, then hold it in front of the right leg, tip down. Lean to the forward right. Look to the lower right. (image 8.12a) Push into the right foot to jump up and spin around to the left. Land the left foot, then the right, forward, bending the right knee forward and straightening the left to take a right bow stance. Circle the blade to the left, up, and over to the left to chop level in front. The hilt is at waist height, the cutting edge down, and the tip points right. Look forward, to the right. (image 8.12b)

Roll over and jump quickly and land firmly. The cutting edge must lead all the way into the chop. When chopping, the cutting edge is down. Chop strongly.

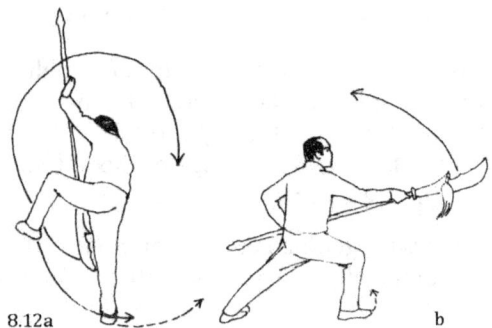

13. Turn Around, Sideways Bow Stance, Present The Blade

zhuànshēn cègōngbù jǔ dāo   转身侧弓步举刀

Without moving the feet, turn the torso leftward and push the right knee to the side. Turn the blade to present it vertically, tip up, cutting edge left, at the right side of the body. Look forward, to the left. (image 8.13)

Complete the turn and the presentation simultaneously.

14. Jump To Bow Stance Chop   tiào gōngbù pī dāo   跳弓步劈刀

Push into the right foot to shift to the left, turning the torso to the left. Step the right foot forward, bending the knee. Hold the blade in front of the body. Look forward. (image 8.14a) Push into the left foot, then the right, to jump forward and up. Look forward. (image 8.14b) Land on the left foot, then the right. Bend the right knee and straighten the left, to take a right bow stance. Chop the blade to level in front. Look forward. (image 8.14c)

Jump forward lightly, and chop strongly.

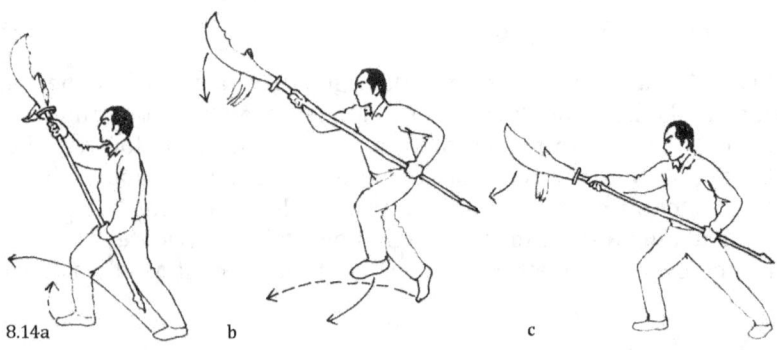

CRESCENT MOON BLADE

15. Left And Right Smears   zuǒyòu mǒ dāo   左右抹刀

Shift back without moving the feet. Smear the blade flat across to the left, turning the torso and the blade cutting edge to the left. Look forward. (image 8.15a) Shift forward, bending the right knee forward. Turn the blade to face right and smear flat across to the right. Look forward, to the right. (image 8.15b)

Turn the cutting edge to face out, in the direction of the smear, for both the left and the right smear. The smearing action is soft.

8.15a   b

16. Empty Stance Covering Chop   xūbù gàipī dāo   虚步挂劈刀

Push into the right foot to shift back, then withdraw the right foot slightly back, shifting forward. Lift the left heel, keeping the ball of the foot on the ground, and turn the torso slightly to the right. Circle the blade down, along outside the right leg to the lower rear. The hilt slants down with the tip angled down. Look to the right side. (image 8.16a) Push into the left foot to shift forward, then step the left foot forward, touching down the foot with the heel lifted, to sit down into a left empty stance. Circle the blade up and over to the front with a covering chop, hilt level, cutting edge down. Look forward. (image 8.16b)

Shift back and forth lightly and with agility, then take a well-defined empty stance. The cutting edge must lead throughout the action of the covering chop.

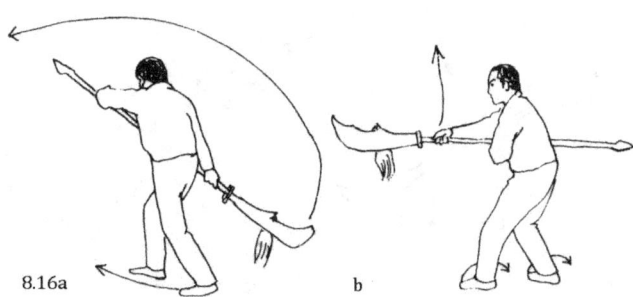

8.16a   b

17. Roll Over To Bow Stance Stab

fānshēn gōngbù zhā dāo   翻身弓步扎刀

Pivot around to the right on both feet, on the spot, turning the body around to the right by rolling into the back. Lift the blade up to the right with the hilt level. Look up. (image 8.17a) Push into the left foot to shift right, then pivot on the right foot to continue to roll over to the right. Then step the left foot forward, bending the knee and straightening the right leg to take a left bow stance. Bring the blade down, then stab directly forward with the cutting edge up, tip forward. Look forward. (image 8.17b)

Roll over quickly, step firmly, and stab strongly.

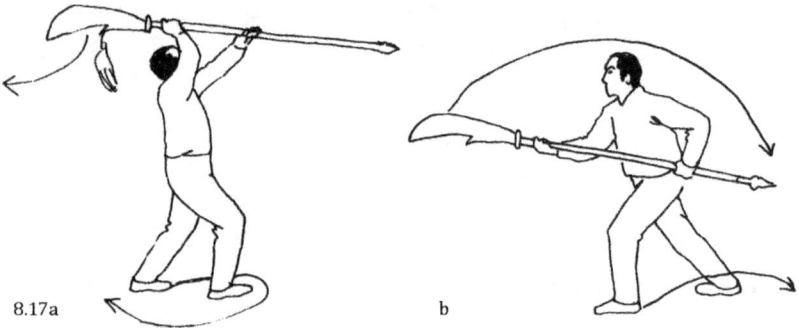

18. Retreat, Slice Up And Chop   tuìbù liāopī dāo   退步撩劈刀

Push into the right foot to shift back, then retreat the left foot behind and turn left. Circle the blade up and over to the rear, taking it through to the lower left, hilt slanting downwards, cutting edge down, and tip to the rear. Look to the rear left. (image 8.18a) Push into the right foot to shift back, turning around to the right, then step the right foot out to the right side. Circle the blade down and along the side to forward, lifting it above the head in the front, edge up, tip forward. Look to the left side. (image 8.18b) Pivot on the spot on both feet to turn right, bending the legs. Circle the blade up and over to chop level at the right, hilt at waist height, cutting edge

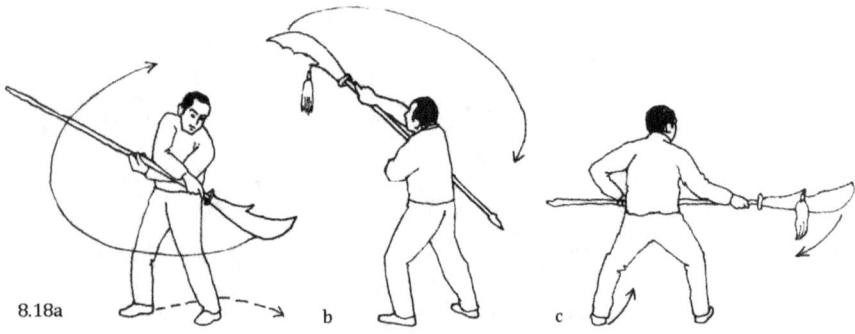

down, tip to the right. Look to the right. (image 8.18c)

Throughout the slice up and the chop, the cutting edge must lead. The slice up is soft, and the chop is done with power. Coordinate the stepping with the turning and the blade techniques.

19. Roll Over, Jump To Bow Stance Chop

    fānshēn tiào gōngbù pī dāo   翻身跳弓步劈刀

Push into the left foot to shift right, and raise the left knee to the side, lifting the right heel. Lower the blade and lean forward to the right. Look forward and down to the right. (image 8.19a) Push into the right foot to jump up and spin around into the back to turn left whilst airborne. Land the left foot, then the right, stepping it forward. Bend the right knee forward and straighten the left, to take a right bow stance. With the jump, circle the blade down, left, and up, to come over and chop out to the right side, edge down, tip slanting to the upper right. Look forward, to the right. (image 8.19b)

Jump and set into the bow stance with good stability. Chop with strength.

Section Three

20. Empty Stance Cradle The Blade   xūbù bāo dāo   虚步抱刀

Push into the right foot to shift back, withdrawing the right foot back a half-step, touching down the ball of the foot with the heel lifted. Bend both legs to sit into a right empty stance. Cradle the hilt in the arms in front of the chest, cutting edge up, tip forward. Look forward, to the right. (image 8.20)

Sit into a distinctly weighted / unweighted empty stance.

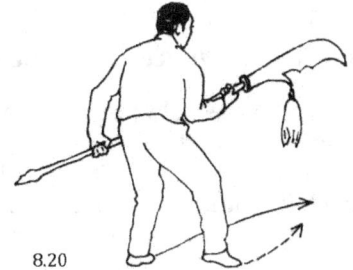

CHAQUAN, VOLUME III

21. Jump To Bow Stance Stab   tiào gōngbù zhā dāo   跳弓步扎刀

Step the right foot forward a half-step. Push off with the left foot, then the right, to jump up and forward without changing the relative position of the hands or the blade. Look forward, to the right. (image 8.21a) Land forward on the left foot, then the right. Bend the right knee forward and straighten the left to take a right bow stance. Stab forward, cutting edge up, tip forward. Look forward, to the right. (image 8.21b)

Jump and land with good stability. Stab strongly.

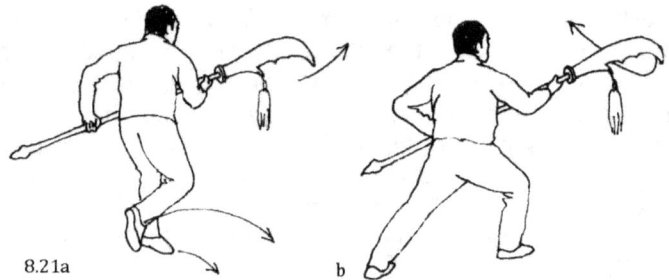

22. Left And Right Smears   zuǒyòu mǒ dāo   左右抹刀

Without changing the stance, smear the blade flat across to the left, turning the torso slightly to the left. Look forward, to the left. (image 8.22a) Still not moving the feet, smear the blade flat across to the right, turning the torso slightly to the right. Look forward, to the right. (image 8.22b)

Turn the blade so that the cutting edge leads into the left smear, then turn it to lead into the right smear. The smearing technique is soft, but with power.

23. Empty Stance Cover And Chop   xūbù gàipī dāo   虚步盖劈刀

Push into the right foot to shift back, and withdraw it a half-step. Circle the blade down and back on the right side, to hold it out at the rear, tip slanting down. Look forward. (image 8.23a) Push into the left foot to shift right. Step the left foot forward and bend the knee. Continue to circle the blade up at the rear, then over to the front to cover and chop. Tuck the left hand into

CRESCENT MOON BLADE

the right armpit. The hilt is at waist height, the cutting edge down, the tip forward. Look forward. (image 8.23b)

When covering, the cutting edge leads. Synchronise the cover with the step.

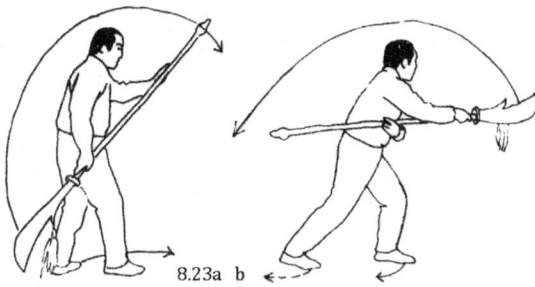

8.23a b

24. Turn Around And Chop   zhuànshēn pī dāo   转身劈刀

Push into the left foot to shift back, and pivot on both feet to turn the body around to the right. Bend the right knee and straighten the left to take a right bow stance. Circle the blade up and over to the rear to chop down. The cutting edge is down and the tip forward. Look forward, to the right. (image 8.24)

Turn quickly. Take a stable bow stance. Do a strong chop.

8.24

25. Walk To Bow Stance Shoulder The Blade
    xíng gōngbù bēi dāo   行弓步背刀

Push into the left foot to shift forward, then move the left foot slightly forward. Lower the blade and circle to the rear, to hold the hilt up at the right side, tip down. Turn the torso slightly to the right. Look forward and down to the right. (image 8.25a) Push into the left foot to shift forward, then step the left foot forward. Circle the blade back and up, then over to the front to hold it level in front. The edge is down, the tip forward, and the left hand tucks the hilt outside the right armpit. Look forward, to the left. (image 8.25b) Push into the right foot to shift forward, then step the right foot forward, lifting the left heel. Do not change the relative position of the hands or blade. Look forward. (image 8.25c)

Push into the left foot to shift forward, then step the left foot forward. Bend the left knee, straighten the right, and sit into a left bow stance. Circle the blade down, past the side to the rear to place is across the upper back, over the left shoulder. The hilt slants from the left shoulder to the rear right, with the tip down. Hold the left hand out to the forward left. Turn the torso to the right. Look back to the right. (image 8.25d)

CHAQUAN, VOLUME III

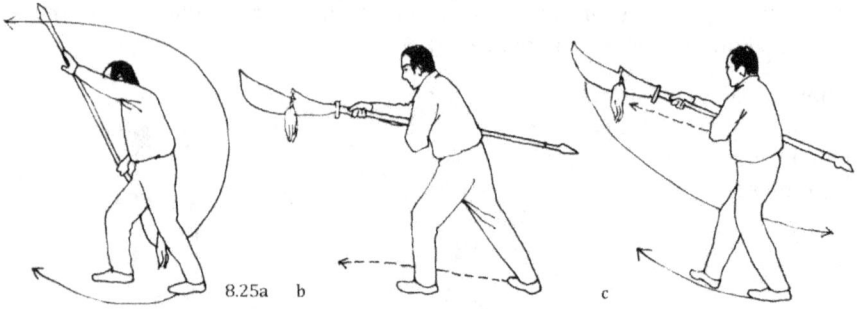

Walk smoothly. Complete the bow stance and the placement of the hilt along the back as one action.

26. Jump To Bow Stance Hack   tiào gōngbù zhǎn dāo   跳弓步斩刀

Push into the right foot to shift forward, and raise the right knee. Circle the blade in the right hand down and forward, then up to cradle it in front of the right side of the chest. Place the left hand on the hilt, towards the base. Look to the lower front. (image 8.26a) Push into the left foot to jump up. Look to the lower front. (image 8.26b) Land forward on the right foot, then the left, bending the left knee and straightening the right, to take a left bow stance. Circle the blade in both hands from above to the right and forward, to hack to waist height at the forward left, cutting edge to the left. Look forward, to the left. (image 8.26c)

Jump forward into the stance with good balance. Hack with power.

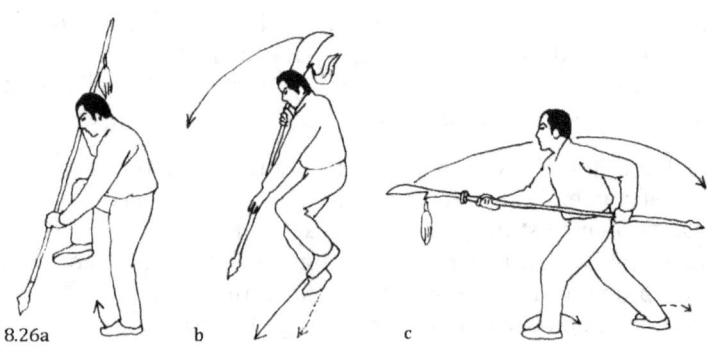

CRESCENT MOON BLADE

27. Turn Around, Smear   zhuànshēn mǒ dāo   转身抹刀

Push into the right foot to shift back, and pivot around to the right on both feet. Bend the right knee and straighten the left to take a right bow stance. Smear the blade flat around to the right in both hands, to the rear. The hilt is at waist height, with the cutting edge to the right. Look forward, to the right. (image 8.27)

Turn quickly. Pivot with good balance. Smear gently.

28. Step Forward, Raised Knee Push   shàngbù tíxī tuī dāo   上步提膝推刀

Push into the left foot to shift forward, then step the left foot forward in front of the right leg, turning it out. Bend both legs, in a crossing step. Bring the blade in to cradle it in front of the chest. Look forward, to the right. (image 8.28a) Push into the right foot to shift forward, and raise the left knee. Turn the torso to the left. Push the blade forward to the right, using both hands. The hilt is at chest height, with the cutting edge to the left. Look forward, to the right. (image 8.28b)

Stand in a stable one-legged stance. Push the blade strongly.

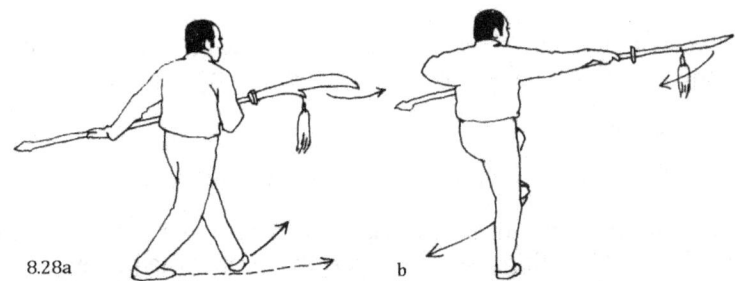

29. Turn Around, Step Forward, Slice Up And Present The Blade (Haul Up A Banner)

zhuànshēn shàngbù liāo jǔ dāo (chě qí)   转身上步撩举刀（扯旗）

Turn left and land the left foot to the left, bending the knee. Lower the blade to in front of the belly, tip back, edge to the left. Look forward, to the left. (image 8.29a) Push into the right foot to shift forward, and step the right foot forward, bending into the knee and turning the torso slightly leftward. Do not change the relative position of the blade. Look forward. (image 8.29b) Push into the left foot to shift forward, step the left foot forward, bending the knee and turning the torso slightly left again. Still do not change the relative position of the blade. Keep looking forward. (image 8.29c)

CHAQUAN, VOLUME III

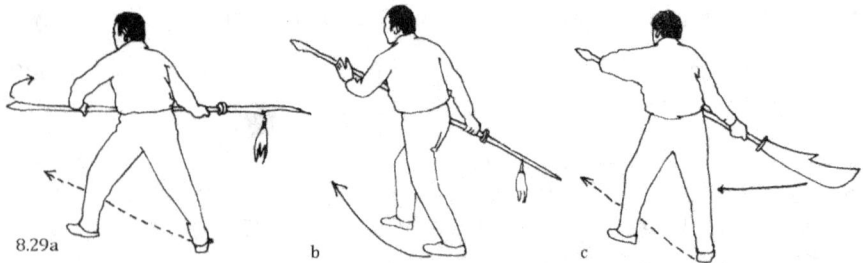

8.29a   b   c

Push into the right foot to shift forward, and step the right foot forward, bending both knees. Turn the torso left some more. Circle the blade down to come forward to hold it outside the right leg. Look to the lower front. (image 8.29d) Push into the right foot to shift to the left, then pivot on both feet on the spot around to the left. Then immediately push into the left foot to shift forward, turning left, and squat on the right leg out to the side. Straighten the left leg to set into a left drop stance. Circle the blade with both hands to the front, then up to slice upwards, then hold it upright. Both hands slide to near the base, the hilt leans a bit to the left, the cutting edge is on the left, and the tip is up. Look to the left side. (image 8.29e)

8.29d   e

First step forward and slice up, then turn and sit to drop stance present the blade. Coordinate all actions to keep the whole move smooth.

Section Four

30. Left Parry And Chop   zuǒ guàpī dāo   左挂劈刀

Push into the left foot to shift right, then raise the left knee. Slide the right hand along the hilt to near the guard, then hold the blade up in both hands at the right side of the body. Look to the left. (image 8.30a) Land the left foot forward, bending into the knee, and leaning the torso slightly forward. Circle the blade with both hands so that it travels down to the left, to parry out to the left in front, tip down, edge up. With the left hand, tuck the hilt into the right armpit. Look forward, to the lower left. (image 8.30b) Push into the right foot to shift forward, turn to the left, then step the right foot forward, bending into the knee. Circle the blade down and across to continue to parry to the rear, then up and over to chop in front. The hilt is at waist height, the edge down, the tip forward, slanting up. Look forward, to the right. (image 8.30c)

The blade spine leads into the parry, and the cutting edge leads into the chop. Chop strongly.

CRESCENT MOON BLADE

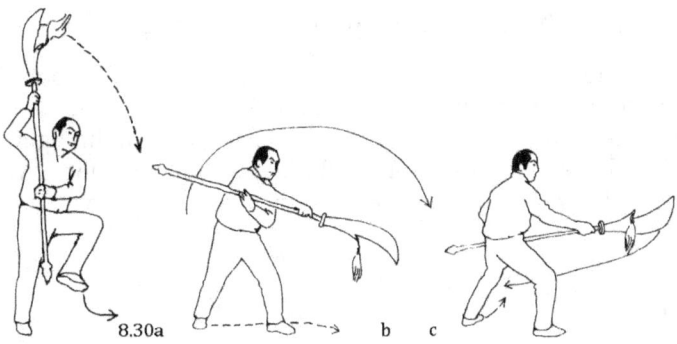

31. Roll Over And Chop   fānshēn pī dāo   翻身劈刀

Push into the left foot to shift right, and raise the left knee to the side, lifting the right heel. Circle the blade down, to bring it across to the left side, tip down. Lean slightly to the right side. Look down. (image 8.31a) Push into the right foot and jump up, rolling into the back around to the left. Land on the left, then the right, foot, bending the right knee forward and straightening the left, to take a right bow stance. Circle the blade up the left side, and over to chop down at the forward right, to waist height, edge down. Look forward, to the right. (image 8.31b)

Jump and spin quickly. Take a stable stance. Chop strongly.

32. Empty Stance Cradle The Blade   xūbù bào dāo   虚步抱刀

Push into the right foot to shift back, then bring the right foot in, touching down the foot with the heel lifted. Bend both legs to take a right empty stance. Cradle the blade slanting in front of the body, with the edge up. Look forward. (image 8.32)

Sit into a distinctly weighted / unweighted empty stance.

33. Jump To Bow Stance Stab   tiào gōngbù zhā dāo   跳弓步扎刀

Step the right foot forward, then push into the left foot, then the right, to jump up. Do not change the relative position of the blade. Look forward. (image 8.33a) Land forward on the left foot, then the right, bending into the right knee and straightening the left, to take a right bow stance. Stab the blade forward with both hands, edge up. Look forward. (image 8.33b)

Jump forward into a stable bow stance. Stab strongly.

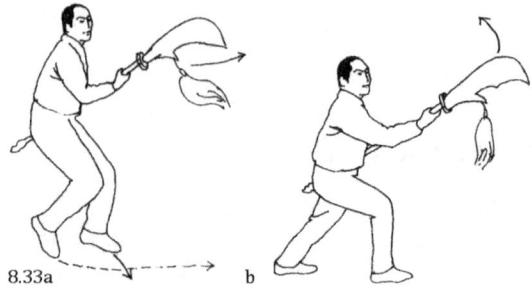

34. Bow Stance, Left And Right Smear

gōngbù zuǒyòu mǒ dāo   弓步左右抹刀

Without changing the bow stance, smear the blade flat across to the left, cutting edge to the left, and turn the torso slightly to the left. Look forward, to the left. (image 8.34a) Still not moving from the bow stance, smear the blade flat across to the right. Turn the torso slightly to the right, and turn the cutting edge to the right. Look forward, to the right. (image 8.34b)

The cutting edge of the blade must lead into the smearing technique to the left and right, so needs to turn over for each one. The smearing action is soft.

35. Empty Stance, Cover And Chop   xūbù gàipī dāo   虚步盖劈刀

Push into the right foot to shift back, then withdraw the right foot behind, bending both legs. Take the blade from in front on the right side, down to outside the right leg, circling it behind on the right with the edge back and the tip down. Look forward, to the right. (image 8.35a) Push into the left foot to shift forward, then step the left foot a half-step forward. Touch down the foot with the heel lifted, and bend both legs to take a left empty stance. Circle the blade up at the back, to come over to cover forward, and chop. Move the left hand towards the base, to tuck the hilt at the right waist. The hilt is level at waist height, cutting edge down, tip forward, to the right. Look forward, to the right. (image 8.35b)

The cutting edge leads into the cover and the chop. Complete the empty stance and the chop together.

36. Turn Around And Chop   zhuànshēn pī dāo   转身劈刀

Pivot both feet on the spot to turn around to the right, then withdraw the left foot slightly to the rear. Bend the right knee and straighten the left, to take a right bow stance. Circle the blade up and over to the rear right to chop flat with the hilt at waist height. The cutting edge is down and the tip forward [tr. note: in the new direction, having turned around]. Look forward, to the right. (image 8.36)

Turn quickly, stand stably, chop strongly.

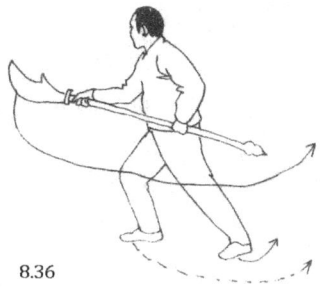

37. Turn Around, Step Forward, Smear

zhuànshēn shàngbù mǒ dāo   转身上步抹刀

Push into the right foot to shift back, then pivot on the left foot to turn around to the left. Then step the right foot behind to the left and continue to turn left. Circle the blade from the front to the left with the turn, to smear flatly to the rear left. The hilt is at chest height, the cutting edge on the left. Look to the rear, at the right [tr. note: back in the previous direction]. (image 8.37)

Turn quickly, and time the smearing with the stepping. The cutting edge must lead into the smearing technique.

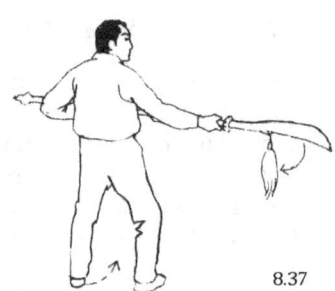

38. Empty Stance, Hide The Blade   xūbù cáng dāo   虚步藏刀

Push into the left foot to shift right, turn the torso left, and bend both knees to take a left empty stance. Circle the blade left and down to the rear right, turning it over to hold it slanting at the waist, tip down, edge up. Look forward, to the left. (image 8.38)

Sit into a distinctly weighted / unweighted empty stance. Coordinate the hiding of the blade with the turn of the body, so that it is hidden behind.

39. Step Forward, Deflect With The Hilt   shàngbù náobà   上步挠把

Step the left foot forward and shift mostly to the left leg. Draw a circle with the hilt to the right, then deflect downwards to the left. Look forward, to the left. (image 8.39a) Push into the right foot to shift forward, then step the right foot forward. Circle the grip to the left to deflect forward and up. Keep the hilt at the right side of the body at an angle, tip slanting down. Look forward. (image 8.39b) Step the left foot forward and hold the base up in front, the hilt slanting down. Look forward. (image 8.39c)

Draw rounded circles with the hilt whilst stepping. Use soft power.

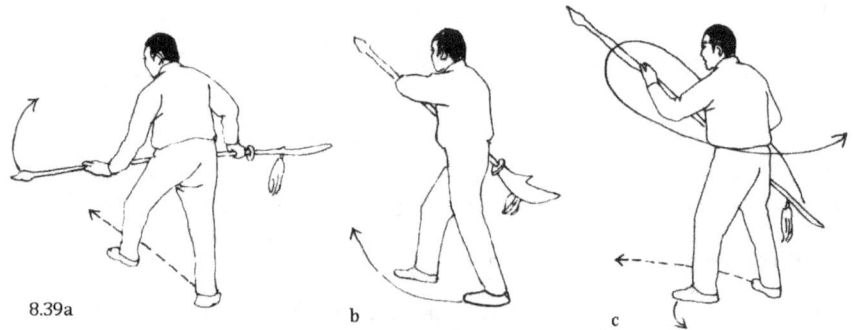

40. Turn Around To Bow Stance Hack

zhuànshēn gōngbù zhǎn dāo   转身弓步斩刀

Push into the right foot to shift forward, pivot on the left foot around to the left, then step the right foot forward [tr. note: in the new direction]. Turn the torso further to the left, bend the left knee and straighten the right, to set into a left bow stance. Bring the blade to the right and across flat to the front to hack across to the rear left, cutting edge to the left, hilt slanting at the left side. Look forward, to the left. (image 8.40)

CRESCENT MOON BLADE

Turn quickly, set to stance stably, hack strongly.

8.40

Section Five

41. Turn Around, Smear   zhuànshēn mǒ dāo   转身抹刀

Push into the left foot to shift back, then pivot on the spot on both feet around to the right. Bend the right knee and straighten the left, to set to a right bow stance. Turn the body around to the right and smear across from the front to the right, towards the rear, with a flat smear. The edge faces right. Look forward, to the right. (image 8.41)

Turn quickly, set firmly into stance, smear into the cutting edge of the blade.

8.41

42. Step Forward, Raised Knee Push

shàngbù tíxī tuī dāo   上步提膝推刀

Push into the left foot to shift forward, then step the left foot forward, turning it out. Cradle the blade in front of the chest with the hilt across at the left side, cutting edge to the left. Look forward. (image 8.42a) Push into the right foot to shift forward, then step the right foot forward. Medially rotate the right arm to turn the blade over, so that the cutting edge is to the right. Look forward. (image 8.42b) Push into the left foot to shift forward, then raise the left knee. Push the blade forward to chest height, edge to the right. Look forward, to the right. (image 8.42c)

Stand firmly in the one-legged stance. Push strongly.

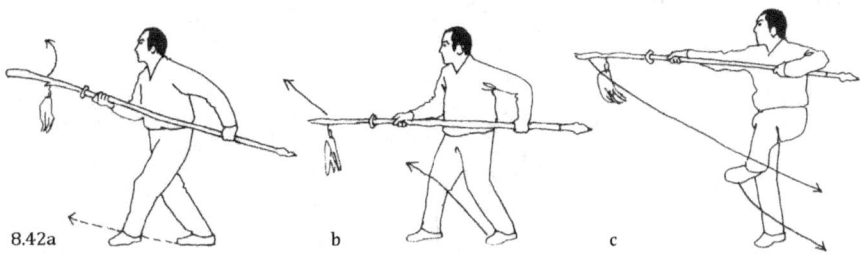

8.42a   b   c

233

43. Turn Around, Slice Up   zhuànshēn liāo dāo   转身撩刀

Land the left foot across to the left side. Circle the blade down and across, to slice to the left, tip angled down, cutting edge to the left. Look forward and down, to the left. (image 8.43a) Push into the right foot to shift to the left, then step the right foot forward, turning the torso to the left. Continue to slice the blade up on the left, to complete a high slice, edge up. Look to the upper front. (image 8.43b) Push into the left foot to shift forward, then step the left foot forward, raising the right knee. Circle the blade in a full circle up and over to the left, to the rear, down, then back up with a high slice in front. Tuck the hilt into the right armpit with the left hand. The hilt is slanting with the cutting edge up. Look to the lower front. (image 8.43c)

The cutting edge must lead throughout the slices. Coordinate each step with each slice up.

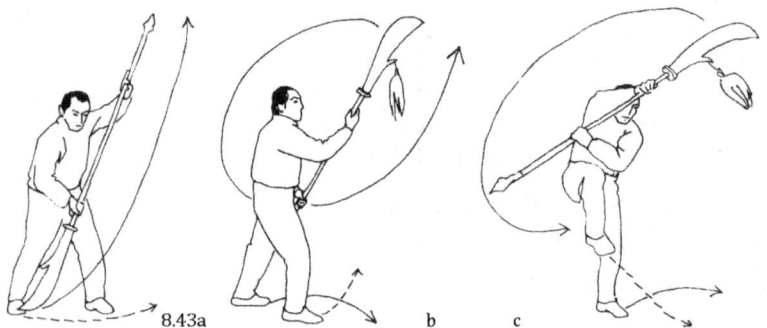

44. Jump To Bow Stance Hack   tiào gōngbù zhǎn dāo   跳弓步斩刀

Push into the left foot to jump up, and land forward on the right foot, then the left. Bend the left knee and straighten the right to take a left bow stance. Circle the blade up and over to the rear, to hold it out at the right side of the body, cutting edge to the left. Look forward, to the right. (image 8.44a) Without moving from the bow stance, circle the blade flat across the front to the left with a flat hack, turning the torso slightly to the left. The blade faces left. Look forward. (image 8.44b)

Jump forward and land stably, hack strongly.

CRESCENT MOON BLADE

45. Closed Stance Push bìngbù tuī dāo   并步推刀

Push into the right foot to shift forward to the left leg, and step the right foot forward, bending both legs. Cradle the blade in front of the belly, hilt along the belly, cutting edge to the left. Look forward, to the right. (image 8.45a) Push into the left foot to shift right, then bring the left foot up to meet the right in a closed stance, and stand up. Turn the torso to the left. Push the blade flat forward with the hilt at chest height, the tip to the right, and the edge turned to the back. Look to the right side. (image 8.45b)

Complete the push as you complete the closed stance. Push with power.

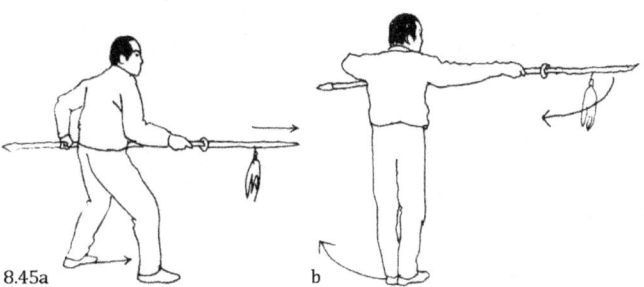

46. Turn Around, Slice Up zhuànshēn liāo dāo   转身撩刀

Step the left foot to the left and bend the knee. Lower the blade at the right, turning the cutting edge down. Look to the right. (image 8.46a) Push into the right foot to shift forward, turn left, and step the right foot forward. Bend the right knee and straighten the left to take a right bow stance. Circle the blade down from the right with the turn, then slice up to the left. The hilt is slanted in front of the body, tip forward, edge up. Look forward. (image 8.46b)

The cutting edge leads when slicing up. Use soft power for the slice.

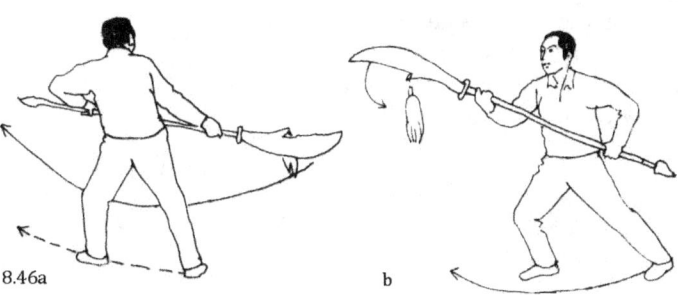

47. Raised Knee Push tíxī tuī dāo   提膝推刀

Push into the left foot to shift forward, then step the left foot forward with the foot turned out. Cradle the blade in front of the body, turning the edge to the left. Look forward. (image 8.47a) Push into the right foot to shift forward, step the right foot forward, turn the torso to the left, and raise the left knee. Push the blade flat out in front to chest height with the tip forward.

235

Turn the edge over to face the right side. Look forward, to the right. (image 8.47b)

Step forward and raise the knee with good balance. Push with good power.

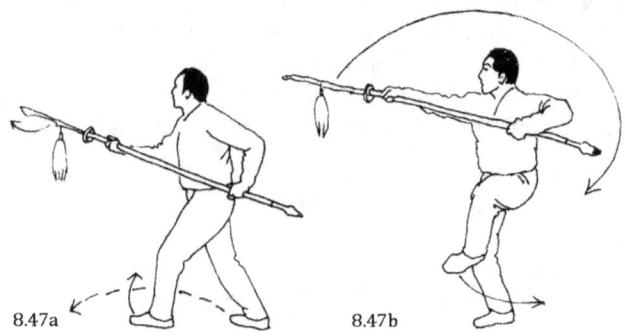

Section Six

48. Turn Around, Parry   zhuànshēn guà dāo   转身挂刀

Land the left foot to the left side, turning it out and lifting the right heel. Circle the blade up and over to the left to parry down on the left, tip down. Turn to the left and tuck the hilt into the right armpit with the left hand. Look to the left side. (image 8.48a) Push into the right foot to shift forward, then step the right foot forward, turning it out and lifting the left heel. Circle the blade to the rear and up, then over to the front to parry down in front, tip down, edge to the rear right. Look forward and down to the right. (image 8.48b)

Keep the hilt tight to either side of the body when doing the turn around and parries to each side. Coordinate each parry with the steps forward.

49. Turn Around, Slice Up And Stab   zhuànshēn liāozhā dāo   转身撩扎刀

Push into the left foot to shift forward, then pivot the right foot on the spot to turn around to the right, lifting the left leg up behind, keeping it straight. Circle the blade down in front to go across to the right to slice up behind, tip down, edge up. Look forward to the lower right. (image 8.49a) Continue to pivot on the spot around to the right on the right foot, turning right, step the left foot forward. Bend the left knee and straighten the right to take a left

CRESCENT MOON BLADE

bow stance. Continue to slice up in front then stab straight, tucking the hilt to the waist, cutting edge up, tip forward. Look forward. (image 8.49b)

Turn quickly, land firmly, stab strongly.

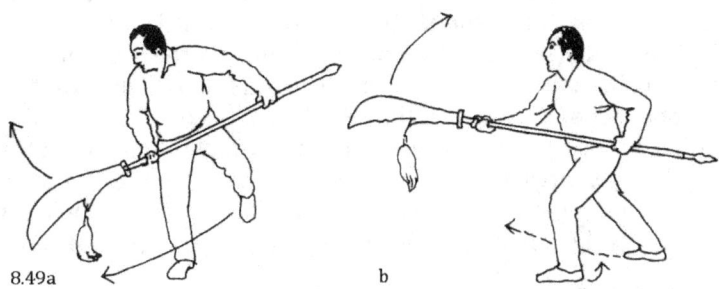

50. Jump To Bow Stance Hack   tiào gōngbù zhǎn dāo   跳弓步斩刀

Push into the right foot to shift forward, and raise the right knee. Cradle the blade in front of the chest, tip up. Look forward. (image 8.50a) Push into the left foot to jump up. Land forward on the right foot, then the left, bending the left knee and straightening the right, to take a left bow stance. Hack forward to the left, angling the hilt to the left side, edge to the left, tip forward. Look forward. (image 8.50b)

Jump forward with good stability. Hack with good power.

51. Turn Around, Smear   zhuànshēn mǒ dāo   转身抹刀

Push into the left foot to shift back, then pivot both feet on the spot around to the right. Bend the right knee and straighten the left to take a right bow stance. As the body turns around to the right, smear to the right in an arcing line with the blade flat, to the rear right. The tip points forward [tr. note: in the new direction] and the cutting edge leads into the cut. Look forward, to the right. (image 8.51)

Turn quickly with a stable pivot. The cutting edge must lead to smear.

237

52. Jump To Bow Stance Hack   tiào gōngbù zhǎn dāo   跳弓步斩刀

Push into the right foot to shift back, and raise the right knee. Bring the blade up, slanting at the right side. Look forward, to the left. (image 8.52a) Push into the left foot to jump up. Land on the right foot, then the left, bending both knees. Bring the blade down to hold it level at the rear right of the body. Look forward, to the left. (image 8.52b) Push into the right foot to shift left, bending into the left knee and straightening the right, to take a left bow stance. Circle the blade across from the rear right to the front, to hack across to the left in front. The hilt is at the left side of the body, the cutting edge faces the upper left. Look forward, to the left. (image 8.52c)

Take a stable bow stance. Hack with power.

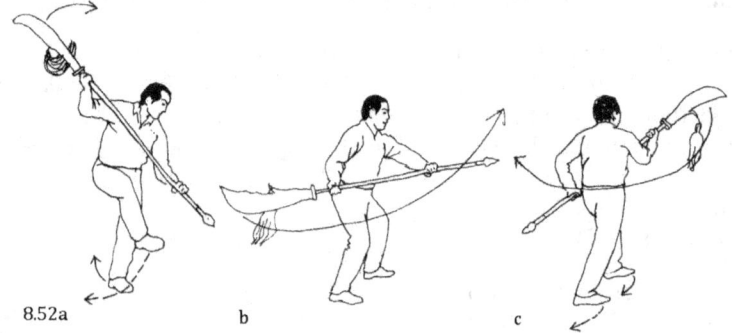

53. Turn Around, Smear   zhuànshēn mǒ dāo   转身抹刀

Push into the left foot to shift back, then pivot on both feet on the spot around to the right. Bend the right knee and straighten the left to take a right bow stance. Smear with the blade across in front and over to the right in an arcing line to the rear right, edge out. Look forward, to the right. (8.53)

Turn quickly, pivoting with good balance. The turn and smear is done softly.

54. Empty Stance Cradle The Blade   xūbù bào dāo   虚步抱刀

Push into the left foot to shift forward, turn to the right, and step the left foot forward. Touch the ball of the left foot down with the heel lifted and

CRESCENT MOON BLADE

bend both knees to sit into a left empty stance. Cradle the blade, crossing to the left side of the body. Look to the left. (image 8.54)

Sit into a distinctly weighted / unweighted empty stance.

8.54

55. Withdraw, Stand The Blade   chèbù lì dāo   撤步立刀

Retreat the left foot to the rear. Raise the blade at the right side, tip up. Look forward. (image 8.55a) Push into the right foot to shift back, then withdraw the right foot to the rear. Look forward. (image 8.55b) Withdraw the left foot to stand beside the right foot in a closed stance. Place the base on the ground with the hilt vertical at the right side. Release the hilt of the left hand and place it at the right hand. Look to the left. (image 8.55c)

Withdraw and place the base on the ground in one coordinated movement.

8.55a b c

56. Closing Posture (Stand To Attention Holding The Blade)

shōu shì (lìzhèng chí dāo)   收势（站立持刀）

Place the left hand at the left side and stand to attention. Look forward. (image 8.56)

8.56

PRONUNCIATION OF PINYIN, THE CHINESE NATIONAL PHONETIC ALPHABET (WITH INTERNATIONAL PHONETIC ALPHABET EQUIVALENTS)

INITIALS (words can start with these consonants, or have a zero initial)

PINYIN	IPA	ROUGH PRONUNCIATION GUIDE
p	p^h	Like English pet with a considerable puff of air.
b	p	Similar to the *pinyin* "p" but without the puff of air (unvoiced, neither English pet nor bet).
t	t^h	Like English tag with a considerable puff of air.
d	t	Similar to the *pinyin* "t" but with no puff of air (unvoiced, not dog).
k	k^h	Like English kill with a considerable puff of air.
g	k	Similar to the *pinyin* "k" but with no puff of air (unvoiced, not English get).
c	ts^h	Like exaggerating English cats.
z	ts	Like the *pinyin* "c" but without the puff of air (unvoiced).
ch	$tʂ^h$	Somewhat similar to English chat with a puff of air, but with the tip of the tongue rolled back.
zh	tʂ	Like the *pinyin* "ch" but with no puff of air (unvoiced).
q	$tɕ^h$	Somewhat similar to English chat with a puff of air, but with the front of the tongue raised and the tip on the lower teeth.
j	tɕ	Like the *pinyin* "q" but without the puff of air (unvoiced).
m	m	Like English met.
n	n	Like English net.
f	f	Similar to English fat, but with the teeth just touching lightly behind the lower lip.
s	s	Similar to English set.
sh	ʂ	Somewhat similar to English show, but with the same tongue placement as the *pinyin* "ch" and "zh".
x	ɕ	Somewhat similar to English shine but with the same tongue placement as the *pinyin* "q" and "j".
h	χ	Raise the back of the tongue and let the breath come through the obstructed passage without vibrating the vocal cords.
l	l	Like English let.
r	ɹ	Like the *pinyin* "sh" but with voicing.

FINALS

n	n	Like English pin.
ng	ŋ	Like English sing.

VOWELS

a	A a ɛ		Usually close to English f<u>a</u>ther (not p<u>a</u>t). Like y<u>e</u>t when written "-ian" or "yan".
e	ɣ e ɛ ə		Usually similar to English p<u>e</u>t, can tend towards a mid vowel.
i	i ⌊ɪ		Usually similar to English b<u>ee</u>. Similar to w<u>e</u>t when written "ui". After c, z, s, ch, zh, sh, and r it is similar to s<u>ir</u>.
o	o u		Usually close to English r<u>o</u>ll. Similar to c<u>ow</u> when written "ao", and <u>owe</u> when in "ou".
u	u y		Usually similar t English o b<u>oo</u>t. After the *pinyin* "x", "q", and "j" and in the vowel groups starting with these consonants, it is pronounced "ü".
ü	y		Similar to French <u>ü</u>. It is written after "n" or "l", because these are the only positions where both "u" and "ü" are possible
y	i		Partially like an English 'y', tending towards i.
w	u		Partially like an English 'w', tending towards u.

INITIAL CONSONANTS

place of articulation	manner of articulation						
	Unaspirated Stop	Aspirated Stop	Unaspirated Affricate	Aspirated Affricate	Nasal	Fricative	Voiced Continuant
bilabial	b	p			m		
labio-dental						f	
dental-alveolar	d	t	z	c	n	s	l
retroflex			zh	ch		sh	r
palatal			j	q		x	
velar	g	k				h	

TONES IN PINYIN			
NUMBER	PINYIN	NAME	RANGE
1	ˉ	high level	55
2	´	high rising	35
3	ˇ	dipping	214
4	`	high falling	51
none	° or blank	neutral	in context

With tone sandhi, tones may change according to the preceding or following tone.

The tone marking is put over the main vowel when there are two vowels written together (usually involving the pronunciation of y or w).

ABOUT THE TRANSLATOR

Andrea Falk has practised external and internal Chinese martial arts since 1972. She has studied Chinese art, geography, history, language, linguistics, literature, philosophy, politics, religion, and sociology since then, as well. She received a Bachelor of Arts majoring in Chinese (1978), a Bachelor of Physical Education (1980) and a Master of Physical Education with an emphasis on coaching science (1990) from the University of British Columbia. She trained in wushu full time on scholarship from 1980 to 1983 at the Beijing Physical Culture Institute, earning an Advanced Studies Diploma in Wushu under the tutelage of Professor Xia Bohua and instruction from Men Huifeng and others. There she learned the basics of Yang and Chen style Taijiquan, Baguazhang, Xingyiquan, Chaquan, Tongbeiquan, and modern Longfist (barehand and four standard weapons). Andrea spent two further extended summers at the Institute in 1984 and 1986.

Starting in 1984, Andrea gradually changed over to learning traditionally, visiting China on extended trips as often as possible to learn in parks, parking lots, and courtyards. She has trained and/or is training Chen style Taijiquan, Baguazhang, and Taiji Changquan as an inside apprentice of the late Huan Dahai (1924-2015) and elder martial brothers in Shanghai; Xingyiquan and Baguazhang as a close student and friend of Di Guoyong in Beijing; and Baguazhang from friends Li Baohua and Lu Yan. When not in China or traveling to teach, she is usually in Québec City or at a cabin in the Laurentian hills, Canada.

Andrea has taught and translated books about Chinese martial arts since 1983. She founded *the wushu centre* in Montreal in 1984, in Victoria in 1992, and in Quebec city in 2007. Andrea has taught Chen Taijiquan, Baguazhang, and Xingyiquan around the world, but mostly in Canada and England.

For years, Andrea translated books for her own students. In 2000, *tgl books* and the website www.thewushucentre.ca were established to bring these translations to a wider audience.

trois gros lapins traversent le chemin

ISBN 978-1-989468-42-5

www.ingramcontent.com/pod-product-compliance
Lightning Source LLC
Chambersburg PA
CBHW071815230426
43670CB00013B/2466